The Existentialist Moment

To Emma, Sebastian and Audrey

The Existentialist Moment

The Rise of Sartre as a Public Intellectual

Patrick Baert

polity

First published in 2015 by Polity Press

Polity Press
65 Bridge Street
Cambridge CB2 1UR, UK

Polity Press
350 Main Street
Malden, MA 02148, USA

ISBN-13: 978-0-7456-8539-7 (hardback)
ISBN-13: 978-0-7456-8540-3 (paperback)

A catalogue record for this book is available from the British Library.

Library of Congress Cataloging-in-Publication Data

Baert, Patrick, 1961-
   The existentialist moment : the rise of Sartre as a public intellectual / Patrick Baert.
    pages cm
   Includes bibliographical references and index.
    ISBN 978-0-7456-8539-7 (hardcover : alk. paper) -- ISBN 0-7456-8539-0 (hardcover : alk. paper) -- ISBN 978-0-7456-8540-3 (pbk. : alk. paper) -- ISBN 0-7456-8540-4 (pbk. : alk. paper) 1. Sartre, Jean-Paul, 1905-1980. 2. Existentialism. I. Title.
    B2430.S34B255 2015
    194--dc23
                                                                                2014043776

Typeset in 10.5 on 12 pt Sabon by
Servis Filmsetting Ltd, Stockport, Cheshire
Printed and bound in the UK by Clays Ltd, St Ives plc

For further information on Polity, visit our website:
politybooks.com

CONTENTS

ACKNOWLEDGEMENTS

I would like to thank Elliott Karstadt, India Darsley and Susan Beer at Polity Press for their help and patience with this project. I am also grateful to John Thompson, who has been encouraging throughout and provided important input at crucial points. I wish to thank Bruno Frère, Marcus Morgan and Flore Cuny for reading the whole manuscript carefully and for suggesting significant improvements. I would like to thank various people who have commented substantially on sections of the book, or on my conference presentations related to the book: in particular, Jeffrey Alexander, Ed Baring, Damian Catani, Randall Collins, Emma Murray, Gisèle Sapiro, Alan Shipman and Darin Weinberg. The comments by anonymous reviewers have been extremely helpful, for which I am most grateful.

Some of the research and writing took place while I visited the Sociology Departments of Brown University and the University of Cape Town, as well as the Centre européen de sociologie et de science politique (CNRS-EHESS-Université de Paris I Panthéon Sorbonne). I am also thankful to staff at the British Library, the University Library in Cambridge and the Bibliothèque nationale de France.

The research leading to these results has received funding from the European Union Seventh Framework Programme (FP7/2007-2013) under Grant Agreement no. 319974 (INTERCO-SSH). This book also benefited from a Leverhulme fellowship (RF-2012-339) and a British Academy small grant (SG102163).

INTRODUCTION

The question

Jean-Paul Sartre achieved an astonishingly high public profile during his heyday. Commentators invariably refer to the huge crowds at his funeral (50,000 according to one estimate), but the evidence for his public standing in France (and indeed abroad) goes well beyond this single event. Sartre's books and plays have been a remarkable success, and once he had come to public prominence he managed to draw large audiences whenever he gave lectures. The amount of sustained media attention and his political influence in France and abroad has been unrivalled.

This book is an attempt to comprehend this extraordinary case of public celebrity. We will not be discussing at length all of Sartre's forays into politics which stretched over a period of nearly four decades; there are many books that have documented this aspect of his biography extremely well.[1] Instead, we will try to focus on the period, in France, when Sartre rose from relative obscurity to public prominence. We call it the 'existentialist moment' because we are talking about a short time span, one in which not just Sartre, but also his philosophy, caught the public's imagination.

Popular conceptions of Sartre tend to locate his rise and that of existentialism in the context of the political turmoil of the 1960s and the student movement, but closer scrutiny shows that this was a period when Sartre's philosophical status – and, to some extent, his public impact – was already on the wane. Sartre came to public prominence much earlier, in the mid-1940s. His popularity and that of his philosophy rose dramatically in a remarkably short space of time, between 1944 and 1947 – especially in the autumn of 1945. This

1

is not to say that there was no interest in his writings before 1944,[2] but it was primarily limited to a specialist audience.[3] By early 1944 Jean-Paul Sartre and existentialist philosophy were still little known beyond a small circle, with his *magnum opus*, *L'Être et le néant*, virtually unnoticed when it was published initially.[4] Yet, within a mere two to three years, Sartre would turn into a major public figure and existentialism would become *vogue*. After 1947 Sartre and his fellow existentialists managed to maintain a high profile, though there was no longer a significant rise in their popularity and their philosophy played increasingly less of a role. Indeed, from the late 1940s onwards, the political issues of the day, rather than philosophy, underscored the public appearances and writings of Sartre, de Beauvoir and Camus, as they, like most other intellectuals in France, became embroiled in the cold war over which they eventually fell out.

The central question, therefore, is twofold: one aspect deals with timing, the other with Sartre's philosophy itself. Firstly, why did Sartre and his philosophical movement gain such rapid intellectual acceptance with an artistic and popular following in France *at this particular time* – between 1944 and 1947, not before or after? Secondly, why during this period was it *Sartre's existentialist movement* that was so successful in gaining popularity? After all, Sartre's philosophical writings were rather opaque and the philosophical current of existentialism had a remarkably small following in France before 1944. Further, the philosophical origins of Sartre's existentialism were distinctly German and were indebted to the work of Martin Heidegger, who had been tainted by his closeness to the Nazi regime during the 1930s.

To make sense of the rapid rise of Sartre in the mid-1940s in France, we will analyse various aspects of the socio-political climate at the time, two of which are worth flagging up here. Firstly, between 1940 and 1945, French intellectuals became involved in intense power struggles in which those seen to be associated with the Resistance were ultimately victorious. In this context, we study the activities of the Comité national des écrivains, the Resistance organization of writers, as well as the purge (*épuration*) of collaborationist intellectuals. We explore how some of the themes that were raised at the trials of collaborationist intellectuals, such as the notion of the author's responsibility, fed into Sartre's existentialist concerns. Secondly, we analyse the role of Sartre in the repairing of severed social ties and the remaking of French nationhood. We argue that the notion of cultural trauma[5] is particularly apt to describe the state of France at the time. Cultural trauma refers to a widespread sense that certain events – in this case, Vichy and the occupation – caused collective distress and irredeemable damage, potentially threatening the social fabric of society. Sartre expressed a sense of cultural trauma – without using those words – but also, crucially, provided a vocabulary to come to terms with it. We argue that it is this dual role that was a key to their success.

In what follows, we will explore how Sartre wrote about the trauma of the war, rather than focus on which events were intrinsically traumatic or were more likely to be experienced as such. So we want to find out how effective Sartre, in comparison with others, was in making his views heard and through which channels his accounts of the war were disseminated. Which types of arguments did he invoke to support their views? Which past events or actions were portrayed as pernicious, and who was to be blamed? According to him, how can the French people move beyond these events? How, in the process, did Sartre position himself?

Exploring, as we do, how intellectuals such as Sartre wrote about cultural trauma – rather than studying the traumatic events as such – is not to deny that what happened between 1940 and 1944 had been exceptionally disruptive, confusing and a harrowing experience for many French people in a variety of ways. Not only did the rapid military defeat come to many as a surprise, with nearly seven million people fleeing southwards to avoid the war zone; as many as 92,000 French soldiers died between 1939 and 1940 and 1,850,00 soldiers ended up in German prisoner camps.[6] Under the conditions of the 'armistice', France was divided up. Alsace and Lorraine were annexed, 'Germanized' and subjected to conscription, resulting in the mobilization of 130,000 men for the German war effort. A large part of France, including Paris, remained under German occupation throughout the war, and even in the South the so-called 'free zone' would eventually – in November 1942 – be occupied as well and divided up in a German and Italian zone of occupation.[7] The term 'free zone' was highly misleading: Pétain's État français (as the Vichy regime called itself) involved active collaboration with Nazi Germany that included the rounding up of political opponents and ethnic minorities, resulting in the imprisonment of more than 130,000 people and the deportation of 76,000 Jews.[8]

Throughout its history, French society had regularly been 'divided against itself', as the aftermath of the French Revolution and the Dreyfus affair testify. The events leading up to the war had already increased political tensions within France, with Léon Blum's Front populaire acting as a focal point,[9] and the Vichy regime accentuated even more what came to be referred to as the 'guerre franco-française' – the internal war within France.[10] Keen to find a scapegoat so as to overlook the strategic errors of the military command, Pétain repeatedly blamed the 'decadence' of the Front populaire for the defeat in the war. With its traditionalism and close links to the Church, Pétain's 'national revolution' was hostile to the values of the French Revolution, and indeed Pétain's dictum 'Work, family, fatherland' ('Travail, famille, patrie') stood clearly in opposition to the republican values 'Freedom, equality, solidarity' ('Liberté, égalité, fraternité'). Jews, freemasons and communists were portrayed as particularly responsible for the national humiliation, and they were excluded from the civil service and professions.[11]

As the war continued, economic tensions rose. Germany's exploitation of the French economy became more apparent, with a considerable proportion of French agricultural and industrial production set to fuel the war economy. Particularly unpopular was the obligatory labour service in France, which was initially set up on a voluntary basis but became compulsory from September 1942. During the war, approximately 700,000 French men were repatriated to work in Germany, of whom a mere 40,000 were volunteers. Under those increasingly problematic circumstances resentment grew and eventually developed into a strong Resistance movement. The activities of the Resistance led to German retaliations, whereby innocent people were taken hostage and executed, something which contributed dramatically to people's antagonism towards the occupying force, but which also divided opinion in France, at least for some time, as to the wisdom and effectiveness of the Resistance. During the war, tens of thousands of members of the Resistance were either killed immediately or deported to extermination camps where most of them died. By the mid-1940s, the heroics of the Resistance were celebrated, with the French Communist Party, which played a central role in the organization, calling itself 'the party of the 75,000 executed people'.[12]

In sum, during the war, France was divided geographically and politically. We will show throughout the book that these political divisions were also played out in the intellectual realm, with collaborationist and Resistance intellectuals pitched against each other and with lives literally at stake. By the mid-1940s, several intellectuals tried to make sense of this confusing episode of French history, a stage in which they themselves had performed many parts. We shall see how the experience of the war and the way in which politicians and intellectuals dealt with it led to a radical reshaping of the intellectual scene, with the curtains finally falling on the dominance by sections of the old literary establishment. It is against this background that we will explain Sartre's rise.

Existing accounts

There is a wide body of academic literature on existentialism, and on Sartre in particular, approaching the topic from a variety of angles. Most secondary sources attempt to elucidate the philosophy or to analyse the novels and plays associated with it. In contrast, little systematic commentary is available on why existentialism gained such prominence when it did. Within this limited body, two sociological types of explanations can be identified: a Bourdieusian perspective and Randall Collins' network approach.

Firstly, some commentators present an analysis that is indebted to the work of the French sociologist Pierre Bourdieu. Anna Boschetti's *Sartre et 'Les Temps modernes'*[13] is one of the most accomplished examples of this genre. Boschetti draws heavily on Pierre Bourdieu's sociological theory of cultural production, and central to her Bourdieusian outlook is his notion of field. She defines the field as any system of social relations that has its own logic; it is precisely this logic that accounts for its specific development.[14] The cultural field is one such field, which, in the case of France, is exceptionally unified, centralized and hierarchical. The French cultural field, like any cultural field, involves a fierce struggle over symbolic recognition. Within this cultural field, only a limited group that is already consecrated itself – a small circle of cultural producers, editors, publishing houses and journals – can bestow legitimacy onto the producers. In this Bourdieu-inspired perspective, some people are better equipped to compete than others, and different fields require different types of resources or 'capital'. Educational or cultural capital proves to be essential in the cultural field in general but there is an added complexity in the French case. In the nineteenth century, the cultural arena was divided between the literary and academic world; they constituted separate fields, each with its own logic. It is only in the course of the twentieth century that the two fields started to intersect, and few people managed to combine the requirements to excel in both fields.

Following Bourdieu closely, Boschetti pointed out that Sartre's profile – his *habitus* and his personal trajectory – is particularly well suited to the fields in which he would later operate and fitted the requirements of the successful intellectual; she refers in particular to his upbringing at home, his entry to the École normale supérieure

5

and the *agrégation*. Those experiences provide him with the necessary skills, confidence and authority to excel. Boschetti was keen to show how Sartre at various stages of his career embodied and benefited from his privileged *parcours*. In addition, Boschetti explained that Sartre's era was different from that of the nineteenth century, which was characterized by a sharp division between novelists and professors. The former were often self-funded and invariably came from privileged backgrounds, whereas the latter went through the meritocratic channels of the École normale. It is only in the course of the early twentieth century that the worlds of novelists and professors would meet, with an increasing number of intellectuals able to cross from one realm to the other. Sartre's popularity can be explained mainly by his unprecedented ability to stand out in those two genres, using them as complementary channels for his ideas, as he managed to compete successfully in both the literary and philosophical fields.[15] In short, Boschetti explains Sartre's success primarily by how he managed to be a total intellectual: journalism would allow him to add another string to his bow. She insists, though, that Sartre should not be seen as a maverick: rather than undermining established models, his trajectory ensures that his practices are perfectly in harmony with the logic of the different fields in which he operates.

Besides the primary explanation, she provides a couple of secondary accounts. Firstly, she asserts that the success of Sartre's existentialist philosophy can be partly explained by the way in which it implicitly propelled the intellectual – depicted as aloof and superior – to the centre stage and was therefore likely to appeal to the rapidly increasing number of teachers and professors.[16] Secondly, towards the latter parts of the book Boschetti draws attention to how Sartre was able to rely on a small circle of intimate friends who were powerful intellectuals in their own right, each occupying editorial positions in literary journals and in newspapers and therefore able to help the others with favourable reviews of their work. It is within this context that she explores the role of *Les Temps modernes*, launched in 1945, which provided the basis for Sartre to establish a hegemonic power base and keep it for a relatively long period of time.[17]

One of Boschetti's strengths lies in analysing the inner logic of the French field of intellectual production, with its distinctive elite institutions such as the École normale. Drawing on Bourdieu's framework, Boschetti also presented a cogent argument as to why, compared to other contemporaries, Sartre was, as an individual, so tremendously successful in advancing his career and public profile. However, although it is true that Sartre managed to excel in various domains and although this might have given him an advantage over others whose activities were limited to one domain, it would be far-fetched to argue that this is the main explanation for why so many people were particularly receptive to his ideas, especially given that in French intellectual history Sartre has not been the only one to combine philosophy, literature and journalism and to do so success-fully. One of the problems with Boschetti's analysis is a tendency to treat the intellectual sphere as a relatively autonomous unity, thereby sometimes ignoring how socio-political factors outside the intel-lectual arena interact with it. In this context, it is interesting to note that Boschetti writes that '. . . Sartre's later success makes it clear that this widespread, tumultuous recognition of his supremacy cannot be explained simply in terms of a particular conjunction of circum-stances at the Liberation'.[18] However, Boschetti's tendency to ignore the wider socio-political context at the time makes it difficult for her to explain why the rise of Sartre and existentialism occurred during this particular period – not before, not after. While methodologi-cally Boschetti is justified in focusing mainly on Sartre, unfortunately her main explanation for his significance occasionally draws on an equally individualistic logic, focusing as it does on his unique and multiple qualities that supposedly gave him a considerable advan-tage over his competitors in the Parisian intellectual field. For all its Bourdieusian terminology and sociological sensibilities, her account sometimes resembles the catch-all explanation that Sartre's success is due to his genius or unrivalled charisma albeit socially induced, and this explains why Jean-François Louette describes her perspective as a thinly veiled 'psychologism'.[19] Boschetti is at her strongest when she discusses broader societal developments that impinged on the cultural sphere (such as the rapid increase of highly qualified teachers and professors in the first half of the century) but she fails to pay sufficient attention to the specific conditions at the end of the war and their dramatic repercussions for the intellectual field.

Drawing our attention now to the network approach, Randall Collins' *Sociology of Philosophies*[20] is an ambitious attempt at a general theory of intellectual change, with a particular focus on transformations within the discipline of philosophy. The theory is applied to no fewer than three centuries of philosophy worldwide, and one of the chapters is devoted partly to French existentialism. Collins' explicitly sociological stance underscores his criticisms of various engrained perspectives on the history of ideas.[21] He is critical of those approaches that conceive of culture – for instance, language – as autonomous of society, and he distances himself from the type of intellectual history that attempts to show, through a detailed investigation of arguments and counterarguments, how one set of ideas brings about another. Collins is critical too of the type of intellectual history that glorifies the individual and his or her creative output, thereby bracketing out the social context in which the production took place. For him, to recognize the situated nature of intellectual activities is not to imply, as 'postmodernist' authors tend to do, the impossibility of making generalizations and establishing causal patterns. Collins insists that generalizations can be made and patterns can be found as long as we build on his general theory of interaction rituals and are sensitive to the distinctiveness of interactions between intellectuals.

Drawing on his wider theory of interaction ritual chains,[22] Collins' core idea is that intellectual creativity and production are embedded in personal relations and networks of face-to-face interaction; those relations transmit emotional energy and cultural capital.[23] Both emotional energy and cultural capital are crucial for creative process; the former because it is a motivating force, the latter because it helps to direct creative output effectively. From this, it follows that it is a mistake to conceive of ideas as rooted in individuals or individual minds; ideas are anchored in networks and motivated to a considerable extent by rivalries between individuals and between groups of individuals. Young aspiring intellectuals are drawn to high-status intellectual groups and are energized when working under or with an important mentor.[24] They compete for the attention of the mentor, with only a few receiving his or her patronage and intellectual direction. Eminent and influential mentors are best placed to provide intellectual guidance to their students, indicating which intellectual avenues are worth pursuing and likely to pay off. These mentors and their students can then form influential schools but there is an upper and lower limit to how many such schools can coexist. Collins calls this the 'law of small numbers', which states that only three to six successful creative schools can exist at one time.[25] Fewer than three is unlikely due to the competitive nature of intellectual life. If more schools emerge, a competitive struggle will eventually lead to the survival of the three to six 'fittest'; the others will be wiped out.

In the chapter 'Writer's markets: the French connection', Collins[26] shows that existentialism was after 1945 one of those competitive creative schools. For him, the French educational system of the 1920s was particularly conducive to the intellectual synergies that later resulted in the existentialist movement. The highly selective, competitive and hierarchical nature of the intellectual field brought together the most ambitious and talented individuals of their generation. Their intense interactions within institutions like the École normale forged the type of networks that are so important for creative intellectual production. By tracing the connections between Sartre, de Beauvoir, Paul Nizan, Georges Canguilhem, Maurice Merleau-Ponty and Raymond Aron, Collins shows that, here again, personal relations and the concentration of emotional energy and cultural capital account for the creative output that took place.[27] This local French network is embedded in a broader German network that includes key phenomenological philosophers like Husserl and Heidegger and importers of German ideas, like Koyré and Kojève. Sartre acts as the 'energy vortex' of the network, benefiting from the unusually high cultural capital that he had amassed at home and at the École normale. However, his considerable educational and cultural resources only explain part of his success; the role of the publisher Gallimard is more important for two reasons. Firstly, the publishing house operated like a 'network centre', putting innovative thinkers in touch with each other and bringing new German ideas to the attention of French intellectuals. Secondly, from the 1930s onwards, Gallimard revolutionized publishing in France by bringing out cheap paperbacks which suited hybrid forms of literature and philosophy like existentialism.

Collins' analysis is particularly persuasive in locating French existentialism within a broader set of intellectual networks going back to the nineteenth century and covering several European countries. Collins' network approach also alerts us to, and helps us to establish, the various personal connections that provided the necessary motivation and sense of direction for Sartre and his fellow existentialists. Collins' explanation of why existentialism came to the foreground is most convincing when he takes into account exogenous forces, which influence the arena of intellectual production, such as shifts within the publishing industry or within the writers' market. The question still remains as to why those personal networks, which he identified, produced ideas that appealed beyond the safe contours of the intellectual elite. Collins might be right that the intensive interaction between students at the École normale is conducive to creative production but his notion of emotional energy remains vague and could be attributed to other *normaliens* as well. Collins' framework is unable to account for why it was Sartre and existentialism – not some other figure or a different intellectual strand – that rose in the mid-1940s and reached a broader audience. Nor does it explain why it was around 1945 – not earlier or later – that Sartre became a public intellectual and existentialist philosophy caught the public imagination. Collins also points out the importance of the arrival of the paperback and a broader mass market, but again other intellectual currents could have exploited these changes just as effectively. Furthermore, the paperback editions only came off the ground in France during the course of the 1950s – several years after Sartre's rise and that of existentialism.

Part of the problem lies in Collins' insistence that the intellectual field is relatively autonomous from other societal developments and, relatedly, in his focus on the inner dynamics of the intellectual world. While in his chapter on French intellectual life he does pay attention to the economic dimensions of intellectual production, his analysis still holds on to the notion that the '. . . distinctive contents of intellectual creativity . . . derive from the inner struggle for attention in the intellectual space'.[28] This makes his approach less suitable for explaining why, at a particular point, some intellectuals, and indeed some intellectual currents, have a broader appeal. More precisely, Collins never properly investigates what he calls the 'distinctive contents' of Sartre's writings, nor does he fully appreciate the extent to which they tied in with the broader cultural climate of the mid-1940s. In our research, we shall analyse Sartre's work during this period, ranging as it did from journalistic pieces to theoretical tracts. We shall see how Sartre reformulated his earlier existentialist position in ways which resonated with the societal sensitivities at the time. It is this affinity that was crucial in Sartre's rise and the dissemination of his ideas.

Besides these two sociological works (Boschetti and Collins), it is surprising that there are no major, well-developed attempts to account for Sartre's rise. Indeed, it is remarkable how few intellectual historians and literary specialists have systematically tried to provide this explanation.[29] One possible exception is Ingrid Galster's edited collection *La Naissance du 'phénomène Sartre'*,[30] with most of the contributions being by trained historians or specialists in French literature. Based on a conference, Galster's volume contains some insightful contributions (including from people who witnessed Sartre's rise first hand or who had worked closely with him), but the chapters are uneven, their article-length limits their scope and significance and there is little that connects then. So the book as a whole does not provide a cohesive argument, and indeed Galster uses the introduction to set out the different perspectives and even to distance herself from some of the contributors.

Nevertheless, there are plenty of secondary sources on Sartre that drop tentative hypotheses as to his success without elaborating or properly defending them. It is worth discussing four of the most recurrent narratives that have become part of the received wisdom about Sartre, if only to show why we regard them as unconvincing or at least incomplete and how our take differs from theirs. The first recurrent explanation that can be found in the literature centres around Sartre's individual qualities. This can take different forms: we are told that his success was due, for instance, to his intellect, his charisma, charm, adaptability, opportunism or simply his determination, ambition and work ethic.[31] While these factors played a role, any such type of explanation in terms of individual attributes, in isolation, is problematic. Take the two characteristics that seem most obviously connected to success: natural aptitude and hard work. There is no doubt that Sartre was very gifted and prolific – later on he would famously resort to amphetamines to enhance his productivity – but many other French writers at the time were talented and industrious. Furthermore, as many writers and artists will testify, work that is later regarded as exceptional can go unseen for decades or even a lifetime. Talent and charisma only come to the fore once recognized by the public, so we need an account for the connection (or lack thereof) between the intellectual and his or her audience. To explain Sartre's rise by referring to his extraordinary abilities risks drawing on a circular argumentation precisely because his success and people's recognition of his abilities are so intertwined. What needs to be explained is why at some point people started to recognize him as a man of talent who had something significant to say. It is the intersection between Sartre and the public that should be our focus of attention, not merely Sartre's idiosyncratic qualities.

A second type of argument focuses mainly, if not exclusively, on the autumn of 1945. Many secondary sources stress the significance of these few months, pointing out that it was at that point that their publications, performances and new ventures accumulated in what became known as the 'existentialist offensive'. Some narrow it down even more and identify Sartre's public lecture *L'Existentialisme est un humanisme* of 29 October 1945 as decisive.[32] Now, it is correct that it was around this time that Sartre and de Beauvoir achieved a celebrity status in France, and we will be discussing this important period (including the lecture) at length in chapter 4. The problem, however, with those accounts that centre round the autumn of 1945 is twofold. Firstly, they tend to remain descriptive, outlining a sequence of events that culminated in the existentialist frenzy, without delving further into the mechanisms that made it possible. Secondly, they bracket out the broader historical context which is so important for understanding Sartre's rise as a public intellectual. To take what is basically a snapshot – the autumn of 1945 – is to ignore the significance of developments in preceding years. It is our contention that by 1945, the experience of the war, with all its trauma and complexity, had already brought about a dramatic and irreversible shift in the political and intellectual scene, and it is this shift which enabled the existentialist offensive to succeed. Sartre's positioning enabled him to tap into complex collective sentiments of guilt, pride and shame which had engulfed the French nation. In sum, to make sense of how, by late 1945, Sartre had managed to connect with the French public and to become a quasi-mythical figure, we need to understand how the war had reshaped the intellectual landscape and, crucially, people's sensibilities and concerns.

A third account suggests that around 1945 existentialist thought became popular because it was associated with the relaxing of morals, did not impose any substantial imperatives and formed a much-needed antidote to the repressive years of Vichy.[33] At the time the portrayal by the popular press of Sartre and the Left Bank helped to consolidate this picture of a carefree generation. This third account is superior to the two other ones in that it focuses on the connection between Sartre and the public and on the significance of the historical context of the occupation and collaboration. It is also correct that Sartre positioned himself strongly in opposition to Vichy and its conservative values. Closer scrutiny, however, shows this explanation to be problematic in a variety of ways. Besides the fact that it is vague and needs further specification, it also rests on the problematic assumption that existentialism hardly imposed any burden on the individual. While it is true that around this time Sartre reformulated his thought and centred it round the notion of freedom, his existentialism, as we shall see, puts a considerable burden on the individuals, forced as they are to take responsibility for all their actions and the consequences of those actions. Also, although Sartre had not yet embraced Marxism, there was already a strong moral voice to his work, siding with the underdog. To suggest that Sartre's existentialism was experienced as a licence for unbridled freedom ignores his strong moral vocabulary at the time and the centrality of the notion of responsibility. While this account rightly hints at the significance of the experience of the war and of the relationship between Sartre's ideas and the existing collective sentiments, we are in need of a more refined and empirically grounded analysis of this process.

A fourth account uses the notion of generation as an explanatory concept. Indeed, a considerable amount of literature in nineteenth- and twentieth-century French intellectual history alludes to the power of generational shifts, especially if the generations concerned experienced very different socio-political developments.[34] The underlying assumption is that shared experiences account for similar sensitivities, possibly resulting in related intellectual endeavours, likes and dislikes. In sum, it is assumed that significant experiences, such as a war, have lasting effects on the collective psyche and therefore the intellectual output. The focus here is mostly on accounting for the causes of the intellectual products rather than their reception, but sometimes the distinction gets blurred and generations are invoked to account for changing sensibilities of audiences. We are not unsympathetic towards this argument, and the central thesis of this book has affinities with it in so far as it allocates a pivotal role to the notion of shared experiences. Indeed, the aim of this book is to demonstrate how the French experience of the Second World War played a significant role in the rise of existentialism in the mid-1940s. But resorting to an explanation in terms of generations is by itself insufficient for two reasons. Firstly, the notion of generation is too blunt an instrument to capture the complex relationship between experience and intellectual sensitivities. If anything, it begs for an explanation rather than providing one – what is it about a particular shared experience that accounts for those sensitivities? Secondly, there is the added complexity that different age groups experience the same significant event such as a war. Of course, significant events might mark younger people more than others as they are still in their formative years, but even that very much depends on a variety of factors such as, for instance, their level of exposure and involvement.

Theoretical orientation and hypotheses

Before we set out our tentative hypotheses, it is worth clarifying some concepts that will be used in what follows. We firstly distinguish 'intellectuals' from 'critics'. By intellectuals, we are referring to those who tend to produce relatively innovative intellectual goods, like plays, novels or philosophical treatises. In contrast, critics, including many journalists, tend to paraphrase and comment on those products in journals or newspapers with a relatively wide circulation. Of course, intellectuals occasionally also comment on the work of other intellectuals in magazines or serials, and, likewise, critics occasionally produce intellectual work of their own. So the distinction is one of degree, but nevertheless of importance because the critic can play the

13

role of gatekeeper, helping or halting the dissemination of intellectual works. We shall see that Sartre and his fellow existentialists, while primarily acting as intellectuals, also regularly took on the role of critics, commenting on each other's work.

Secondly, we distinguish between the 'intra-intellectual arena' and the 'public intellectual arena'. Within the intra-intellectual arena, professional intellectuals address mainly other professional intellectuals. One of the defining features of the intra-intellectual arena is that it is mainly governed by the intellectuals themselves. The public-intellectual arena is quite different, admitting a degree of validation by the 'consumers' of knowledge as well as the producers. Public intellectuals, by definition, address a broader audience, and the success of public-intellectual output is determined not solely by intellectuals, but also by the media – professional journalists and commentators – and publishers.

Three additional clarifications need to be made about the distinction between the intra-intellectual and public intellectual arena. The first clarification concerns the precise nature of the intra-intellectual arena and its relationship to the academy. The self-regulatory principle of the intra-intellectual world is epitomised by the Humboldtian notion of the university according to which the academic world is largely managed by the academic producers themselves: they set the agenda, comment and adjudicate on the writings and careers of their colleagues.[35] The intellectual status of theories and evidence is established by academic peer review, not public accessibility, acceptance and popularity. Even if increasing government interference, a rising audit culture and budget cuts have meant the gradual erosion of the Humboldtian vision,[36] universities still operate with a certain level of autonomy. However, the intra-intellectual domain does not have to be limited to the realm of the academy. It can also refer to writers who operate outside the contours of the university but whose writings are read by a limited group of other specialized producers. Like many other writers of his circle, Sartre never held an academic position; he was a secondary school teacher until the early 1940s. His philosophical essays of the 1930s and his *L'Être et le néant* – the former are to a certain extent precursors to the latter – made him a respected figure among a small specialized public. While he had published *La Nausée* and *Le Mur* before the war and had staged *Les Mouches* under the occupation, his existentialist philosophy did not reach a wider public until the end of the war.

The second clarification about the typology concerns its resemblance to Bourdieu's distinction between the field of restricted

14

cultural production and the field of generalized cultural production.[37] For Bourdieu, in the field of restricted production producers address other producers and defy an economic logic; in the field of generalized production producers address a broader public and embrace a business model. There is a subtle difference, though, between Bourdieu's distinction and the one which we use here. His typology reflects his presupposition about how the two fields bring about different cultural products: he believes that the field of restricted production encourages innovative high-brow products and the field of generalized production generates medium-brow replications of a set format. We make no such assumption and focus instead on the dissemination of intellectual ideas from one arena to the other.

The third clarification concerns the relative coverage of the intra- and public intellectual arena in the sociological literature. The intra-intellectual arena has been the subject of extensive sociological analyses.[38] Over the last couple of decades, an impressive body of research has emerged, ranging from theoretical reflections on the hegemonic force of elite academic institutions[39] and the dispositions of university professors[40] to carefully crafted reconstructions of the strategies of academics within their institutional context.[41] However, there are limits to the usefulness of this research for understanding the public intellectual arena because the latter operates according to a distinctive logic. Being less sealed off and addressing a broader audience, public intellectuals are more dependent on the media and critics. They can sometimes use a public audience to overcome resistance from a sceptical intellectual elite, appealing to the public 'over the heads' of academic peers. Whereas there are plenty of general accounts of the phenomenon of the public intellectual,[42] sociological accounts of the public intellectual arena are surprisingly scarce, and they often centre on the debate about the public sphere and its possible decline.[43] In this context, both historical sociologists[44] and historians with a sociological bent[45] tend to invoke a supposedly golden era of the public intellectual, while lamenting its alleged decline.[46] Although there can be virtue in this sociological reflection, if only to warn academics of the possible caveats of excessive professionalization,[47] it does not always provide empirically substantiated insights into the workings of the public intellectual arena and into the conditions under which it may flourish.[48] A recent survey of the little research about public intellectuals that is available shows the situation, at least in the US, to be more diffuse and certainly less apocalyptic than Jacoby and Posner suggest.[49] Among the few excellent studies that do contribute to knowledge about the public intellectual sphere is, for instance, Michèle Lamont's article on Jacques Derrida's impact both within the academy and beyond, Swartz's piece on Bourdieu's foray into the public realm and Misztal's study of Nobel Peace Prize winners.[50] In a similar vein, we shall aim to further our understanding of the public intellectual sphere through a case study, one which in some respects involves a public-intellectual arena in its most archetypal form, as represented by mid-1940s France. While focusing on the case of Sartre, the broader underlying question is under which conditions ideas are likely to spread from the intra- to the public intellectual arena.

In what follows, our approach will differ substantially from those perspectives on intellectual life that are predominantly text-based and that are preoccupied with motives and strategies of individual thinkers. Indeed, sociologists and historians of intellectual life often explore the motives and strategies which individuals developed in a given academic context. On a related note, they tend to treat the intellectual field as in relative isolation from external factors. As the focus here is on the diffusion of a set of ideas from the intra- to the public intellectual domain rather than on the intentions of those who spread the ideas or on the precise meanings of the ideas, it becomes particularly important to broaden our perspective well beyond the safe contours of texts and individual strategies and to be sensitive to the broader institutional and cultural dimensions that have bearing on the intellectual field without being confined to it. Without necessarily siding with all dimensions of actor-network theory as defined by Bruno Latour,[51] the approach adopted here has affinities with one aspect of it in so far as it consciously avoids imposing too rigid a theoretical framework from the outset and it makes an effort not to exclude *a priori* any factors that might have been constitutive of the making of the existentialist movement.

While avoiding a rigid frame of reference, we nevertheless adopt a theoretical orientation. This introduction is not the place to elaborate on the perspective underlying this research, except to say that it centres round the idea that through their work writers position themselves intellectually and that this positioning affects whether their ideas are taken up by others and, if successful, how they are adopted. For those readers interested in the theory, we refer to the final chapter where we expand on this idea and where we revisit some of the empirical material in the light of the new theory proposed. For now, we shall clarify some of the hypotheses which provide a guiding framework for this study.

Our starting assumptions are threefold. Firstly, ideas are more likely to spread from the intra- to the public intellectual domain if they are 'packaged' in terms of a coherent intellectual doctrine and 'labelled'. Writings, public performances and critics help to position the author and present the ideas in a unified fashion and as part of a coherent doctrine. Furthermore, while the spread of the intellectual doctrine or school will undoubtedly depend on the charismatic qualities of those who promote the doctrine and their determination and skills in promoting it, it will also crucially depend on the structural relationship of those intellectuals *vis-à-vis* the intellectual establishment, the publishing industry and the critics. Finally, whether or not a doctrine manages to enter the public intellectual domain will depend on whether it manages to resonate with recent socio-political experiences and, crucially, whether it does so better than older, established ideas.

On this basis, five concrete hypotheses will guide our research. Firstly, ideas spread more rapidly if their intellectual proponents manage to develop intricate connections within the world of critics. Sympathetic critics will then be able to report favourably and promote the distribution of the writings and the ideas within them. Successful intellectuals tend to have a good rapport with the journalistic world, often taking on the role of commentating themselves. Secondly, the ideas spread more rapidly if the established ideas have lost credibility within society, either because the ideas no longer resonate with a larger public or because the 'carriers' of the ideas have lost legitimacy or have diminished authority. Thirdly, the ideas spread more effectively if the publishing industry caters for a 'high-brow' mass market, and if the intellectuals are in a relatively strong position *vis-à-vis* the publishing industry. This strong position enables them to push through their agenda and publicize their ideas. Fourthly, the ideas are more likely to spread if the intellectuals involved use additional communication channels like public lectures and radio or television appearances. The phenomenon of public lectures goes back a long time and became widespread in the course of the nineteenth century, whereas French intellectuals started appearing regularly on the radio as early as the 1940s and on television during the next decade. Fifthly, the ideas will disseminate more effectively if they resonate with the broader cultural climate among the educated classes. The ideas need to strike a chord with their potential audience, allowing them to make sense of their current or recent experiences. The most sophisticated ideas will fail to penetrate the public-intellectual arena if they do not manage to connect with the recent and present experiences of the people involved.

17

Dreyfus and the notion of the intellectual

As a final introductory point, it is important to dispel a few possible misunderstandings. We are not arguing that Sartre was the first French philosopher to gain public prominence. Henri Bergson, for one, was famous at his time[52] and his lectures at the Collège de France attracted huge crowds, especially after the publication of *L'Évolution créatrice*.[53] More importantly, we are not asserting that all aspects of Sartre's existentialism were exceptionally new or ground-breaking in the French intellectual context at the time, nor are we positing that the broader historical trajectory in the preceding half century proves irrelevant for understanding the rise of existentialism in the mid-1940s. Rather, existentialists revisited historically rooted views about intellectuals and their political engagement – views which acquired a renewed significance at the end of the war. In what follows, we acknowledge the continuity or resemblance between earlier notions of the role of the intellectual and Sartre's reflections on the same issue, but we focus our attention on those conditions at the end of the war which account for why his particular take on these notions resonated with a wider public and broke through to the public intellectual domain.

It is indeed worth recalling the specific socio-political and intellectual trajectory of France from the late nineteenth century till the end of the war so as to situate the subsequent surge of French existentialism in a broader context. In this period of half a century, one feature stands out as significant for our discussion: the emergence of the modern notion of the intellectual. Intellectual historians tend to agree that the modern concept of the intellectual gained currency especially during the Dreyfus affair in the 1890s, although the term had already been in use slightly earlier.[54] While the political divisions between Dreyfusards and anti-Dreyfusards were not as straightforward as previously assumed,[55] the term 'intellectual' played a pivotal role in the conflict between the two groups. In 1898 a group of academics, students and writers signed two *protestations*, denouncing the violation of the law in the Dreyfus and Estherházy affair. Contrary to received wisdom,[56] the petition was not explicitly a defence of Émile Zola's 'J'accuse!', but it did express similar concerns.[57] Shortly afterwards Georges Clémenceau, a defender of Dreyfus, referred to this petition approvingly as the 'Manifesto of the intellectuals'. One week later the anti-Dreyfusard Maurice Barrès published a little article, entitled 'La Protestation des intellectuels!', in which he mocked the use of the term. This acerbic piece popularized the notion, and from then onwards anti-Dreyfusards used it pejoratively and invariably with a sarcastic undertone. For them, 'intellectuals' were outsiders, who drew on abstract thinking and who were therefore out of touch with the historical roots of French culture and language. Anti-Dreyfusards also considered intellectuals to be 'pretenders': that is, not the genuine article but would-be cultured people, often of foreign extraction and therefore unable to match the cultural and aesthetic attributes of those with a long French ancestry. However, the anti-Dreyfusards were not the only ones using the term. Those Dreyfusards who were targeted swiftly adopted the notion of the intellectual themselves, stripping it of its negative connotations, and using it with pride to refer to themselves as principled defenders of true French values of justice and truth. The intellectual became a self-congratulatory concept. As the Dreyfusards were ultimately victorious, it is no surprise that their notion of the intellectual – and not the pejorative one – became more influential throughout the twentieth century even to the extent that some writers on the right labelled themselves in this fashion.

Important for our concerns are two observations. Firstly, what is particularly striking about the 'Manifesto of the intellectuals' is the implied assumption on the part of the signatories that their professional status allowed them to exert authority over the wider public even when they were commenting on a phenomenon well beyond their expertise or specialism.[58] Indeed, by the end of the nineteenth century a considerable number of academics and writers appeared convinced that their opinions about socio-political matters were sufficiently important to matter to a broader audience, thereby invoking scorn on the part of anti-Dreyfusards like Ferdinand Brunetière who argued that being an expert in one field does not make you an authority in another. Secondly, the image of the intellectual, invoked by both camps during the Dreyfus affair, is one who is actively engaged in the world, in particular involved in the politics of the day. In that sense, the term 'intellectual', as introduced in the late nineteenth century in France, corresponds to the current Anglo-Saxon notion of a 'public intellectual'. More specifically, this intellectual is tied to the republican cause and defends progressive values based on abstract principles of truth and justice.[59] L'intellectuel is therefore situated on the left of the political spectrum, although subsequent attempts have been made by right-wing intellectuals to appropriate the term. Finally, intellectuals are anti-conformists who distrust le pouvoir; they present themselves as the voice of reason against government forces.

It is this picture of the intellectual – as authoritative, politically engaged, left-leaning and in opposition to the government – which remained an important feature of the intellectual landscape of the first half of the twentieth century and which eventually fed into the frenzy of the later stages of the Second World War and the liberation. This is not to say that the notion of a committed intellectual had remained uncontested in the first three decades of the twentieth century. For instance, Julien Benda's *La Trahison des clercs* famously accused intellectuals of abandoning reason and universal principles in exchange for passion in the pursuit of particular causes (socialism and nationalism), prompting Paul Nizan, a close friend of Sartre, to write *Les Chiens de garde*, a harsh critique of Benda and a fierce defence of progressive political commitment.[60] The 1930s was characterized by a similar ambivalence: while various authors (including Sartre) expressed disillusionment with society and politics and toyed with the idea of art for art's sake, political events surrounding the Popular Front and the Spanish Civil War sparked off considerable engagement.

We shall see, however, that by the mid-1940s the idea of political engagement had become the new orthodoxy. Key features of the Dreyfusard image of the intellectual reappeared in Sartre's writings about literature and writing, which explains why some commentators refer to Sartre as a 'Dreyfusard *après la lettre.*'[61] Just as the petition was associated with the birth of the modern notion of the intellectual, petitions became the hallmark of the era of the *intellectuel engagé* with Sartre as one of the keenest and most prolific signers. However, we should be careful not to overstate the continuity between the views of the Dreyfusards and Sartre's thought because the latter presented a coherent philosophical doctrine in which the role of the intellectual was only one, albeit important, ingredient. As we shall see, Sartre incorporated his notion of the engaged intellectual within a much broader existentialist vocabulary that enabled sections of French society to articulate and assimilate the war experience. Therefore, the similarities between Sartre's views and those of the Dreyfusards are not sufficient to explain why his existentialist framework moved from relative obscurity to prominence between 1944 and 1947, and it is to this question that we aim to provide a multi-layered answer.

Just as Sartre's notion of the committed intellectual built on an earlier notion of the Dreyfusard intellectual, Sartre's broader worldview, as it developed in the 1930s and early 1940s, was not entirely unique. Some of his ideas were shared by others who were equally marked by the harrowing experience of the First World War. The Great War had brought earlier confidence and optimism to an abrupt halt, and many French writers in the 1930s expressed ideas similar to those that appeared in, for instance, Sartre's novel *La Nausée*. Absurdity and contingency were shorthand for feelings of despair that had engulfed the intellectual scene. As far as philosophy is concerned, Sartre was certainly not the first French intellectual to show systematic interest in existentialism and phenomenology. In the 1920s and 1930s, German philosophy was regarded in high esteem in France, and many major French intellectuals, such as Lévinas and Aron, had research spells in Germany where they became acquainted with the intricacies of Husserl and Heidegger's philosophy. It was indeed Aron, on his return from his research stay, who prompted Sartre to study in Berlin and continue his research on Husserl. French intellectuals did not even have to go to Germany to learn about these ideas: Alexandre Kojève's lectures at the Sorbonne (1933–9) introduced Hegel from a Heideggerian perspective to a new generation of intellectuals.[62] Around the same time, some of Heidegger's texts were available in French, due to Henry Corbin's translations.[63] In sum, not only were Sartre's publications of the 1930s, addressing phenomenological questions, in sync with the French intellectual scene at the time, but so was *L'Être et le néant*, published in 1943, engaging as it did with Hegel, Husserl and Heidegger. Several others had been concerned with existentialist themes, notably philosophers such as Gabriel Marcel and Jean Wahl who integrated ideas first developed by Kierkegaard and Heidegger.

What was distinctive, however, was Sartre's particular appropriation of phenomenological and existentialist ideas. Sartre's doctrine stood out in a variety of ways. Whereas in France existentialist concerns had often been associated with a Christian or Jewish outlook, we shall see that Sartre promoted an overtly atheist version. By the mid-1940s, Sartre would rebrand his philosophy in a more digestible manner. Sartre was particularly skilful in reformulating earlier existentialist themes more positively, allowing his readers to make sense of a traumatic episode of French history.

Structure of the book

The book consists of seven chapters, with the first two setting the scene against which Sartre's rise will become intelligible. Chapter 1 depicts the unusual context of the occupation of France, from mid-1940 until mid-1944, and it explains how the occupation and collaboration altered the cultural arena substantially, accentuating already existing divisions within the intellectual community. Chapter 2 analyses the purge of French collaborationist intellectuals, especially in 1944 and 1945, and it also pays attention to the intellectual debates surrounding the trials of collaborators. Chapter 3 explores the intellectual shifts that took place in France in conjunction with the purge; it also shows how Sartre's journalistic pieces of 1944 and 1945 tapped into those changes and resonated with the spirit of the time. Chapter 4 elaborates on what Simone de Beauvoir called the 'existentialist offensive', the sudden rise of existentialism in the autumn of 1945; it focuses particularly on how the launch of the journal *Les Temps modernes* and Sartre's public lecture *Existentialisme est un humanisme* enabled him to position himself as an engaged intellectual with Resistance credentials. Chapter 5 explains how, in the course of 1946 and 1947, Sartre consolidated his position as a committed intellectual by publishing two major works: *Qu'est-ce que la littérature?* and *Réflexions sur la question juive*. Whereas the former is a comprehensive theoretical treatise centred round the notion of engagement, the latter applies this perspective to the problem of anti-Semitism, a case of central importance at the time. Chapter 6 summarizes the arguments set out in the book, providing a multi-levelled account for the rise of Sartre. It also provides an explanation for why, from the early 1960s onwards, Sartre and existentialism gradually lost their central position within the French intellectual scene. Chapter 7 elaborates on the theory underlying this book, outlining a performative perspective for conceptualizing intellectual interventions. While drawing on examples from the previous chapters, we also try to demonstrate the broader applicability of this theory, well beyond the Sartre case.

— 1 —

OCCUPATION, INTELLECTUAL COLLABORATION AND THE RESISTANCE

To make sense of Sartre's rise at the end of the war, we shall have to retrace the complex, and at times confusing, trajectory of France under German occupation. In this chapter, we shall discuss how the reality of the war and occupation had significant repercussions for the cultural and intellectual field, redefining its configuration and in the process creating an irreparable schism between two politically opposing factions within the writers' profession. While this juxta-position had deeper historical roots, the political context of the war accentuated it and gave it new meaning. It also meant that the oppos-ing factions had very different working conditions and led very dif-ferent lives. It is important to grasp the intensity of this rift, as well as the unique dilemmas that the war brought about, because they would affect the distinctive cultural sensitivities of the immediate aftermath of the war into which Sartre was able to tap. For this, we will first examine the broad changes brought about by the German occupation and Vichy and then investigate their specific effects on the cultural and intellectual field.

German occupation and Vichy

May and June of 1940 were traumatic for the French population, not least because the initial military stalemate with Germany was followed by a surprisingly swift defeat at the hands of what was supposed to be a technologically inferior army. France and Britain declared war on Germany in September 1939, and then came the so-called Phoney War[1] – a period of eight months of military inactivity – which lasted until 10 May 1940 when suddenly Germany invaded the Netherlands,

Belgium and Luxemburg, thereby avoiding the Maginot line. Within less than forty days the German forces had penetrated French territory. On 5 June 1940, confronted with the capitulation of Dunkirk and heavy casualties, an exasperated Prime Minister, Paul Reynaud, reshuffled his War Cabinet and brought three army men in to reinvigorate a dwindling morale. Besides General Maxime Weygand, the Commander-in-Chief of the French army, the trio included the newly promoted Brigadier-General Charles de Gaulle and the ageing Marshal Philippe Pétain. For ten days, these men would share the same cabinet table, before opting for dramatically opposed choices. With German soldiers entering Paris on 14 June and six million French people fleeing to the South (plus an additional two million non-French people on the move), their government moved to Tours and then Bordeaux. Two days later, faced with further French capitulation and with ongoing disagreements with Weygand, Reynaud gave way to Pétain who would become the last Prime Minister of the Third Republic and would also be responsible for dissolving it.

The trauma of the First World War was still fresh in the minds of members of the highest ranks of the French military establishment. They were elderly, had experienced the Great War first hand and were anxious to avoid further casualties on that scale. Both Weygand and Pétain decided to renege on the Anglo-French agreement of March 1940 according to which neither France nor Britain would seek an armistice or peace treaty with Germany. Not only did neither trust Britain as an ally, both had little faith in Britain's ability to withstand the German war machine. On 17 June, Pétain announced the armistice, while de Gaulle, together with other senior officers, left for London and set up the 'French free forces'. The next day, de Gaulle made his famous broadcast through the BBC, rejecting the armistice and calling on the French to continue the fight against German occupation. After short spells in Bordeaux and Clermont-Ferrand, Pétain's cabinet eventually settled in the quiet spa town of Vichy, which gave the government its name. The armistice was signed on 22 June and handed Germany control over the North and West of the country, including the complete Atlantic coastline, though in practice the administrative jurisdiction of Vichy would often extend beyond the 'unoccupied zone'. Besides the occupied and unoccupied zone, there was the 'forbidden zone': comprising the Northern departments of Nord and Pas-de-Calais, it was strategically important and under control of the German High Command in Brussels. Finally, there was the annexation of Alsace and Moselle in Lorraine; this part of France is now 'returned' to Germany.

This situation would last until November 1942, when Germany finally seized control of the whole of France, prompted by fear of an Allied invasion from North Africa, but even then Vichy continued to administer the country. Pétain's well-publicized meeting with Hitler on 24 October 1940 conveyed to the French public his commitment to a close relationship with Nazi Germany, and indeed six days later he acknowledged that he had accepted the 'principle of collaboration'.[2] Although this was the first time the notion of collaboration was used so publicly, Pétain only expressed one of the major tenets of the armistice, with article 3 stipulating that the French people ought to 'collaborate' with the occupying power.[3] Initially this notion of cooperation faced remarkably little resistance: the propaganda reiterated that the war with Britain would be brief, that Germany would be victorious, and that an alliance with the latter would help to maintain internal order. Britain was portrayed as an aggressive imperial power willing to sacrifice French lives for strategic purposes: the assault by the Royal Navy on the French fleet in Mers-el-Kébir in early July 1940 further fuelled this belief. At the beginning of the occupation, some conservatives were concerned that the Nazis might join forces with the French Communist Party, but it soon became apparent, long before the German invasion of Russia made this alliance impossible, that the Germans had no such intentions.

So, early on, collaboration was widely seen as the least of all evils, the possibility for peace and internal stability. Vichy had broad support and was seen as an opportunity for a fresh start. It soon transpired, however, that this collaboration came at a heavy price, literally as France had to cover the occupation costs and had to give up Alsace and Lorraine, but also in numerous other ways: food shortages made everyday life harsh; very few of the 1.6 million French prisoners of war were released; the French army, rebranded as the Army of the Armistice, was substantially reduced and put under control of the German force; French administration as a whole was subject to German control; and eventually more than 600,000 French men were compelled to go and work in Germany after a voluntary system proved unsuccessful. It was particularly this Service du travail obligatoire which made the German occupation unpopular.

On 10 July 1940 the National Assembly voted for its own dissolution, the legal basis of which has been hotly debated ever since. A couple of days later, Pierre Laval became Pétain's deputy, a position he lost in December of that year but regained in April 1942. The constitutional acts of 11 and 12 July 1940 provided a legal framework for the new French nation. They also gave Pétain a wide range of powers, including the legislative, judiciary and executive, and officially he became 'Chief of the French nation'.[4] Pétain's Vichy obtained a certain amount of international recognition, something which would be emphasized by defence lawyers during the trials of Vichy politicians and collaborators. No fewer than forty countries, among them the United States and Russia, recognized Vichy as a legitimate government. However, only six countries bothered with an embassy in Vichy but, again, the US was one of them.

Pétain was held in high esteem because of his role in the First World War, in particular his success in the battle of Verdun. The ill-fated Maginot line had been his idea but this seemed hardly to dent his reputation; nor did the fact that his overall military vision in this war had been old-fashioned. Eighty-four years old when he headed Vichy, he adopted, from the outset, a fatherly role towards the French people, describing his new position as 'the gift of my person (to the nation) so as to attenuate her suffering'.[5] This grandiose statement set the tone for things to come: the idolatry surrounding his person as well as the Catholic themes of suffering and repentance would become central to the Vichy ideology. Pétain's tours around the country, the carefully orchestrated rallies in his support, and his rigid control of newspapers and radio maintained a remarkable personality cult which only waned in the latter stages of the war. He portrayed the armistice as a desperate but necessary measure to avoid a repeat of the massacre of the First World War and to protect the French people against the malaise of foreign occupation. The media played a central role in promoting the idolatry surrounding Pétain. Whereas in the occupied zone the Propaganda–Abteilung Frankreich controlled Radio-Paris, in the unoccupied zone la Radiodiffusion nationale promoted the Maréchal and his conservative values.

Very early on, Pétain promoted the 'National Revolution',[6] a conservative ideology reminiscent of the 'moral order' of the 1870s. The term 'National Revolution' had been in vogue since the 1930s, and although not frequently used by Pétain himself, it became associated with his vision for France. This ideology occupied a central role in the first couple of years of Vichy, and it declined in importance in the latter stages. Its motto 'work, family, fatherland' purposefully mirrored 'liberty, equality, fraternity'[7] of the French Revolution, thereby making clear its attempt to reverse republican values. 'Discipline' was another catchword used by Vichy to sum up the new ethos of physicality and restraint that would replace the era of supposed idleness, indecision and decadence. The National Revolution promoted traditional family values, a strong work ethic and respect for hierarchy and authority, and it often brought up nostalgic images of harmonious rural community life. Only a few days after signing the armistice, Pétain already spoke about the treaty as 'first and foremost an opportunity for a moral revival'. The recent defeat to Germany was depicted as a rightful punishment for a 'decadent' nation that had lost its way in the eternal squabbles of a parliamentary democratic system and in the pursuit of secular and republican values. Now was time for the French population to repent for the degeneracy of the Third Republic and especially for the socialist policies of the 'Popular Front'. Vichy vigorously promoted Catholicism, and in return the Catholic Church hierarchy was supportive of the regime. Above all, Vichy ideology was hostile to the Enlightenment, which, by promoting abstract principles like liberty and equality, supposedly undermined the moral fabric of the French nation.

Vichy relied on *préfets* – unelected officials – to implement its policies in the various *départements*. The ideology of Vichy was put into practice in a variety of ways. The police force was expanded; Vichy promoted paramilitary organizations especially for the young; it dismantled labour unions and employers' organizations and created a corporate structure to end class antagonisms; and it provided financial incentives for women to stay at home. Above all, Vichy enacted a set of laws, which acted in conjunction with Nazi ordinances. Within the first couple of months, people with a foreign father could no longer be employed by the state; naturalization laws and laws against anti-Semitism were reversed; reform camps were introduced for dealing with misbehaving adolescents; 'secret societies' were banned; and freedom of expression was curtailed.[8] The Statutes on Jews[9] of October 1940 and June 1941 involved a set of discriminatory laws against Jews, which included depriving them of their full citizenship and excluding them from the army and the civil service, business, teaching and other professions. This was a prelude to tighter anti-Semitic laws and discriminatory measures against Jews: in 1941 their businesses were seized and from 1942 they were subjected to a curfew and were forced to wear yellow stars. This persecution eventually culminated in the French-assisted deportation of 75,000 Jews to German concentration camps of which around 2,000 survived. As the war progressed, Vichy became more visibly repressive, fascist and anti-Semitic, a process accelerated by the arrival of the Milice, although the Berlin-imposed reinstatement of Laval in 1942 is widely seen as a watershed. Faced with increasing repression and the increasing likelihood of German defeat, the Resistance became more popular. Resistance activities led to harsh reprisals and more visible repression.

With the French defeat, the German occupation and the installation of Vichy, the cultural and intellectual landscape altered quickly as a significant number of artists and writers fled abroad. Between 1940 and March 1942, 1,500 intellectuals managed to leave the country with the help of organizations such as the Emergency Rescue Committee, an American outfit based in Marseille. Most would go to the Americas or the UK. Among the individuals the ERC helped to escape were André Breton, Jules Romains, Antoine de Saint-Exupéry, Jacques Maritain, Claude Lévi-Strauss and Raymond Aron. Those who stayed behind did not always look favourably at those who had left, even if they shared an anti-German and anti-Vichy outlook. Some expressed disappointment: they felt that abandoning France in its hour of need was unpatriotic and would leave scope for the Germans to reshape the cultural and intellectual landscape.[10] Of course, the escape turned out to be a matter of life and death for intellectuals of Jewish descent such as Lévi-Strauss and Aron. Nevertheless, those who remained in France sometimes acted as if they had the moral high ground over those who had gone into exile. They certainly faced a tough balancing act, trying to reconcile their desire to speak out and act with the reality of the German censor and repression. For Jewish intellectuals who stayed in France, there was soon little choice but to remain silent or anonymous. A clear example is Julien Benda who retreated in the unoccupied zone and wrote under a pseudonym in clandestine publications.

The defeat changed the cultural and intellectual scene considerably in other ways too. In the occupied zone, the Ministère de l'information of the État français set in place institutions to encourage the National Revolution and to censor intellectual or artistic activities that did not comply with the Vichy orthodoxy. It also provided practical and financial assistance to journals, such as the fascist *Idées* or the conservative-Catholic *Demain*, which promoted views perceived to be more or less in line with the reigning ideology.[11] Given the shortage, the paper distribution proved a powerful instrument of control, with collaborationist journals invariably receiving more paper. Several contributors to those reviews also occupied roles in the Vichy propaganda machinery. They tended not to belong to the meritocratic elite, counting very few *normaliens* among them; Vichy offered them a fast-track career which otherwise would probably not have been available to them. Unsurprisingly, they were particularly hostile to the *concours*[12] – and more generally towards the Grandes écoles – openly despised the meritocratic channels of the Third Republic and were sceptical of the role of the intellect in French society.[13]

Although Vichy was an authoritarian regime with conservative and fascist writers at the service of a relentless propaganda, non-collaborationist intellectuals who lived in the unoccupied zone had more freedom than their northern counterparts. Some journals which did not toe the party line managed to survive, notably *Les Cahiers du Sud* (Marseille), *Poésie* (Villeneuve-lès-Avignon), and *Confluences* (Lyon), and some writers who might have been arrested in Paris were not in the occupied zone. Even after 1942, when the Germans occupied the South following the progress of the Allied forces in North Africa, the repression remained less visible and less pervasive in the Southern zone. It would be wrong, however, to overplay the differences between Vichy and the occupied zone. In practice, Vichy did not act autonomously; neither in general policies nor in the intellectual realm. It had to operate largely in conjunction with the occupying forces, and it was in the running of cultural and intellectual matters often subordinated to German demands.[14] Further, Paris remained the cultural and intellectual centre, especially given Vichy's anti-intellectual stance. This meant that the peculiar conditions of the Parisian intellectual arena reverberated well beyond the occupied zone.

In the occupied zone, the Germans quickly moved to control carefully the intellectual and artistic production. As in other occupied countries, this task was mainly allocated to the Propaganda-Abteilung, but France was unique in that the German embassy also played a role, with Otto Abetz, the German ambassador, as a key person. The German strategy was for Parisian intellectual life to remain active. Abetz's role was to promote a vision of a larger Europe, led by Germany of course, in which the French and German people would be able to live harmoniously side by side, appreciating each other's culture. Abetz was in many respects an obvious choice to lead this cultural strategy and embark on a charm offensive. Prior to the war, he had spent many years in Paris and already had contacts in the local intellectual and artistic circles. There were also personal touches: he was a Francophile, spoke the language fluently and, above all, his wife was French, which helped him alleviate lingering suspicions from the local population. Once ambassador, Abetz became personally involved in the shaping of cultural and intellectual affairs, making sure, for instance, that his friend Drieu la Rochelle took over the editorship of the prestigious *La Nouvelle Revue française*. With Abetz in charge, cultural life in the French capital appeared to remain as vibrant as before, but with clear restrictions: anti-German sentiments and anti-fascist political messages were forbidden, and any

Jewish traces were removed. So the main theatres in Paris, such as the Comédie française, soon reopened, but they were no longer allowed to employ Jewish actors and directors, nor were they able to perform works by Jewish playwrights. Picture houses reopened, again with restrictions to which films could be shown.

Under Abetz, two principal institutions were meant to secure cultural hegemony: l'Institut allemand (or Deutsches Institut) and the Informations-Abteilung, with the former intended to woo the intellectual elite and the latter targeting a broader audience. In conjunction with those two, there was also the Amt Schrifttum,[15] which was designed to promote German literature but which turned out to be less significant. Headed by Karl Epting, l'Institut allemand organized German courses, Franco-German conferences, musical concerts, plays and films. It also set up a French–German bookshop and distributed a 'liste Matthieu' of 'recommended' German books, organizing their translations.[16] Rudolph Rahn was in charge of the Informations-Abteilung, a large organization with over 1,000 employees and which organized high-profile exhibitions, such as the anti-freemasonry exhibition of autumn 1940, 'La France européenne' of 1941 and 'Le Juif et la France' of 1941–2. It also set up new journals and magazines, such as *La France au travail*, and replaced editorial staff in existing ones such as *L'Illustration*. It took over some publishing houses such as Le Pont et Offenstadt, Calmann-Lévy, Nathan and Ferenczi, and managed to control a variety of newspapers and magazines such as *Aujourd'hui* and *Les Nouveaux temps*.[17]

In practice, Abetz had to navigate a complicated setting, having to accommodate Goebbels and the Propaganda-Abteilung. They were sometimes at loggerheads. Several high functionaries in Berlin, including Goebbels, felt that Abetz had virtually gone native or at least was too lenient. It is in this context that Abetz was recalled at the end of 1942, although he was able to resume his post one year later. It would be a mistake, however, to portray the German control of intellectual and cultural production as simply one of persuasion and seduction; it also used coercion. We already mentioned some of the anti-Semitic policies in the cultural realm. They were part of a broader cleansing strategy. The German occupying forces imposed strict censorship and compiled various lists of banned books: after an initial 'Bernhard' list of 143 forbidden titles, then followed in September 1940 the infamous 'Otto' list with more than 1,000 titles.[18] This list was updated in 1942 and 1943, eventually banning more than 1,500 books. Books written by Jewish or so-called anti-German authors, ranging from Sigmund Freud to Charles de Gaulle, were to be destroyed. The Propaganda-Staffel stipulated that publishing companies should not publish Jewish or anti-German books. In cases of uncertainty the manuscript was to be sent to Propaganda-Staffel, which would decide whether or not it was publishable. Bookshops were subjected to a similar control with clear instructions about which books should not be sold. Some bookshops were closed and hundreds of thousands of books were burned. Various newspapers and magazines disappeared, among which were *La Lumière*, *Les Nouvelles Littéraires* and *Marianne*.

Intellectuals and collaboration

If we define collaboration as cooperation with an occupying force, then in the case of France during the Second World War it manifested itself in different and sometimes nebulous forms. The Vichy administration represented its most straightforward, and indeed most political, type, as the notion of collaboration was intertwined with the armistice. Official, overt collaboration took a sinister turn with the arrival of the Milice, a paramilitary organization set up in January 1943 to combat the Resistance and round up Jews. Other forms of collaboration were less clear-cut, however. Towards the end of the war, the term was often used to refer to those who had profited financially or career-wise from the occupation. In some cases individuals were involved in clear-cut collaboration of this kind but other cases were less straightforward as it was not always clear whether the individuals involved had helped the occupying force more than other people had. The difficulties arise from the fact that, because of the structural dependency produced by the occupation, most French people could not avoid having to serve or assist the occupying force in some capacity.

Collaborationism, as a doctrine in support of collaboration, was easier to detect not least because it often took a written form. From early on collaborationist authors sided with the Vichy in attributing the military defeat to republican sections within French society, but whereas Pétain mainly accused left-wing politicians of the Third Republic, the intellectuals who supported Vichy or Nazi Germany often pointed fingers at other intellectuals. For them, various literati and thinkers, from Jean Cocteau to André Gide, supposedly had corrupted the youth or had misled their readers by putting talent and abstract intellect above virtue and national pride.[19] Ever since the late nineteenth century, literary figures of all political persuasion, as well as sociologists and social philosophers, had regularly described

31

French society as in a state of moral decadence or 'anomie', lacking the erstwhile vigour and 'national energy'. In the course of the 1930s writers of all political persuasions wrote about the lack of the nation's vitality. After July 1940 several intellectuals, again not all on the right, identified national decay as one of the main causes, if not *the* cause, of the military defeat. Supporters of the new regime were quick to identify the causes of the nation's decadence – parliamentary democracy, republican values and unfettered individualism – and to emphasize their Anglo-Saxon roots.[20] Some conservative intellectuals close to Vichy criticized in particular the notion of art for art's sake, which in their eyes was a recipe for frivolity and degeneracy, although this moralistic view was not shared by all collaborationist intellectuals and certainly not by those who were anxious to preserve intellectual and artistic autonomy. Most collaborationist intellectuals were united around an anti-Enlightenment stance, denouncing those who prioritized science and specialized expertise. They were hostile to the *normaliens* and academics, as both were, in their minds, associated with the emptiness of specialization, the absence of creativity and the mediocrity of meritocracy.[21] They were in search of a new type of intellectual who in some respects embodied its antithesis: no longer ethereal and cerebral, these new intellectuals were supposed to be virile and passionate, in touch with their physicality and instinct.[22]

Even non-collaborationist intellectuals, like André Gide, were initially taken with the assumption of a decadent Third republic and a rampant individualism and the need for a temporary (French) dictatorship that would restore discipline and cohesion.[23] From the very beginning of the war and of the occupation, then, the trauma of the defeat was played out within the intellectual arena, with collaborationist intellectuals initially taking on the mantle of the accuser. It took François Mauriac to question the outrageous assumption, held by the accusers, that the intellectual interventions of their opponents could possibly have been so important as to affect the nation's morale and ultimately the military outcome. Throughout the war, many intellectuals on both sides of the struggle – collaborationists and Resistance intellectuals – would subscribe to this presumption of the all-importance of intellectual work and in particular its significant socio-political impact. Very soon Resistance intellectuals, as will become clear, would also take on the role of accusers, attributing at least as much responsibility to collaborationist intellectuals as they had done to others. The notion of the author's responsibility would play a central role in the trauma work in which both factions were involved.

Within the group of collaborationist writers, it is important to draw a distinction between intellectuals like Jean Luchaire and Charles Maurras who were broadly supportive of Vichy and intellectuals like Marcel Déat, Jacques Doriot and Lucien Rebatet who heralded the values of Nazi Germany and fascism. The former felt strongly about patriotism and tradition, whereas the latter embraced the revolutionary spirit of fascism and were critical of Vichy. A similar distinction applies to collaborationist newspapers and weeklies: for instance, the newspaper *L'Action française* espoused Pétainist views, whereas the politico-literary magazine *Je suis partout* and the newspaper *L'Oeuvre* took a pro-fascist and pro-German stance. This distinction was intertwined with opposing sections within the political elite as reflected in the tense relationship between the two main political figures: when Pétain dismissed Laval in December 1940, the latter joined forces with Doriot and Déat who wanted a closer relationship with Nazi Germany. The institutional structure of Vichy also reflected this juxtaposition, with the Légion française des combattants loyal to a Pétainist line and the Milice exhibiting all the hallmarks of fascism.[24] This is not to say that, intellectually, the two types of collaborationist doctrine had no affinities: fascist writers like Rebatet and Brasillach had been influenced by Maurras' *L'Action française*. Maurras himself, however, remained hostile towards German aggression and sceptical towards its brand of fascism – something which he would use in his defence at the end of the war – and some former members of his organization even joined the Resistance.[25]

There was another difference between the Vichy-supporters and the ardent fascists: the former were more likely to change their political stance *vis-à-vis* the occupation and the war, whereas the latter had an entrenched position. As the war progressed in favour of the Allied forces (and as Vichy and the German occupation became more visibly repressive and exploitative), some of the early Pétain supporters distanced themselves from the regime. In the beginning of Vichy, the Catholic writer Paul Claudel wrote his infamous 'Paroles au Maréchal' (widely known a 'L'Ode à Pétain'), praising him in coming to France in her hour of need, but he soon altered his stance. The École de l'Uriage provides another striking example: initially set up to train the next generation of Vichy intellectuals and officials, its teachers and students eventually abandoned their pro-Vichy and pro-Pétain stance, and many of its members, including the philosopher Emmanuel Mounier, joined the Resistance. Initially these Catholic radicals, centred round the journal *Esprit*, had interpreted the military defeat as a judgement of the Third Republic and its rampant individualism,[26] but eventually they allied themselves with intellectuals who represented the Republican, secular tradition. Most dramatically, the poet Claude Roy, active in *L'Action française* before the war and a contributor to *Je suis partout* until 1941, became quickly disenchanted with Vichy and joined the Resistance and the French Communist Party.[27]

This is not to suggest that the people associated with the fascist cause were always politically straightforward. Communism could have served their anti-democratic and anti-bourgeois stance sentiments well, and some of them had flirted with communism in the past.[28] Many fascist intellectuals hankered after the idea of a strong and decisive leader, which they could find in Stalin as much as Hitler. Exalted by the idea of the subordination of individuals to a single leader and by their integration within a collective entity, they were fascinated by the large rallies which again took place in Russia as well as in Germany. Even Robert Brasillach, an ardent fascist, wrote openly that he understood the appeal of communism, and towards the latter part of the war Drieu la Rochelle, by now fully aware of the possible defeat of Germany, hoped for the surge and total victory of the Russian army. Although their attitude towards communism might have been at times ambiguous, most remained steadfastly anti-democratic and loyal to Nazi Germany at least until its defeat became imminent.

It was, at the time and retrospectively, relatively straightforward to identify those who promoted the doctrine of collaborationism during the war. Some had taken a pro-Nazi or fascist stance before the war broke out: on the eve of the war Brasillach's *Les Sept Couleurs*,[29] Drieu la Rochelle's *Gilles* and Céline's *Bagatelles pour un massacre* and *L'École des cadavres* all expressed admiration for fascism, with the latter being particularly anti-Semitic. At the beginning of Vichy, several books came out praising Pétain, including Georges Suarez's *Le Maréchal Pétain* and his *Pétain ou la démocratie? Il faut choisir*. Charles Maurras' *La Seule France* and Henri Massis' *Les Idées restent* reiterated their anti-parliamentarian position, whereas Lucien Rebatet's *Les Décombres* and Céline's *Les Beaux Draps* were clearly fascist and anti-Semitic works. Collaborationist intellectuals were given airtime to express their views, and they were able to publish books or articles in newspapers and magazines.[30] In the context of paper shortage, collaborationist publications were not subjected to the same restrictions as others.[31] As mentioned earlier, their newspapers or journals often received financial support from the authorities or various pro-German organizations: the Ministry of Information and the Cercle européen (to which we will return later) both provided financial assistance to Châteaubriant's *La Gerbe*. The Propaganda-Abteilung helped collaborationist authors by including their names and works in its list of recommended authors and books.

Officially, most publishing houses remained neutral, although a few, such as Denoël, Grasset and Mercure de France, clearly promoted collaborationism and were known for doing so. This was a time when the owners still put their personal stamp on their publishing houses and cultivated personal relationships with their authors. Both Robert Denoël and Bernard Grasset were openly supportive of Nazi Germany and they made sure that their companies (Denoël and Grasset) published collaborationist material by Céline, Rebatet and Drieu la Rochelle. While not as ideologically committed, most other publishing houses were equally willing to publish collaborationist material and generally complied with German demands. Indeed, they also actively cooperated with the German authorities: besides Denoël and Grasset, twelve other publishing houses, including Gallimard, cooperated with the Propaganda-Abteiluing to bring out luxurious editions of collaborationist writers. Likewise, key publishers like Plon cooperated with l'Institut Allemand to translate German books of the 'liste Matthieu'.[32] In some cases it is appropriate to talk about coerced cooperation. Gallimard in particular was under pressure to comply with German demands; it had a reputation of publishing books by left-wing authors and was at the beginning of the war under threat of closure. In this context Gaston Gallimard accepted the controversial appointment of Drieu la Rochelle at the helm of *La Nouvelle Revue française*.[33]

Most overtly collaborationist newspapers and journals were based in the occupied zone with notable exceptions such as *Candide* (Clermont-Ferrand), *Gringoire* (Marseille) and *Action française* (Lyon). As mentioned before, the Germans controlled large daily newspapers like *Paris-soir*, *Le Matin* and *Le Petit Parisien*, though collaborationist intellectuals also wrote for smaller politico-literary journals. Robert Brasillach and Lucien Rebatet wrote for the pro-German weekly *Je suis partout*, whereas Alphonse de Châteaubriant and Abel Bonnard published in the equally partisan *La Gerbe*. Some of the collaborationist intellectuals managed to occupy positions as gatekeepers by holding key editorial positions in established journals: Drieu la Rochelle, with the help of the German ambassador, took over from Jean Paulhan as editor of the prestigious *La Nouvelle Revue française*; Georges Suarez took the helm of *Aujourd'hui* after its founder Henri Jeanson refused to comply with German demands;

and Marcel Déat became editor of a revamped *L'Oeuvre*. Others launched new journals: in 1940 de Châteaubriant started the politico-literary weekly *La Gerbe* with the financial assistance of the German embassy, in the same year Jean Luchaire founded *Les Nouveaux Temps*; and in 1943 Brasillach became editor of *La Chronique de Paris* after stepping down from *Je suis partout*.

Some of the collaborationist writings might have helped the occupying forces or Vichy by altering the views of the French people. This was more likely to be the case for writers who published in major newspapers such as *Le Matin* or for well-known novelists who could count on a large readership: Rebatet, for instance, wrote for the daily *Le Petit Parisien*, of which up to 500,000 copies appeared daily, for *Je suis partout*, of which at some point more than 200,000 copies were sold, and for *La Gerbe*, with a circulation of 140,000 copies, and his virulent anti-Semitic novel *Les Décombres* sold 65,000 copies in the occupied zone.[34] It might have been less obvious for those writers who were not so well known or who wrote for more specialist magazines like *Comoedia* which sold not more than 50,000 copies or *La Nouvelle Revue française* with a circulation at some point as low as 5,000. What is clearer, however, is that well-known collaborationist writers were paid handsomely, especially if they wrote for the popular press. Among those who remunerated their star authors particularly well was, for instance, the collaborationist and overtly anti-Semitic magazine *Gringoire*, now based in the occupied zone and with a circulation of more than 300,000 copies more than capable of rewarding its celebrity contributors.[35] As we shall see in the next chapter, evidence of high payments would play a crucial part in the prosecution of collaborationist intellectuals at the end of the war as they were seen as evidence of a corrupted soul and lack of authenticity.

Besides writing and editing, collaborationist writers also exhibited their support for Nazi Germany or Vichy in other ways. They socialized with Germans and attended social events organized by the occupiers, something which was publicized in daily newspapers and used by Nazi Germany for propaganda purposes. Their attendance legitimized the German presence and provided an air of normality. When Céline attended the opening of the Institut des questions juives in Paris in May 1941 he gave credibility to an institution dedicated to presenting a warped view on the Jewish people. Particularly symbolic was the acceptance by seven collaborationist writers to the European writers' congress in Weimar in the autumn of 1941. The invitation came from Goebbels himself; Robert Brasillach, Abel Bonnard, Jacques Chardonne, Drieu la Rochelle, André Fraigneau,

Marcel Jouhandeau and Ramon Fernandez were among the French attendees and founded the European Writer's Union. On their return a reception at the German embassy followed, attended by Parisian journalists who duly reported the 'fruitful' visit and the enthusiasm of those who attended the Congress. The following year a similar congress was organized, with Drieu, Chardonne and Fraigneau again among the attendees.

Equally significant was the Groupe Collaboration, set up in the autumn of 1940 by Alphonse de Châteaubriant with the aim to establish 'cultural collaboration' between Germany and France. The Groupe Collaboration was close to l'Institut allemand and they organized conferences together. From the end of 1941 onwards, the Groupe Collaboration also operated in the occupied zone, and this provided a useful outpost for l'Institut Allemand. Finally, there was also the Comité d'honneur du cercle européen, a similar organization to the Groupe Collaboration. It aimed at facilitating 'European cooperation' and brought together people in business and intellectuals.

As we shall discuss in the next chapter, by mid-1944, any war-time membership of these organizations or any attendance at their social events (or indeed at conferences or meetings sponsored by them) could be held against writers, and many intellectuals from a wide political spectrum were open to this accusation. When interrogated in 1945 Otto Abetz commented on the willingness of non-collaborationist writers to attend receptions at the embassy, he was obviously trying to portray his own role during the war in a positive light, but there was also an element of truth in his version of the events, partly because the intellectual circles were inevitably intertwined and partly because of the ambiguous position of some of the German officials and the people surrounding them. For instance, both Gerhard Heller, who was in charge of the literary censor at the Propaganda Staffel, and Karl Epting, the director of the Institut Allemand, were on surprisingly good terms with a wide range of writers, some of whom were not committed to collaboration.[36] On the whole, though, they were more likely to form closer friendships with collaborationist intellectuals, which occasionally led them to intervene on behalf of detained Jews or Resistance fighters. A close friend of the collaborationist author Marcel Chardonneau, Gerhard Heller from the Propaganda-Staffel secured the release of Chardonneau's son who had been detained because of Resistance activities. Suzanne Abetz, the French wife of the German ambassador, intervened personally to secure the release of Maurice Goudeket, Colette's Jewish husband.

37

Sacha Guitry and Arlette managed to persuade Otto Abetz to release the Jewish playwright Tristan Bernard.[37]

Intellectuals, non-collaboration and Resistance

In the beginning of the occupation, organized resistance against the occupier, including that by intellectuals, consisted of various small groups which operated relatively independently and in an amateurish manner. One of the first resistance organizations by intellectuals was the réseau du Musée de l'Homme, also known as the RMH, initiated in the summer of 1940 by a group of scholars mainly in the area of ethnology and sociology. Another example of such an organization, even less professional and certainly more marginal in the history of the resistance, was Socialisme et liberté. It was led by Jean-Paul Sartre and Simone de Beauvoir and it was founded in early 1941, shortly after Sartre's release from a German prisoner-of-war camp. Both organizations were short-lived: key members of the RMH were arrested in early 1941, whereas Sartre and Co dismantled their organization after a couple of months for fear of being caught. The crucial difference for the organized resistance against Germany came with the German assault on Russia in June 1941 which broke the non-aggression pact between Hitler and Stalin. This brought Russia into the war and, crucially, activated the French Communist Party. The Communist Party was an organized and disciplined outfit, which subsequently played a pivotal role in coordinating the different groups and building up a central structure. The Resistance, as it became known, was this central unit. The Communists were also key players in the formation of the Comité national des écrivains, the clandestine organization of writers (of which more later). Crucially, the Communists also had an important say in the recruitment by the Resistance. For instance, they were sceptical of Sartre's political credentials, and this partly explains why he did not join the movement before 1943.

Among those intellectuals who did not promote collaborationism, it was difficult, at the time and subsequently, to identify those who compromised themselves through their writings. During the war, non-collaborationist writers expressed different, even opposing, views as to what was regarded as permissible. Some writers took the position that any form of official publication during the German occupation and Vichy was an act of collaboration. Different reasons were given: some intellectuals argued that the German or Vichy censor would compromise writing, whereas others like Jean Guéhenno[38] felt that any form of cultural participation would legitimize the regime, providing a sense of normality. They pointed out that the German occupiers wanted to create this false illusion of normality so that writing in official outlets assisted the occupiers precisely as they intended. This is not to say that this act of self-censorship was without its own compromises. Having now to rely exclusively on other sources of income, many intellectuals including Jean Guéhenno held full-time teaching posts which required taking the oath to Pétain and being subjected to some monitoring.[39] Nor is it the case that everybody who decided to abstain from writing in legitimate outlets did so out of conviction. Some Jewish intellectuals, like Benda, were concerned about their safety and withdrew from public life. Even if they wanted to publish, they found it difficult to find a willing publisher and to bypass the censor.

More was at stake, however: the act of silence acquired a special significance at the time. Already in June 1940, it occupied a central place in *La Nouvelle Revue française*: in the last issue under his directorship Jean Paulhan wrote 'L'Espoir et le silence' in which he stressed the dignity and power of silence in the face of the aggressor.[40] Soon, in everyday life, the German occupation would magnify the political significance of silence: people were anxious not to be seen as interacting too much with the occupier, and this non-engagement became a symbolic act of rebellion.[41] It is indicative that silence played such a central role in Vercors' famous Resistance novel *Le Silence de la mer*[42] which appeared in 1942 and in which two members of a French household – an older man and his niece – refuse to speak to their self-imposed lodger, a German officer. If in this clandestine novel silence was a symbolic act of non-compliance, it mirrored the significance of silence in reality: members of the Resistance had to be discreet so as not to be caught, and it was crucial for them not to reveal any information when caught and interrogated by the Germans. Silence became associated with not succumbing under torture; it was essential to the survival of the Resistance and acquired a heroic status. Resistance writers knew about the dangers and the need for secrecy, not in the least because some left-wing intellectuals who were involved in early resistance movements or publications were arrested and executed. Among them were various members of the RMH (réseau du Musée de l'Homme) such as Anatole Lewitsky, and founders of the clandestine publications *L'Université libre*, *La Pensée libre* and *Les Lettres françaises* such as Jacques Decour, Georges Politzer and Jacques Solomon.

Official silence by writers was often accompanied by their clandestine publications: clandestine publications were directly associated with the act of silence as they often came with a heading or warning not to read them out loud, nor to pass them to people you cannot absolutely trust.[43] In 1942 the Catholic writer François Mauriac appealed for 'the trial of silence' and started contributing to the clandestine *Les Lettres françaises* which appeared in the occupied zone and was in the hands of the Comité national des écrivains (henceforth CNE).[44] Initially called the Front national des écrivains, the CNE was an underground organization of writers with strong ties to the French Communist Party, with as central figures party member Louis Aragon in the unoccupied zone and the more pluralistic Louis Paulhan in Paris. A relatively small organization, with at most forty members at each time, the CNE managed nevertheless to occupy an important role in the intellectual field. The first issue of *Les Lettres françaises* contained the Manifesto of the organization, condemning those who write for official outlets and explaining the rationale behind the publication. Publishing in official newspapers or magazines amounted to an act of treason. Only those in support of the occupiers are allowed to write and speak, hence the need for a clandestine journal.[45] Resistance writers often used clandestine publications to denounce collaborationist writers. In December 1941 *L'Université libre*, an early clandestine outlet, attacked the German writers who had visited the writers' congress in Berlin. Likewise, *Les Lettres françaises* regularly denounced collaborationist writers and exposed German attempts to co-opt French culture.

Even those non-collaborationist writers who decided to publish in official outlets often wrote for clandestine magazines and newspapers as well. There were many such options. Besides *Les Lettres françaises* in Paris, the CNE published *Les Étoiles* in the unoccupied zone. Several underground journals and newspapers emerged, the names of which – *Combat*, *Résistance*, *Cahiers de la libération*, *La Pensée libre*, *Franc-Tireur* and *Défense de la France* – reflected the Resistance spirit. With time, the production increased both for specialized and non-specialized outlets. Always catering for a niche market, *Les Lettres françaises* distributed 4,000 copies in 1943 but managed fourfold that figure one year later. In 1944 Camus' *Combat* sold 250,000 copies fortnightly. Clandestine publishing houses were set up, with Louis Aragon behind both *La Bibliothèque française* and *Hier et aujourd'hui*. The largest and most influential clandestine publishing company was *Les Éditions de minuit*, launched in Paris early in 1941 by Jean Bruller and Pierre de Lescure. The first novel, Vercors'

Le Silence de la mer, appeared in February 1942, and by the end of the war *Les Éditions de minuit* had published twenty-five books, including works by significant authors like Paul Éluard, François Mauriac and Aragon.[46] On average *Les Éditions de minuit* printed 1,000 copies of each book and these were distributed from person to person. Some books published by *Les Éditions de minuit* arrived in England and the United States. *Le Silence de la mer* was reprinted in London and the copies were sent back to France.[47] Sometimes the books that arrived in London were used for propaganda purposes, broadcasted to the French public by the BBC. These BBC adaptations were possibly less dramatic than the millions of copies of Éluard's moving poem *Liberté* which were dropped by the Royal Air Force on French soil, but the symbols were similar, linking French literary prowess to the Allied forces.

One of the central themes in clandestine Resistance writings concerns the French cultural patrimonium. French literature in particular was invariably portrayed as encapsulating the spirit and essence of the French people. It was depicted as the driving force of French Resistance, but was also in grave danger of being annihilated. In the next chapters, it will become clear that, after the liberation, Sartre would continue and further elaborate on this theme of French literature encapsulating the nation. But what is important to note is that this complex portrayal of French literature – in terms of essence, strength and fragility – was already central to Resistance writings, as exemplified, again, in *Le Silence de la mer*. Most of the action in this quintessential Resistance novel takes place in the main sitting room which also acts as a library where the uncle and niece read. The well-meaning German officer repeatedly stresses how much he respects the vast cultural heritage of France, respectfully referring to and consulting the books in the shelves. Once this 'good German' visits Paris, however, he becomes aware of the real motives of his German colleagues who are bent on destroying French culture in its entirety. No longer willing to be complicit in this cunning, pernicious plan, he decides to leave this comfortable setting and heads for the Eastern Front, fully aware of the dangers this entails.

The plot of the novel gives some indication of how, for a significant number of Resistance writers, French literature was intertwined with the survival of the nation, and the act of writing was a key weapon against the German occupation. It is worth mentioning that few Resistance writers were involved in the armed Resistance, opting for literary Resistance only. Hence a predilection for a view that sees Resistance writings, not merely symbolically, but on a par with armed Resistance. Just as collaborationist intellectuals causally linked 'degenerate' literature with weak national morale and lack of military prowess, clandestine publications emphasized the political significance of literature, especially in the circumstances of the war and the occupation. They portrayed their own writings as genuine and effective acts of resistance while conversely depicting collaborationist writings as no less than acts of treason. Not only did they regularly denounce collaborationists for their writings and for consorting with the enemy, but they would also, especially in the latter stages of the war, discuss at length the legal (and other) measures that might become available in a future liberated France to punish collaborationist writers.

It goes without saying that writers who on the whole restricted themselves to clandestine publications tended to be known for certain as Resistance intellectuals only to a limited circle of like-minded, often clandestine, writers. For security reasons, the articles in clandestine publications were anonymous or signed with a pseudonym. The wider public knew very little about Resistance publications, let alone anything about the precise identity of their authors, until the end of the war. With the additional London copies of *Le Silence de la mer*, Vercors had obtained a minor cult status among the literati with Resistance sympathies, but even he did not reach a broader audience. Ironically, during the war clandestine Resistance writers became known as such once collaborationist intellectuals 'outed' or attacked them. Aragon's political leanings were widely known, but it was Drieu la Rochelle's virulent attacks on him, rather than his underground writings, that initially positioned him as a Resistance hero. It is only at a later stage, when it was safe to do so, that the clandestine publications could be showcased as proof of one's Resistance credentials.

If some writers were reluctant to publish in official outlets and had the opportunity to publish unofficially, in practice the act of withdrawing from official publishing was not always as straightforward. Writers were sometimes entangled in networks that crossed political divides, leading to conflicting motivations and contradictory choices. Those intellectuals who preferred not to write in official reviews themselves did not necessarily resist aiding the publications by others, even in compromised outlets. The most intriguing case concerns Jean Paulhan. After stepping down as chief-editor of *La Nouvelle Revue française*, he encouraged writers to contribute to the journal and generally assisted his successor, Drieu la Rochelle,[48] even when it became apparent that the latter was taking the journal in an unequivocally pro-German direction. This is all the more remarkable given Paulhan's political orientation and his contributions at the same time to the clandestine *Les Lettres françaises*.

Many non-collaborationists continued to write for official publications. Generally, publishing in outlets that appeared in the unoccupied zone seemed to be regarded as more acceptable, just as writing for Radio-Vichy was seen as more palatable than for Radio-Paris. If so many decided to write for non-clandestine publications, the justification for doing so varied. Some provided an instrumental justification: they had no other financial means or, more controversially, unlike say Gide and Duhamel, they still had to make their name and were therefore not in a position to abstain from writing. Some asserted that writing was tied up with their identity and was innocuous enough to be continued.[49] Others, however, presented a political argument, for instance expressing the view that any writing, as long as it did not promote Nazi or Vichy principles, was an expression of the French spirit and therefore commendable.[50] Writing, as mentioned earlier, was widely seen as an act of defiance: France might have lost the war but fought on in other ways. A significant number of writers went even further, arguing that writing could be used to convey political messages, albeit in a coded manner to defy the censor. These cryptic messages would galvanize support for the Resistance. Some forms of writing were more suited to this than others: poetry in particular seemed to be well suited. The *poésie de contrebande* bypassed the German censor, appearing in journals such as *Poésie*, *Confluences* and *Fontaine*.

In an effort to convince the doubters, many writers at the end of the war attempted to show the hidden political message of their wartime writings, whether in the form of literature, plays, poetry or journalism. Take, for instance, Sartre, who combined clandestine writings with the publication of 'official' material vetted by the occupier. This official material included *L'Être et le néant*, published in 1943 and read at the time by only a small group of people; it also included two plays that reached a larger audience. After the war, he presented his play *Les Mouches*,[51] staged in 1943 in Paris, as a thinly disguised critique of the occupation that urged French people to stand up against the German occupying force. Such revisiting of previous writings was not without problems: if the German censorship had not identified the political message in this way or at least not seen it as a sufficient threat, then the question arises how clear it would have been to readers or viewers at the time and what would have been its effectiveness altogether. In the play Orestes is involved in a double murder to avenge his father, something which, Sartre subsequently argued, showed, at some level, that it was right for French people to assassinate German soldiers.[52] But in the play the citizens of Argos refuse to condone his actions, so it would be equally plausible to conceive of this work as a condemnation of anti-German actions. Sartre's other wartime play, *Huis clos*,[53] depicts three people, who are dead, but who are faced with each other's company *ad infinitum*. Again, Sartre later depicted the play as forcing people to recognize that they need to resist German occupation, but it is very difficult to see how this quintessentially existentialist play could be conceived in such distinctly political terms. Very few critics did so at the time.

Given the constraints at the time, plays with the most transparent political message tended to be pro-German or pro-Vichy. They did not have to use coded messages to avoid the censor. The other playwrights faced a more difficult task, attempting to convey a message while bypassing the censor. Sometimes the same play was interpreted very differently by commentators with opposing political perspectives. Claude Vermorel's *Jeanne avec nous*, staged in 1942, loosely based on the story of Joan of Arc, was seen by Rebatet as an ode to fascism, but de Beauvoir thought at the time that it was very difficult not to see it as unequivocally anti-German and anti-Vichy. On other occasions, the meaning of a 'Resistance' play was only transparent to the initiated; that is, to those in the know, who were likely to be part of the author's circle. Only to this section of the audience, which had a more intimate knowledge of the author and his intentions, did the play appear like an unequivocal critique of the occupation. To the others, various interpretations were available.

Non-collaborationist authors who decided to write 'officially' faced a variety of ethical dilemmas. The non-collaborationist writers who published openly had to navigate carefully especially when dealing with the press. When Simone de Beauvoir's *L'Invitée*[54] was shortlisted for the Prix Goncourt, Sartre conveyed that the CNE did not object as long as she did not give an interview to the press or write an article about it.[55] Non-collaborationist writers had to be mindful about where to publish, not only avoiding collaborationist journals or reviews, like *Je suis partout* or *Les Cahiers franco-allemands,* but also more subtle outlets such as the weekly literary review *Comoedia* which was based in the occupied zone and which published material by collaborationist authors such as Jouhandeau and Chardonne. Indeed, Sartre was later criticized for publishing a piece on Moby Dick in the first issue of *Comoedia* under the occupation, but he was not the only non-collaborationist author to contribute to the journal: Éluard, Desnos and Paulhan had also published in it. Edited by René Delange, *Comoedia* committed itself to 'French–German collaboration' on a cultural level, though in practice it operated on a pluralistic basis. In addition, writers had to be careful because the tenor of a journal could change dramatically with the appointment of a new editor. The most obvious example is the change in *La Nouvelle Revue française* once Drieu la Rochelle took up the position of editor. He managed at first to persuade Gide, Valéry and Éluard to publish in his journal, but soon they distanced themselves from it and Drieu faced an uphill struggle finding high-calibre contributors. The journal became known as 'NRBoche' with pro-Nazi contributors such as Abel Bonnard, Lucien Combelle, Bernard Faÿ and Ramon Fernandez.[56] Within the political minefield of the occupation, Drieu la Rochelle found it difficult to steer the journal: even the revamping of an earlier apolitical stance – Gide's art for art's sake – was seen as complying with German strategies. Without quality names and increasingly pro-German connotations, interest in the journal dropped: whereas in 1941 it still had a circulation of 11,000 copies, it was down to 5,000 in early 1943 and in June of that year Drieu was forced to abandon the project.[57]

The ethical dilemmas went even further, however. Even if non-collaborationist writers managed to avoid publishing in tainted journals, their writings often came out with publishing houses which also published pro-fascist or at least pro-collaborationist material. Aragon, Sartre and Camus published with Gallimard alongside, for instance, Drieu la Rochelle. Numerous other compromises were made, partly because the censor curtailed what could be written. Mindful of the German obsession with expelling any Jewish traces from writing, Camus removed references to Kafka from his *Le Mythe de Sisyphe* so that the latter could be published.[58] Anxious to save *Annales d'histoire sociale*, Lucien Febvre controversially persuaded his Jewish colleague Marc Bloch to allow the removal of his name from the journal. By this time Bloch had already lost his post at the Sorbonne and had moved to the unoccupied zone, from which he continued to write for the *Annales* under a pseudonym.[59] The removal of Jewish references was not limited to the text itself. In 1943 Sartre's play *Les Mouches* was performed in what used to be called the Théâtre Sarah Bernhardt but had now been rebranded as the Théâtre de la Cité; its director was on very good terms with the occupiers.

The latter example already gives some indication of how the circles of collaborationist and non-collaborationist intellectuals intersected. Regardless of their political orientation, intellectuals tended to come from similar backgrounds and had gone through similar educational establishments such as the École normale. Indeed, some non-collaborationist intellectuals continued to engage with political opponents because of old ties. Paulhan and Malraux continued their friendship with Drieu la Rochelle, who in 1943 even became a god-father to one of Malraux's children. Drieu la Rochelle and Paulhan both worked at Gallimard, and in 1941 Drieu helped with the release of Paulhan after he was arrested for his connections to the Musée de l'Homme. Paulhan continued his friendship with Marcel Jouhandeau, and Marguerite Duras remained a close friend of Ramon Fernandez.[60] Occasionally Resistance intellectuals used their contacts or positions to infiltrate collaborationist circles: Robert Desnos continued to write for *Aujourd'hui* even after the arrest of its founding editor Henri Jeanson, from which point the journal took a distinctly collaboration-ist line; Desnos passed on useful information to the Resistance group Agir in which he was heavily involved.[61]

Concluding comments

So far we have provided a sketch of the complex socio-political situ-ation in France between 1940 and 1944 and how this affected the cultural and intellectual scene at the time. In this broad picture, five points are worth emphasizing, partly because they are important for what happened subsequently.

Firstly, under Vichy and the German occupation the intellectual arena was reshaped considerably. This restructuring took place espe-cially in the occupied zone, but also in the South. It affected the public intellectual arena as well as the intra-intellectual arena. There was not only the closure of several publishing houses, newspapers and maga-zines, but also the 'hostile takeover' of many others, accompanied by the swift arrival of new editors, willing to toe the new party line or at least accommodating to the new regime. In the occupied zone the German censor of cultural and intellectual production, as well as the numerous translations and the promoting of German or pro-German material, led to a radical reshaping, and to a certain extent homogeni-zation, of the official intellectual scene. Moreover, Jewish and 'anti-German' writers were no longer able to publish or occupy editorial or ownership positions. Some of them emigrated when they still could; the lives of those who remained in France would soon be in danger.

Secondly, initially few intellectuals took a clear stance against Vichy. In this respect, they were not very different from the wider French public, which was in the early stages positively disposed towards Vichy and Pétain. The lack of critical distance *vis-à-vis* Vichy at the time can be explained in a variety of ways. The trauma of the First World War played a role; many wanted to avoid the repeat of a massacre on a similar scale and were therefore willing to accept, however grudgingly in some cases, the idea of an armistice. We should also not forget that in the course of the 1930s dissatisfaction had already built up with the Third Republic, together with a widespread belief that democracy is unlikely to provide a stable, secure government. Crucially this belief was not limited to the political right, and many bought the Vichy ideology that its government was an opportunity for a new beginning, free from what was perceived as the indecisiveness and divisiveness within the Third Republic.[62] Another factor explaining the relative popularity of Vichy in the earlier stages lies in the lack of clarity as to what the new regime would entail. Only later, when the Vichy policies came into force and German demands increased, did the general public – and the intellectuals – take a more critical distance. It is at that point that the opposition between collaborationist and Resistance intellectuals came to the fore. At the end of the war, some writers would brush over this earlier period of indecision and passive acceptance, portraying 1940 as a watershed moment which triggered off their political engagement or intensified their already existing commitment. In the context of the purge, however, this earlier period came to haunt some writers, who were now at risk of being blacklisted or even prosecuted just for been mildly supportive of Vichy in the early stages. This would eventually undermine the credibility of a section of the literary and intellectual establishment, a factor which, as we shall see later, helped Sartre's rise.

Thirdly, many collaborationist intellectuals sided with the official Vichy line, helping to articulate the trauma of the unexpected, rapid defeat at the hands of the Germans. Like Pétain they blamed the alleged 'degeneracy' of the Third Republic, but rather than accusing the politicians of the Popular Front, they focused their attention on the limited circle of intellectuals, targeting socialist writers or 'irresponsible' exponents of 'l'art pour l'art'. Pétainist intellectuals tended to moralize, whereas pro-fascist writers often attacked the politicized writings on the left. Particularly striking is this process of translation: that is, turning a broader societal issue at the time – the predicament of the war and the occupation – into one that concerned only a limited group of writers. This translation was tied to the notion of responsibility, with collaborationist intellectuals placing the blame squarely on other intellectuals. Writing in clandestine publications, Resistance intellectuals quickly retaliated, accusing collaborationist intellectuals of treason and holding them responsible for their writings and for other compromising activities. By doing so, they too reduced the broader issue of the war into a narrower dispute among intellectuals. Both camps – collaborationist and Resistance intellectuals – tended to emphasize the significance of writings within the wider political and military context. Resistance writers went even further by depicting French literature as the essence of the nation – the way in which it was able to fight on. Attributing power to intellectual production would reach a climax during the subsequent purge of collaborationist intellectuals, in some cases with devastating consequences. We shall discuss in the next chapter how, during the purge, the notion of responsibility, now used against collaborationist intellectuals, acquired an unprecedented centrality in the cultural sphere, a shift into which Sartre tapped.

Fourthly, those intellectuals who were not supportive of Vichy or Nazi Germany, and especially those who were hostile to the occupation, faced difficult choices which they did not have to make before the war broke out. Shall I write in official outlets? If not, what other compromises will I have to make to stay afloat financially? If so, where shall I publish? Given the censor, how can I convey what I want to say? These are just some of the decisions which these writers had to make on a regular basis. This peculiar context – for most of the individuals were involved in an unprecedented situation – made them particularly sensitive to the political dimensions of writing and to the elements of choice and responsibility involved in their profession. It also led to a heightened sensitivity to the performativity of writing: no longer merely the material trace of something ethereal, writing was now seen unequivocally as an act which *does* something: writers became conscious of how their writings positioned them, refuting or justifying the occupation, and this by the mere fact of being published at all, by being published in a particular outlet or by some subtle innuendo. For Resistance intellectuals, this preoccupation with performativity even extended to the notion of silence which soon acquired heroic connotations. It became associated with purity, strength and resilience against the occupying forces. The cult of official silence accompanied the publication of clandestine publications as they were seen as the only ones allowing for pure, untainted and uncensored expression. We shall see in the next couple of chapters that, with the end of the occupation, this view changed. While the performative view of writing would persist, silence would no longer be portrayed quite as vividly in heroic terms. Its exact opposite – the act of speaking out – would become highly valued. Sartre would contribute to bringing about this transformation, while also benefiting from it.

Fifthly, while politics might have played a significant role in their writings, remarkably few of the collaborationist intellectuals operated at the centre of the political life of Vichy. Very few influenced Vichy politics, with the exception possibly of Marcel Déat who combined his journalistic work at *L'Oeuvre* first with attempts to unite collaborationist parties under one umbrella and later on in the war with a ministerial position under Laval. Even he was generally disliked and shunned by the other Vichy politicians. Conservative in spirit, Vichy was naturally sceptical of intellectuals and they played little role there, with most collaborationist intellectuals congregating in Paris where they held various editorial and journalistic positions. On the other side, very few of the Resistance intellectuals were involved in the military Resistance, concentrating their efforts instead on writing and distributing clandestine publications. So on both sides of the political spectrum, the actions of intellectuals were limited to writing. While it is true that publications *can* affect the morale and influence people's views and actions, there is no strong evidence in the case of France that either group of writers – collaborationist or Resistance – actually had a significant effect on the course of events. This is worth mentioning, not only because both camps put so much emphasis on the political efficacy or responsibility of the author, but also because those same themes resurfaced at the end of the war and played a crucial role in the way in which the trauma of the war became articulated.

— 2 —

THE PURGE OF
COLLABORATIONIST
INTELLECTUALS

The previous chapter depicted the intellectual landscape in France during the occupation. It showed how from mid-1940 until mid-1944 collaborationist intellectuals had the upper hand in a variety of ways. They were able to speak and write freely, and they controlled the means of symbolic production. They managed to occupy major editorial positions, exemplified by Pierre Drieu la Rochelle's appointment as chief editor of the prestigious *La Nouvelle Revue française* in 1940.[1] Also, in 1940 the Germans put in place a series of measures that curtailed intellectual production. For instance, the Propaganda Staffel stipulated that publications which undermined German interests would be forbidden; and the use, sale or distribution of any book on the infamous Otto list would be banned.[2] Many anti-collaborationist intellectuals were forced underground, writing in Resistance publications like *Cahiers du Sud*, *Les Lettres françaises* and *Combat*. Alternatively, they had to express their ideas in a disguised manner to bypass the censorship.[3]

By the summer of 1944, however, the tables were turned. With the liberation, the censorship was lifted and anti-collaborationist authors used their radically improved resources and their considerable wartime credentials to attack and discredit collaborationist intellectuals, in some cases hoping to bar them from the profession. As in other countries that had been occupied by Germany, the prosecution of collaborators operated along both official and non-official lines: while the French provisional government made a concerted effort to instal an official purge and to follow correct procedures, it could not halt the *épuration sauvage* – the many *ad hoc* 'tribunals' and executions that took place around the country.[4] Like other formerly occupied West European countries at the time of the liberation,

France managed to impose a legal route to deal with its collaborators, resulting in a rapid decline of summary executions. What was distinctive about France, however, was that the purge also included legal procedures against a significant number of authors and editors. In no other country at the end of the war were intellectuals targeted as they were in France. As a group they were over-represented; some collaborationist writers would end up serving harsh sentences and a few were even executed.[5] We will now turn to this period of prosecution – and indeed at times persecution – of collaborationist intellectuals; these events changed the intellectual landscape in a variety of ways, which eventually helped to propel Sartre and existentialism.

The trials of writers were intertwined with intense power struggles within the intellectual sphere: non-collaborationist intellectuals played a crucial role in the trials of collaborationist intellectuals, feeding arguments and meta-arguments to the prosecution, while presenting a distinctive narrative of the Vichy years and the role of the writer in that context. This was one of the avenues that anti-collaborationist intellectuals used against their collaborationist counterparts. In addition, anti-collaborationist intellectuals also attempted to 'out' collaborationist intellectuals, hoping to bar them from publishing. Chronologically these attempts at naming and shaming pre-dated the formal procedures. So it makes sense to turn to them first before elaborating on the trials.

Antecedents and developments of the professional purge

The previous chapter explained that, as early as 1941, Resistance writers formed the Comité national des écrivains, a clandestine organization of anti-fascist authors, henceforth referred to as CNE. This group developed initially out of the Front national des écrivains which was controlled by the French Communist Party (PCF). With key members such as Jacques Decour and Louis Aragon, the CNE maintained a close link with the PCF but it also included writers such as Jean-Paul Sartre who were not members of the PCF. As mentioned earlier, the CNE published an underground journal *Les Lettres françaises*, which contained political as well as literary essays, and in which, crucially, collaborationist authors were denounced on a regular basis. From the very beginning, the journal not only identified these authors but also argued that they should ultimately be punished for their writings. The November 1943 issue of *Les Lettres françaises* proposed that, after the liberation, a committee of writers and legal experts investigate the wartime efforts of various writers, plus allocate appropriate sanctions and advise on court cases.

When the liberation came, the question arose of how to put a system of punishment into practice. Legal proceedings would be one course of action, but it was clear that this would only affect a small number of authors. In addition, the CNE decided to hit collaborationists where it hurt most by making it difficult, if not impossible, for them to publish; and the members of the CNE decided that, by virtue of their star quality and Resistance credentials, they, as a collective body, had enough clout to enforce this. It is in this context that the first non-clandestine issue of *Les Lettres françaises* of 9 September 1944 published a statement in which the CNE declared that its members would refuse to publish for any newspaper, magazine or edited collection that published the writings of collaborators. With an uncanny resemblance to the purging mentality underlying the Otto list, the CNE made available a list of collaborationist authors, among whom were the names of explicitly fascist or pro-Vichy authors such as Robert Brasillach, Louis-Ferdinand Céline and Pierre Drieu la Rochelle. Some of them would also be prosecuted at a later stage; others would not. The list was extended to include 94 authors or editors. A final list, published on 21 October 1944, included no fewer than 158 names, some of whom had clearly published openly fascist material, but others were not as easily classifiable.[6] Very soon, some prominent intellectuals spoke out against the list, pointing out that it included relatively innocent authors, or alternatively pleading that people, especially young people, should be allowed to make mistakes. Others argued that the list would be ineffective, because the authors who signed up did not have sufficient power or authority over the publishers, who were likely to resume the publishing of the 'blacklisted' authors. Those who signed the list would, then, have to give up their principles and publish in the 'tainted' outlets or end up being victims of their own blacklist. As it happened, those sceptics were right and very soon the blacklisted authors were able to publish.

The CNE was also meant to target publishers who were responsible for publishing fascist material, and a special commission for the purge of publishing was set up in February 1945.[7] This commission investigated various publishing houses but with little effect. Targeting publishers turned out to be more difficult than punishing authors, not least because pro-Nazi and Resistance authors sometimes shared the same publisher.[8] This was the case for Gallimard, which published Camus, Sartre and Aragon, but had also continued to publish *La Nouvelle Revue française* under Drieu la Rochelle. Several authors with Resistance credentials, including Sartre, came to Gaston Gallimard's rescue.[9] Of all major publishing houses, only Grasset was found guilty by this committee, possibly because of Bernard Grasset's own avowed pro-Nazi sympathies.[10] At the end of the war, therefore, several publishers were indebted to members of the CNE for protecting them against further reprisals for collaboration, and this put the intellectuals in an unusually powerful position *vis-à-vis* their publisher. As we shall discuss later, this partly explains Gaston Gallimard's willingness in 1945 to help launch Sartre's journal *Les Temps modernes* which, although ostensibly pluralistic, became an important outlet for the popularization of existentialist philosophy.

While the purge caught the public eye because of the major court cases, it is also worth mentioning two decrees which affected many publication outlets and writers. The decree of 30 September 1944 banned newspapers or periodicals which had emerged during the occupation or which had continued to appear two weeks after the armistice or two weeks after Nazi Germany moved into Vichy in November 1942. In addition, it suspended any newspapers or periodicals published by individuals who were being prosecuted for their wartime activities. The decree set stringent conditions: newspapers or periodicals that showed 'weak patriotism' or insufficient independence towards the enemy could be banned. In these unique circumstances, some newspapers and periodicals managed to survive the war unscathed (*Le Figaro, Le Populaire, L'Humanité*) but others did not. A vacuum was created in which new newspapers and periodicals could emerge, some of which had Resistance credentials (*Combat, Franc-tireur, Libération, Défense de la France*). Indeed, several previously clandestine publications became 'official', whereas others positioned themselves in line with the Resistance spirit. It is in this distinctive context that Sartre and his colleagues would launch *Les Temps modernes*, which, as we shall see later, clearly positioned itself in line with the Resistance spirit.

The decree of 30 May 1945 stipulated that writers and artists who had collaborated with the enemy would be purged. The underlying idea was twofold. It was, first and foremost, regarded as morally unacceptable that writings which had helped Nazi Germany would continue providing financial resources for the person who created them. In addition, it was also considered appropriate, as a punishment, that those artists or writers who had colluded with the enemy should be banned from exhibiting or selling any of their work for a certain period. A special Comité national d'épuration des gens de lettres, auteurs et compositeurs was placed in charge to investigate various authors. It relied to a certain extent on the blacklist of the CNE, but also sent questionnaires out to various writers and artists in which they were asked to identify any actions during the war that might have compromised them. This committee was less effective, not only because it relied on self-identification but also because it decided not to investigate authors who were due to have a trial.[11]

The trials: context and complexities

After the liberation, legal procedures were launched against individuals who had collaborated with the enemy. Some writers argued that the purge was necessary to overcome the traumatic and divisive experience of the war: for instance, Jean Lacroix wrote in *Esprit* of February 1945 that French society had been torn apart to such an extent that a 'surgical operation' was needed to restore 'social health'.[12] But from the very beginning, the views about the purge varied: whereas the rhetoric of the French Communist Party was one of revenge, moderate forces saw it as a necessary evil and called for calm.[13] With time, there was less appetite to inflict heavy sentences and scepticism about the purge grew.[14] Most significant trials of collaborationist intellectuals took place in the second part of 1944 and the first part of 1945. It is important for us to have a closer look at the legal proceedings, not least because the legal arguments proposed in the trials tied in with broader intellectual debates, ranging from the status of literature to the political dimension of writing and the responsibility of the author.

The accusations against individuals ranged in their severity: some were accused of bringing about 'national indignity' whereas others were accused of committing 'treason'. While the former was a lesser crime, the latter was punishable with the death penalty. As many as fifteen intellectuals or editors were prosecuted for treason according to article 75 of the 1939 French Code pénal. The crucial section of Article 75 stipulated that a French citizen is guilty of treason and punished by death if he colludes with a foreign power to help the enemy in its hostilities towards the French nation.[15] Compared to the few who were accused of treason, substantially more people (and, indeed, more intellectuals) were prosecuted for national indignity, relying on Article 83 of the Penal Code. As time progressed – and as the mood changed – individuals were more likely to be tried for national indignity than treason, although technically, the legal case for this type of prosecution was particularly problematic for two reasons. Not only was Article 83 of the Penal Code introduced as late as August 1944 and therefore a retrospective law, but the 'crime' of national indignity did not refer to the breaching of a previous penal law as such but referred to a 'clear unpatriotic act' by which the person had 'dishonoured' himself and put shame on the French nation.[16] Consequently, what constituted 'national indignity' remained vague and was open to various interpretations. This lack of clarity meant, among other things, that what distinguished it from treason was not as clear cut.

As for the accusation of treason, the collaborationist nature of the Vichy regime created an additional problem. In most cases, the defence argued that complicity with Vichy could not constitute an act of treason because it was the legitimate government of France at the time, and indeed several foreign countries treated Vichy as such. Later critics of the purge, like Maurice Bardèche, would reiterate this legal point.[17] In several trials of collaborationist intellectuals, the defence argued that there could not be 'collusion with the enemy' given the armistice, or that at least the court case should be adjourned until Pétain and Laval's trial because the latter would provide clarity as to the legality of Vichy.[18] The prosecution counteracted by pointing out that the Provisional Government of France had already treated Vichy as illegitimate, that an armistice is a convention in which two hostile nations suspend – not cease – hostilities, or, more controversially, that undermining the very idea of France, with its emphasis on political freedom and humanitarian values, could be deemed to constitute treason.

However, legal proceedings against intellectuals added other complications. To what extent can writings or speeches constitute collusion with a foreign power and help to initiate hostilities against the nation? How can we establish the causal link between a piece of writing and its alleged consequences? How can we find out the meaning of a piece of writing? The last question may explain, firstly, why most of the legal cases tended to focus on journalistic, rather than literary, writings in so far as it was possible to make the distinction. With literary genres, there would possibly be more scope for debate as to what was really meant. Indeed, as we shall see, in their defence collaborationist intellectuals often played on the distinction between fiction and reality. Secondly, it may also explain why prosecuting lawyers would sometimes make an effort retrospectively to trace coherence in the ideas expressed by the defendant, demonstrating how his fascist ideas might have pre-dated the war.[19] Coherence or consistency, if found, could help solidify allegations regarding intent. On a related point, the question about the meaning of a text inevitably comes down to context, and collaborationist intellectuals sometimes argued that reading out in court snippets of their work, as the prosecution did, was unfair because they were taken out of context.[20] They only made sense within the broader context of the work from which they were lifted or of the whole *oeuvre*.

Among the most publicized trials involving intellectuals were those of Georges Suarez, Henri Béraud, Charles Maurras and Robert Brasillach. Of the four, Suarez was probably the least eminent but his trial received considerable attention because he was the first writer to be prosecuted for treason committed during the Second World War. While before the war his political views had oscillated between left and right, by the early 1940s he had become the chief editor of the collaborationist journal *Aujourd'hui* and author of a sympathetic biography of Pétain. His trial, on 23 October 1944, only lasted one day, at the end of which he was found guilty and later executed. Henri Béraud's trial took place on 29 December of that year. He was an accomplished novelist who wrote a series of highly charged articles in the collaborationist journal *Gringoire*, and whose pro-Vichy stance seemed to be particularly fuelled by an intense hatred of the British. The jury found him guilty of collusion with the enemy, but François Mauriac – by then already sceptical of the purge – pleaded on his behalf, and de Gaulle commuted the sentence to life imprisonment. He was eventually released in 1950.

The two most sensational trials involving writers – the trials of Maurras and Brasillach – took place in January 1945. Charles Maurras' trial took place over four days, starting on the 24th. By the time of his court case, he was elderly. A fervent anti-Dreyfusard in his youth, he had been in charge of and was the chief ideologue of the far-right *Action française*, which interestingly did not curb him from repeatedly expressing anti-German views. He too was found guilty according to Article 75, but, like Pétain[21], his death penalty was commuted into a life sentence ('réclusion à perpétuité') because of his advanced age. The most controversial case, however, was the trial of the novelist and journalist Robert Brasillach. Editor of the fascist *Je suis partout*, he had called for the execution of left-leaning politicians and Resistance fighters. The trial took only one afternoon – on 19 January 1945 – at the end of which he was found guilty of treason. Like Suarez, he was executed, in spite of a petition circulated by François Mauriac and signed by major literary figures like Jean Anouilh, Albert Camus, Paul Claudel and Jean Cocteau. The petition asked de Gaulle, by then Chairman of the Provisional Government, to change the death penalty into a life sentence, something which he refused to do.

The verdict in the Brasillach case shook the Parisian intellectual world. He was relatively young and he was the only son of an army officer who had died in the First World War (the petition on his behalf focused on this latter point). Above all, he had gone through the elite channels of French education and was a well-known intellectual. Although despised by many for his political outbursts, he was also a respected literary figure. It is the Brasillach case which sparked off a debate among intellectuals about fairness (or lack of it) of the *épuration*. However, he and Suarez were not the only ones to receive such harsh verdicts: of all the trials of collaborationist intellectuals, ten intellectuals received the death penalty. Of these, four were executed – besides Suarez and Brasillach, there were the lesser-known Armand Chastenet de Puységur and Paul Chack – whereas three death sentences were commuted to life sentences and three were condemned to death *in abstentia*.[22] Many others received long sentences, forced labour or forced reclusion, although in the course of the 1950s most of these, if still alive, would receive an amnesty. Other potential celebrity trials involving intellectuals did not take place at the end of the war: on 15 March 1945 Drieu la Rochelle committed suicide, while Céline escaped via Germany to Denmark, sentenced *in abstentia* five years later and subsequently pardoned.[23] If both had been sentenced around the same time as Brasillach, it is not inconceivable that they too would have received a harsh sentence. It is certainly a fact that earlier trials – in particular those which took place in 1944 and early 1945 – were more likely to lead to harsher sentences than the ones which took place later.

There was immense media interest in the trials of collaborators. All newspapers reported the major court cases, including the trials of collaborationist intellectuals. The emotive style of reporting gives some sense of the experience of trauma that had engulfed the nation and to which the media would contribute. Very few newspapers opted for a neutral tone, with the surprising exception of *Combat*, which for each trial factually reported the case for the prosecution and defence. It is worth paying attention to *Le Figaro* and *L'Humanité*. They both used emotive language, albeit from different political angles.

Le Figaro used a melodramatic writing style, portraying in lyrical terms the tense atmosphere of the trials. In comparison with *L'Humanité*, it opted for a more conciliatory tone, often expressing pity for the accused and describing their fragility. Remarkable given the circumstances, *Le Figaro* described the trial of Suarez as a 'dialogue' between different 'voices' – between two perspectives, so to speak – one represented by the presiding judge Ledoux and the other by Suarez. *Le Figaro* insisted that it was important for France to hear this dialogue but it implicitly acknowledged that Ledoux and Suarez did not speak from a position of equal strength: Ledoux was described as speaking 'firmly' and 'assured', whereas Suarez was 'hesitant', sometimes 'deaf' and occasionally 'violent.'[24] The same style, focusing on the physical and psychological frailty of the defendant, continued in the reporting on Brasillach's and Maurras' trials. It portrayed in detail the physical appearance of Brasillach – now no longer assured and jovial, but an emaciated and diminutive character. Maurras was described as looking dishevelled and old.[25] In both Brasillach and Maurras' case, the language used by *Le Figaro* suggested they were first and foremost sad cases, carried away by their own rhetoric. Crucially, they were, at least during the war, not quite aware of what they were doing: Brasillach seemed oblivious to his own tendency to conflate literature and politics, whereas Maurras never seemed to think through properly the effects of his writings.

L'Humanité took a much harsher position. Tied to the French Communist Party, it took a partisan line, especially for the earlier trials. Reporting on Suarez's trial, the newspaper published a piece, titled 'Finally a little bit of justice outside the provinces; Georges Suarez, the Gestapo journalist, will pay with his head'.[26] The author applauded the verdict, but deemed it unacceptable for the trial to take so long – half a day – to arrive at this judgement as, so it was argued, one only needed a quarter of an hour to read a few extracts from his writings and arrive at a sound judgement. The article also deplored the fact that Suarez would not be executed immediately, but it ended triumphantly with the statement that others will be facing the same verdict.[27] By the end of 1944, however, *l'Humanité* somewhat changed its tone, reporting on the trial of Béraud, albeit one-sidedly, less passionately.[28] The title of the article described him as a traitor and denouncer[29], highlighted the case of the prosecution and played down the arguments of the defence, but the overall tone had become certainly less vengeful. Likewise, the article on the trial of Brasillach, roughly one month later, was also, although biased, more moderate in tone.[30] It focused on Brasillach's wrongdoings, ignored the intricate details of his own defence and ended with a disapproving note on those who turned up to support Brasillach but the overall tone remained *sachlich*. Maurras' trial, however, led to acerbic comments reminiscent of the commentary on the Suarez case. In the article 'Maurras, the murderer, will live!'[31] the author expressed astonishment that Maurras, of all people, was spared the death sentence. The piece described the trial as badly conducted, leading to an 'indulgent verdict' that is deeply unpatriotic.[32]

This brief excursion into the media reports on the trials shows that emotions ran high during this period. In particular, the earlier trials aroused passions and acted as a vehicle through which the trauma of the war was revisited and expressed. We shall discuss in the next chapter how around this time Sartre published several pieces in which he tapped into this mood and tried to make sense of the occupation, Resistance and collaboration. For now, it is important to delve further into the arguments used during the trials because they tied in with a broader cultural shift which eventually helped to propel Sartre. Indicative of this shift was, again, the media reporting at the time.

The trials: prosecution and defence

The arguments and meta-arguments presented in the major trials of writers, both by the prosecution and defence, give us a particularly vivid insight into the power struggles that took place between the intellectuals concerned.[33] Two issues are worth distinguishing: the opposing claims regarding the function of writing; and the claims on both sides regarding purity and patriotism. We will take each theme in turn and elaborate on how both were raised by the prosecution and defence. We shall explore how these legal issues and arguments fed into the broader intellectual arena at the time, prompting intellectuals like Sartre to revisit the war and reformulate their own philosophy.

Responsibility

Invariably, the prosecution of collaborationist intellectuals argued that writings of intellectuals should not simply be regarded as opinions without further consequences. Consistent with the views expressed earlier in clandestine Resistance publications, they argued that writings are consequential. According to this position, writing or public performances imply an audience: it is one thing to have opinions, but it is an altogether different thing to express thoughts within a public arena. Writing is public, and the audience can be persuaded by it. In this context, Simone de Beauvoir refused to sign the petition to save Brasillach's life on the grounds that he, like anyone else, was responsible for his writings. If, as the prosecution argued, writers have an impact on their readers, then it follows that they bear responsibility for what they have written and for its role in the causal chain of events. The media certainly took this position. Commenting on Brasillach's trial, *Le Figaro* wrote that he had played with ideas and words as if they were toys whereas they were obviously not – they could hurt and even kill people.[34] He did not distinguish properly between fiction and facts.[35] Regarding Maurras, the same newspaper commented that he failed to realize the consequences of his writings.[36] As suggested earlier, *Le Figaro* held that Brasillach or Maurras were guilty but not on the grounds that they had been fully aware of their actions and consequences. It was their wilful oblivion – their choice not to see when it mattered – that made them particularly guilty.

However, two qualifications need to be made. The first qualification relates to the content of writings what made some pieces more consequential than others. While it was not uncommon for the prosecution to argue more generally that the German war strategy included propaganda and that therefore any pro-German piece constituted a potential act of treason[37], prosecuting lawyers were keen to focus on texts which were more visibly linked to particular atrocities. In particular, the prosecution focused on writings which allegedly had called for the execution or deportation of political opponents. The prosecution's case against Maurras centred round an article in which he had asked about the whereabouts of the Worms family, the father of which was subsequently murdered.[38] Likewise, the case against Brasillach was partly based on his repeated calls for the rounding up, revenge and murder of political opponents.[39] The media too paid particular attention to these acts of denouncing, their possible lethal consequences and the responsibilities this entailed. Commenting on the case, *Le Figaro* discussed those articles by Maurras in which he had called for Resistance fighters to be killed, in particular a piece in which he had denounced members of the Fournier family.[40] *Combat*, again eager to report factually and evenly, also explained the rationale of their defence: both Maurras and Brasillach pointed out that the Resistance murders of German soldiers had led to harsh reprisals and that they had wanted to put a stop to this endless cycle of violence.[41] The same newspaper even reported Brasillach's daring, if not provocative, argument that Resistance fighters too should be held responsible for their actions on the grounds that they should have known – or arguably knew – that their actions would lead to massive reprisals.[42]

The second qualification refers to the status of the writer and his appeal to and authority over a larger public. Sometimes the prosecution focused on the type of publication outlet: publishing in large newspapers, rather than specialized magazines with a sophisticated readership, made you more likely to influence a gullible audience. Often, however, the argument went further, focusing on the intrinsic abilities of the writer. The prosecution held that authors with exceptional talent were particularly responsible for their writings: their rhetorical skills managed to persuade the most vulnerable, especially the youth. The prosecution of Maurras developed the argument further: talent provides an aura, authority or seductive style that helps to persuade readers and guides them towards unspeakable crimes.[43] Likewise, the prosecution in the Brasillach trial emphasized his undoubted literary talent, which, so it was argued, made him particularly responsible compared to lesser intellectuals: he had managed to influence the youth who subsequently joined the collaboration.[44] Interestingly, Brasillach's lawyer tried to reverse the argument when he defended him by arguing that someone with his extraordinary talent should be spared the death penalty.[45] Tellingly, in his memoirs de Gaulle explained that he decided not to pardon Brasillach precisely because of the burden of responsibility that accompanied his literary talent. Like the prosecution of Brasillach, de Gaulle focused on the effect talented writers have on an amenable audience and the extent to which it compels some readers to commit terrible crimes. 'For in literature, like anywhere else, talent comes with a responsibility.'[46] Likewise, the newspapers discussed extensively the issue of talent and the responsibilities it entailed, even when dealing with court cases of 'lesser' intellectuals: *Combat* emphasized that the presiding judge in the Suarez trial commented on his literary talent and deplored the misuse of his obvious abilities,[47] while *Le Figaro* stressed that the prosecution against Béraud centred around his talent.[48] But especially in the case of a high-profile figure like Brasillach did the issue of talent come to the forefront: *Le Figaro* described him as 'gifted', but misguided by his desire to excel ('briller') and by his sectarianism.[49] Even *L'Humanité*, notoriously unforgiving towards collaborationist intellectuals, commented on his abilities, depicting him as a 'talented writer and critic'.[50]

If the prosecution emphasized that writing has consequences and therefore implies responsibility on the part of the author, the defence unsurprisingly took the opposite stance and made this the cornerstone of its plea. Writers, so they argued, have the freedom to express their opinions and that is what they are: mere opinions. In Jacques Isorni's defence of Brasillach, he lamented that the trial was a *procès d'opinion*: the main accusations, so he argued, do not stand up, so all we are left with is a trial of opinions.[51] His line of argument was abundantly clear: you might disagree with Brasillach's writings, you might find them unpleasant, but they are opinions, worthy of expression. Accordingly, this reasoning, centred round the principle of freedom of expression, received considerable attention in the press. For *Le Figaro*, for instance, this principle was at the heart of Béraud's defence: he now regretted some of his writings, but as a 'free writer' ('écrivain libre'), he had written what he felt at the time and he had been carried away by his own polemics ('emportements de polémiste').[52] While the defence lawyers relied on this notion of the 'free writer' and newspapers emphasized it, it was certainly not the only argument used by the defence in court. Surprisingly some lawyers argued that the prosecution of their clients went against the spirit of the French Revolution, which was ironic given the anti-Republican stance of their clients. Whether appealing to the French Revolution or not, the defence in the various trials tended to hold on to a sharp distinction between art and literature on the one hand, and politics on the other, arguing that the blurring of that distinction would be dangerous. Whereas progressive intellectuals saw writing as political, the right often embraced the notion of *art pour l'art* during this period, thereby exonerating their wartime activities. This is not to suggest that during this time collaborationist intellectuals were in a position to openly advocate this view or elaborate on it. They had little authority; if they were not in the dock, they were at risk of being prosecuted, and very few of them found publishing outlets. While they developed meta-theoretical arguments regarding the separation of art and politics well before the trials, by the time of the purge their position was too weak to propagate these views and it was therefore up to lawyers to make the case. Nevertheless, in prison (often await-ing trial), the writers repositioned themselves as apolitical: their intellectual activities had become esoteric and devoid of contempo-rary political significance. They managed to do this, for instance, by focusing their energies on translating Greek poetry. It is only a couple of years after the purge – when the mood had settled and doubts had been raised about the purge – that collaborationist intellectuals found the confidence to speak out.

In the context of the construction of cultural trauma, the trials are also illuminating, not just for what they considered as punishable but also for what they ignored or obfuscated. Given the focus of the trials on the responsibility of writers, one could reasonably expect attention to have been given to their involvement in genocide. However, the notion of crimes against humanity was not part of French law.[53] So in contrast with the Nuremberg trials, none of the major French trials, including those against intellectuals, centred round crimes against humanity.[54] This meant that the *épuration* overlooked, for instance, the French collusion in the Holocaust. While the Vichy regime had from the very beginning implemented discriminatory laws against Jews and subsequently deported Jewish people to Germany, the prosecution tended to ignore this and, instead, focused on actions that colluded with a foreign power against the French nation. Likewise, very few court cases against intellectuals focused on the anti-Semitic material, which is particularly striking given the overtly anti-Semitic tone of most collaborationist writings. Rather than exploring the complicity with genocide, the *épuration* helped to shape the view that it was very much the French nation that had been violated and that, consequently, it was France, its dignity and cohesion that needed to be restored, a narrative which was promoted by de Gaulle and the Provisional Government. It was not until 1946, when Sartre published his *Anti-Semite and Jew*, that there was a proper discussion of the issue of anti-Semitism in relation to the war, and, even then, the exploration of the French involvement in the Holocaust remained limited.[55]

Purity and patriotism

We have mentioned how, as part of their defence, collaborationist intellectuals often held on to the separation between politics and art. But this was not a consistent strategy across the board. Collaborationist intellectuals also contended that their intellectual interventions had political consequences. Indeed, some of them argued both: while they saw the intellectual and political realms as separate entities, they also held that their own writings had helped the French nation. To understand this complex scenario, we need to explore how intellectual purity and patriotism were central to the legal proceedings and to the intellectual discussions that accompanied them.

In the power struggle between the two factions of the French intelligentsia, both laid claim to purity of a kind. Both argued that their writings remained untainted. The defence by collaborationist intellectuals centred round purity in relation to national pride. Maurras claimed that throughout the war his intentions had remained honourable as he had been always preoccupied with the well-being of the French nation and had remained as hostile to Germany as to the Anglo-Saxon threat. Brasillach's arguments were similar: while conceding that in retrospect he might have been mistaken, he insisted that throughout the war he had remained true to his intentions and to the

French cause. Brasillach maintained that collaborators in France and Gaullists in London had similar concerns – protecting France – but operated in different circumstances. As for cultural collaboration, he dismissed his visits to the Institut allemand and the Libraire Rive gauche as insignificant, but depicted his trip to Weimar as another patriotic act – to maintain the intellectual presence of France. The press paid particular attention to these arguments about purity and national pride. *Le Figaro* gave a *verbatim* report of Maurras' bombastic defence according to which nothing had given him more satisfaction than to sacrifice himself for the good of the nation.[56] Reporting on the Brasillach trial, *Combat* contrasted his comparison between collaborators and Gaullists with his earlier writings in which he had depicted de Gaulle as a 'traitor' and Gaullists as 'bandits'.[57]

If the defence focused on the purity of intentions, it is because the prosecution attempted to show the opposite. The prosecution argued that collaborationist intellectuals had benefited financially from their wartime activities, thereby tarnishing them even more.[58] To make the case less abstract, prosecutors often provided precise figures of the remuneration associated with particular articles. In the case against Béraud, the prosecution pointed out that he was paid 600,000 French francs per year for his editorial duties at Gringoire and was therefore the best-paid journalist of his time.[59] To make the case more emotional, the prosecution depicted collaborationist authors as having led a lavish, luxurious lifestyle, in contrast with the vast majority of French society – including of course the Resistance writers – who lived a modest existence. The defence claimed the opposite was true: not only was there a clear separation between their writings and the political realm, but their work also remained untainted by economic interests.[60] In this view, financial gain had never been a motivation; they had not benefited from their writings; they led a simple lifestyle; they had remained sincere; and so on. For example, in his defence, Brasillach claimed that he left his important position at *Je suis partout* due to patriotism just when it would have become lucrative.[61]

The newspapers spent considerable time discussing the issue of impure motives. Commenting on the trial of Armand-Louis-Marie Chastenet de Puységur, a collaborationist writer and journalist, *Combat* focused its reporting on his possible financial gains during the war.[62] *Combat* and *Le Figaro* elaborated on how during the cross-examination Suarez had to admit that he received 65,000 French francs per month for his editorial work at *Aujourd'hui*[63] and how he defended himself by pointing out his various expenses.[64] *Combat* and *L'Humanité* gave precise figures for Béraud's remuneration:

1,200,000 French francs for thirty articles.[65] *L'Humanité* remained of course the most vitriolic: in its article about Béraud's trial, the newspaper introduced him as a 'salaried corrupter of French opinion'.[66]

During the purge old divisions within France were played out and references were made to the theme of internal divisions within French history. In their defence most collaborationist intellectuals drew parallels between their predicament and the unfair treatment of some authors, like André Chénier, under the terror of the 1790s.[67] Making the comparison with the 1790s had dramatic appeal: it invoked images of kangaroo courts, injustice, arbitrariness and brutality. But it was not just the terror that was invoked; references to the Dreyfus affair were rife. After hearing his verdict, Maurras famously shouted that this was Dreyfus' revenge,[68] thereby implicitly complying with the view of Resistance intellectuals that Vichy, with its anti-Semitism and fervent Catholicism, was broadly speaking an anti-Dreyfusard plot. Collaborationist intellectuals found particular affinity with the anti-Dreyfusards and their appeal to loyalty to the nation over individual rights:[69] they too, so they claimed, had expressed extreme loyalty to the French nation. Some collaborationist intellectuals would look much further in the past and indeed beyond French borders and, for instance, compare their situation with Socrates. The message was loud and clear: do not expect justice from the legal system; the legal system is politicized; do not expect to be rewarded for speaking the truth.

Both collaborationists and Resistance intellectuals portrayed themselves as the true patriots. If the prosecution made the case for treason, the defence invariably focused on the legal ambiguity of Vichy. In this context, the defence portrayed Vichy as a legitimate government or at least as a government which appeared legitimate at the time. The legality of the armistice and Vichy was at the core of Suarez's defence, according to commentators at the time.[70] From this perspective, collaboration with Vichy appeared like a patriotic act, rather than an act of treason, and to condemn collaborationist authors was to employ retrospective justice. Within this defence, two strands can be distinguished. The first group of writers argued that France and Nazi Germany were so intertwined that patriotism manifested itself in pro-German attitudes. This pro-Nazi argument was in line with the collaborationist ideology, as expressed during the war. Most of the authors who were being investigated or prosecuted had subscribed to the idea that France had become a degenerate nation and that the solution lay in the alliance with Nazi Germany.[71] From this viewpoint, leaving aside the legality of Vichy, the armistice could not be a betrayal of the French nation; it was essential to its restoration. The second strand of argument was quite different. Writers within this group were keen to stress their consistently anti-German stance. While conceding that they had been Vichy supporters, they argued that they had remained hostile to Nazi Germany. It is this second strand which received considerable press coverage. *Le Figaro*, for instance, commented on how Béraud pointed out that his attitude had always been both anti-German and anti-British[72] and how Maurras too stressed his persistent anti-German attitude.[73]

If patriotism was central to the defence, the prosecution was set on undermining the claim that Vichy supporters were the true defenders of the French nation. For this purpose, they sometimes used sexual metaphors and analogies, and they did so in ways that are shocking to the contemporary reader. The prosecution of Brasillach used his writings to allude to his alleged homoerotic fantasies about German soldiers. His alleged love and desire for the occupiers was very much used against him. Brasillach was an obvious target for this: there had been speculation about his sexuality for some time, and some of his writings about the occupation were indeed suggestive. Brasillach was not an isolated case. Throughout this period, the Resistance was regularly referred to as masculine, virile and assertive, whereas the collaboration was depicted as feminine, weak or homosexual.[74] The true France was portrayed as pure and virginal, and the occupation as rape and, sometimes, as one in which the rape victim appeared as an accomplice.[75] As we will discuss later, Sartre's description of collaborators followed the same line: alluding to Brasillach and Drieu la Rochelle, he observed that homosexuals were proportionally over-represented among collaborators (without providing empirical evidence for this) and that their relationship with the occupier had strong homoerotic and sadomasochistic qualities.

Concluding comments

The prosecution of collaborationist intellectuals occurred within a broader framework of the purge. People from other sections of society were put on trial as well, including some high-ranking members of the military, senior civil servants, businessmen and of course politicians like Laval and Pétain. It would be a mistake to conceive of the prosecution of collaborators in purely legal terms, especially given the fervour of the purge. The humiliation of the rapid defeat and long occupation, the exploitative relationship between Germany and

France, the ambiguity of French officials, the complicity of Vichy – all these factors had made for a traumatic experience which in what still amounted to the age of nationalism called for a strong public reaction. The purge was this reaction – a collective, visible effort to deal swiftly with four years of trauma and confusion. The purge of writers was part of this broader attempt by some sections of French society to deal with the recent, traumatic past, identify the culprits and take revenge on them. The question remains, however, why the writers were treated so severely. Why were they treated more severely than, say, civil servants in the Vichy administration or people in business who had collaborated with the Germans and who had benefited from the occupation?

Some commentators provide an obvious explanation: compared to, say, economic collaboration, it is relatively easy to 'prove' intellectual collaboration given the multiple copies of the texts which are available.[76] But this explanation only goes so far: intellectual products are not always reliable sources for conviction as they can be and were interpreted in different ways. Further, in comparison with economic, political or military action, it is difficult to establish whether a particular intellectual product has aided the enemy significantly (just as, conversely, it is hard to determine whether it has undermined the enemy). Indeed, it is often difficult to prove a causal chain between the publication (or speech) and effects of this kind, even in cases where there is little uncertainty as to the message that is being conveyed. We will, therefore, need to provide a different explanation for why, among collaborators, intellectuals in particular were targeted. The fact that the writers on trial were treated harshly and that their texts were thought to amount to treason gives some indication of the significance attributed to writing in France at the time. For educated sections of the population across the political spectrum, writing and literature were integral to French national pride and hope. During the war Resistance writings had further enhanced this mythology of writing as embodying the French spirit: literature in particular was depicted as allowing the continuation of the fight through other means, but also as under threat by the occupying forces. The power of this myth – writing as all-important, encapsulating the essence and strength of the French – goes some way towards explaining the frenzy surrounding the purge of intellectuals as well as the absence of sound judgement during the trials. It is against the background of this myth that writing can be seen as treason and that literally 'selling out' (writing for the enemy while receiving remuneration for it) can become a legal argument. From this point of view, collaborationist writers had used writing – this sacred entity which makes the French nation what it is – against itself. It was the ultimate act of betrayal.

The initial blacklists of intellectuals and the subsequent legal cases against some of them helped to position and reposition them within the political and intellectual field. The trials in particular can be seen as sites of struggle over positioning, whereby defence and prosecution lawyers employed arguments and meta-arguments which located the defendant within the socio-political and intellectual spheres at the time. Against the background of national fervour, the prosecution positioned the writers on trial as traitors responsible for some of the atrocities that took place, while the defence attempted to depict them as genuine patriots who kept up the French spirit in difficult circumstances. Both the prosecution and defence also employed meta-arguments; that is, abstract propositions which reflected on the phenomenon of intellectual production itself. These meta-arguments employed during the trials touched upon broader issues about the nature of intellectual work and its relationship with the political sphere and with the author's responsibility. Both prosecution and defence were concerned with the purity of the author and national pride and both made the connection between those two. There were also subtle differences, however: whereas the prosecution invariably portrayed an intricate link between writing and politics, the defence often took contradictory positions. On the one hand, they drew a clear dividing line between writing and the polity. On the other hand they argued that the content of their writings had been hostile to Germany or that the act of writing as such – regardless of its content – constituted a form of French Resistance.

In the trials of collaborationist writers the notion of responsibility occupied a central role. It always does in legal cases, but it did so here in a unique fashion. Authors were held responsible mainly for their writings, especially for the alleged consequences of those writings. In some cases other activities of symbolic significance were brought up. For instance, Brasillach was held responsible for attending the Writers Congress in Germany or events at the German Institute and for having occupied a senior position in the Librairie allemande, key to German propaganda.[77] But overall the written texts were decisive in the case against them. Firstly, it was argued that the more talent you have, the more notoriety; and the more notoriety, the more people can be persuaded by your arguments and might act upon them. With talent comes responsibility, so the argument went. More significant authors can influence people more than minor ones so they bear the brunt of responsibility more. Secondly, it was implied that authors have the responsibility, at the time of writing and publishing, to think ahead and conceive of the possible effects of their intellectual products. They ought to have realized, for instance, that some forms of writing could incite hatred which in turn might lead to atrocities. Authors were meant to be aware and conceive the possibility of those consequences. With this legal platform, the notion of responsibility would become central to the intellectual field in the mid-1940s. The defence, on the other hand, tended to rely on the assumption of a separation between art and politics, between writings and reality. It showed remarkable similarities with notions of art for art's sake and the autonomy of art, associated with Gide and Drieu. This notion of *art pour l'art* was now associated with the extreme right, which would make it an untenable position in the intellectual landscape of the aftermath of the Second World War. As we shall see, this cultural shift, whereby responsibility became the catchword, would play a significant role in Sartre's rise.

If the trials are to be seen in terms of positioning, then it is important to conceive of how they affected not just the positioning of collaborationist writers but also of Resistance intellectuals. The trials consistently demonized collaborationist writers, attributing immense responsibility to them for the possible consequences of their newspaper articles. This implied that the act of writing – whether as literature, articles in *revues* or pieces in newspapers – was all-important. But if writing was now regarded as so significant and if the internal fight against the occupier was seen as so decisive (as it was by so many French people), then it is perfectly comprehensible that the people who had written against the oppressor when it really mattered now gained in status. So the trials implicitly glamorized the intellectuals associated with the Resistance. We have seen in the previous chapter how during the war Resistance intellectuals were convinced of the significance of their work. Now, with the trials of collaborationist intellectuals, this view, hitherto limited to a minority of Resistance writers, became widespread. So the myth of the Resistance writer was born. As we have seen, the trials were public events, commented upon by the press, and it was this reporting which contributed to the myth of the Resistance writer. The spread of this idea, from a minority view to a widespread notion, was accompanied by a shift in meaning. Whereas during the war Resistance heroics were associated with the art of silence, it was now speaking out which was seen as a valiant act.

The trials of intellectuals are also interesting for what they tended to ignore or failed to address. Very little, for instance, was said about the anti-Semitism of the writers on trial, even during the later court cases when the knowledge of the Holocaust was in the public domain. Neither side – prosecution nor defence – elaborated on the anti-Semitism of the defendant. There were a few exceptions to this rule – the prosecution in Brasillach's trial focused momentarily on his infamous call to '. . . separate ourselves from the Jews *en bloc* and not keep the little ones . . .'[78] – but overall this lacuna is striking. When the anti-Semitism of a writer was mentioned, it tended to be brief and was part of a whole list of allegations. This lacuna is remarkable given the legacy of the Dreyfus affair, the atrocities to which Jews had been subjected during the war, the complicity by Vichy officials and the overtly anti-Semitic outbursts in the writings of many defendants. The explanation for this void might partly lie in the fact that the main themes – writing, the nation, responsibility – tended to overshadow other concerns. But it might also lie in the fact that anti-Semitism had, prior to the war and during it, not been restricted to the circle of fascist and pro-collaboration writers, and the case for the prosecution was more compelling by focusing not just on what was problematic about collaborationist writings but also what was distinctive about them. Furthermore, Vichy's discriminatory treatment of the Jews and its complicity in their deportation made for a particularly shameful episode which was difficult to revisit especially at the time when societal renewal was on the agenda. Indeed, the trials of Laval and Pétain too paid little attention to the anti-Semitism of Vichy. It was not just in court that the issue of anti-Semitism remained absent; the topic was hardly addressed in intellectual debates at the time, something which would only change with the publication of Sartre's *Réflexions sur la question juive*.

The *épuration* led to a reshaping of the French intellectual field in two ways. Firstly, the blacklist and the trials meant that several members of the intellectual establishment could no longer be regarded as credible authoritative figures. Not only did the purge lead to the elimination of some prominent fascists (either because they were executed or assassinated or because they opted for suicide to avoid prosecution), others were now seen as tainted by their war efforts or, in some cases, by the lack of those efforts. While the blacklist failed in its intention to discourage editors from publishing the named authors, it did succeed, at least temporarily, in discrediting a considerable section of the intellectual elite, not just openly fascist sympathizers, but also writers like Pierre Andreu and Jean Giono who were not as easily classifiable and whose main mistake, it now seemed, was not to have taken a firmer stance when it mattered most.[79] Some prominent intellectuals were publicly discredited: Ferdinand Céline, Henry de Montherlant and Charles Maurras. Elderly people like Maurras would not have time to recover the lost ground and for those young enough to do so it would still take many years to find a position in the competitive intellectual landscape of post-war France. Secondly, some intellectual currents – and to a certain extent the people associated with them – were now, in the context of the purge, regarded as irrelevant if not pernicious. The trials, in particular, popularized the notion that any piece of writing is a political act and that to deny its political connotations is irresponsible at best and an apology for fascism at worst. The notion of art for art's sake, therefore, which had been popular before the war in some circles, was now moribund. In sum, this dual process, with the public degradation of several hitherto authoritative intellectuals and of previously influential artistic and intellectual strands, led to a temporary vacuum which would be readily exploited by new intellectuals who were able to tap into the new sensibilities.

While the purge hurt a large section of the intellectuals, it didn't affect the publishing houses to quite the same extent. The previous chapter elaborated on how the opposing intellectual circles often overlapped within the same publishing house, and it is this intersection which partly explains why so few editors were targeted. The interests of those Resistance intellectuals who sat on the investigating committees were intertwined with those of the major publishing houses that had published collaborationist material. Although publishing houses like Gallimard had cooperated with the occupiers and had published openly fascist tracts, it was not in the interest of Resistance intellectuals to pursue a witch hunt or assist a legal case against them. On the contrary, they made a concerted effort to protect their own publishers. The case of Gaston Gallimard is interesting because he would soon, as head of his publishing house, occupy an important position in the intellectual field in the immediate aftermath of the war. He had powerful protectors in the committee: Aragon and Sartre were relentless in defending his war record. It was not so difficult for them to make a case for Gaston Gallimard: before the war he had built up a reputation of publishing left-leaning authors and it is this reputation which had made him particularly vulnerable during the war and more open to pressure. The purge did mean that a small group of writers including Sartre obtained, at the time, a powerful position *vis-à-vis* their publishers. From this position of strength Sartre would be able to persuade Gallimard to publish his flagship journal *Les Temps modernes*, launched in October 1945. For Gallimard this journal, with its Resistance connotations, was ideal to draw a line underneath the war period and to re-establish himself as a leading publisher of progressive authors.

— 3 —

INTELLECTUAL DEBATES
AROUND THE PURGE:
RESPONSIBILITY, PURITY,
PATRIOTISM

The intellectual climate immediately following the liberation

In the previous chapters we learned that during the war the notion of the writer's responsibility quickly became a key element in the rhetoric of Resistance intellectuals, especially in relation to their fight against collaborationist intellectuals. Whereas during the period of the war the circulation of this concept of responsibility took place largely through underground publications, the subsequent trials of collaborators and the media attention they received meant a much broader audience became acquainted with and sensitized to the notion of responsibility. From 1944 onwards, the educated echelons of French society, which regularly followed the reporting of the trials in the newspapers and especially the cases involving intellectuals, became interested in this notion, particularly in relation to the experience of the war. In conjunction with the trials, various discussions took place particularly among Resistance intellectuals about the responsibility of the writer, both in specialized literary journals and in more popular outlets.[1] The notion of responsibility became central to the vocabulary used by former Resistance intellectuals to express the trauma of the war, to identify both perpetrators and victims and to seek resolution through legal means. In this process Resistance intellectuals tended to interpret the larger societal issue of collaboration as a narrower issue of intellectual collaboration. Contributors to the Resistance journal *Les Lettres françaises* reiterated that writing is an act, which like any act, entails consequences and therefore responsibility. In the context of the trials, *Combat* called in October 1944 for a 'politics of responsibility', urging the French to be brave, make difficult decisions and implement harsher sanctions if necessary.[2] In Camus' editorials in November of the same year, the notion of responsibility looms large again: Camus wrote about the need for a new morality of the press, which should educate and pursue truth rather than entertain.[3]

Most telling of the mood among former Resistance intellectuals at the time was the exchange in the Resistance journal *Carrefour* in 1945. At the beginning of that year, the editorial team of the journal decided to invite writers to comment on the notion of responsibility because it had become so topical. A clear pattern emerged among the articles that were sent in. Contributors tended to articulate and justify the case of the prosecution: they argued that writers are legally responsible for their writings and for the acts that might have resulted from those writings.[4] Several contributors went further by making a distinction between the degree of culpability of collaborationist writers and those of other collaborators.[5] Vercors' piece was a prime example of this argument. Vercors (Jean Bruller), the author of *Le Silence de la mer*, drew a sharp distinction between industrialists who collaborated and collaborationist intellectuals: the actions of the former only concern themselves whereas the writings of the intellectuals affect others. Comparing the two, so he argues, is like '... comparing Cain with the Devil: Cain's crime stops with Abel whereas the peril of the Devil has no limits.'[6] Also, he argued that the freedom of the writer goes with responsibility for the consequences of his actions. Normally the author shares the responsibility with his or her readers, but in a police state, where the readers are not able to express their opinion, the responsibility lies solely with the author. This means that an author needs to justify him- or herself before a court not just for what he or she has written but also for the actions which his or her writings elicited.[7]

If as a result of the trials the author's responsibility took centre stage in intellectual debates at the time, there was also rather quickly a growing disquiet about the purge which fuelled intellectual debates about the validity of the trials and the appropriateness of the reprisals. Through his columns in *Le Figaro* the Catholic writer François Mauriac was one of the first publicly to condemn the trials, leading to an acrimonious dispute with the Communist-leaning atheist Camus which lasted from September 1944 until January 1945. Very few former Resistance intellectuals would have sided with Mauriac during this period, but the tide turned shortly afterwards and eventually even Camus would come round to Mauriac's position. Brasillach's trial was a watershed moment: whereas in 1944 only a few isolated individuals like Mauriac expressed concerns about the fairness of the trials and the appropriateness of the sentences, Brasillach's death sentence and execution shook the literary and intellectual world and led more writers to condemn the excesses of the purge. The large number of writers who signed the petition to commute his death sentence to life imprisonment was indicative of this shift. Interestingly, though, the arguments presented at the time centred round his family (his father had died as a soldier in the First World War) rather than the severity of the punishment. The broader intellectual debate about the purge, which started with the Mauriac-Camus controversy, saw two opposing factions. For Mauriac and Paulhan, for instance, writers, like anyone else, should be entitled to make mistakes in life, we should learn to forgive, and this charitable attitude is essential to national reconciliation. On the other side, Camus, Julien Benda and others close to the Communist Party defended the trials on the basis that writers, like other people, should face up to their responsibility. Benda's special preface to the 1946 edition of his book *La Trahison des clercs* should be seen in this light, emphasizing as he did the premeditated nature of writing and therefore the culpability of those who had erred.[8] As we said before, however, very soon even the strongest defenders of the purge would be appalled by the disproportionate, erratic and unfair nature of the verdicts, and within a couple of years the purge would be seen as an unfortunate episode. For now our discussion focuses on the period between mid-1944 and the end of 1945. As we shall see in this chapter, Sartre during this period reformulated his philosophical position, making it less abstract, attributing centrality to the notion of responsibility and speaking directly to the experience of the war.

Besides the focus on the author's responsibility, the myth of *résistantialisme* was another distinctive feature of the French political and intellectual landscape during this period. We discussed earlier that the French experience of the war had been particularly traumatic in a variety of ways. Not only was the military defeat, and the speed of it, devastating to morale, but so were the occupation and the Vichy regime, characterized by widespread inaction of many French people and active collaboration of the French authorities with the occupiers. Furthermore, national pride was dented by the way in which Pétain depicted German victory as a rightful punishment for French sins.[9] Towards the end of the war, various attempts had to be made at rebuilding French pride and repairing and reunifying the nation; and the transmission of what Maurice Halbwachs termed 'collective memory' played a central role in this.[10] This collective reconstruction of recent history overplayed the extent of French Resistance and downplayed collaboration as an activity of the few. Different parts of the political spectrum would embrace this *résistantialisme*, a compelling reconstruction of history, according to which most French people actively fought the occupier but were betrayed by sections of the political class.[11] De Gaulle's speeches of the mid-1940s were quintessentially *résistantialiste*, elaborating on the heroics of the French fight against the German occupation and portraying a unified picture of a defiant nation. His famous speech at the liberation of Paris, reported in all the major newspapers, portrayed France and its capital in lyrical terms. Paris, so he said, was liberated by its 'own people', and the 'whole of France' – 'eternal France' – fought the occupier.[12] Whereas de Gaulle's speeches tended to *imply* this portrayal of a united and resilient France rather than advocate it, various newspapers *explicitly* described the Resistance as representing a large constituency.[13] Communists would also subscribe to this picture: given their central role in the Resistance, the *résistantialiste* account of history implied that the French Communist Party embodied the will of the French nation. This helped the party to achieve a central role within the post-war political landscape and to gain electorally. It is only at a later stage – in the 1960s – that *résistantialisme* would be questioned, but in 1945 it was the dominant narrative.[14] We shall see that some former Resistance intellectuals, and in particular Sartre, played a significant role in promoting and perpetuating this myth and that Sartre's role in this helped him gain stature in the post-war political and intellectual field.

The myth of *résistantialisme* also tied in with attempts on the part of the provisional government to provide a broad platform that would unite and give purpose to a previously divided country. For four years the French had been divided between those who, whether in the occupied part or under Vichy, collaborated with Nazi Germany and those who continued to fight the Germans in France or from abroad. It would be a mistake to interpret this 'internal' conflict as confined to the war situation; the divisions between the opposing factions ran much deeper and had a long history. The conflict between Republican and anti-Republican forces in France were long-standing and had flared up repeatedly, notably during the Dreyfus affair. When Maurras at the end of his trial shouted bombastically that the verdict was 'Dreyfus' revenge', he reminded those who followed the legal proceedings of how the opposing strategies during the war tied in with historically embedded fault lines within French society. Aware of the history of these opposing factions and of the acuteness of the situation at hand, General de Gaulle and his staff put a substantial effort into implementing a sense of societal solidarity, and the intellectuals, wittingly or not, played a vital role in this collective healing. *Résistantialisme* was part of this collective endeavour to create a sense of cohesion and to lay the blame on a small group. We shall see that Sartre in particular not only promoted a *résistantialisme* view, but also emphasized the need in the current circumstances for the French to embrace a newly found commonality.

To make sense of Sartre's sudden popularity in the aftermath of the war, it is important to read closely some of his key texts during this period and to put them in the intellectual and socio-political context which we have outlined so far. We will see that during this period Sartre rearticulated his philosophical position and made it pertinent to the situation at hand, providing a vocabulary that expressed and reframed the experience of the war in ways that helped to express and alleviate the trauma and helped sections of French society to move forward. Sartre's articles showed a possibly unrivalled feel for the sensibilities and emotional needs at the time and an ability to express them vividly and lucidly, outlining his existentialist position while using non-technical language. If in these articles Sartre drew partly on *L'Être et le néant*, the content and tone differed substantially. The articles address a broader audience so it is no surprise that the abstract and turgid style of *L'Être et le néant* has given way to a lively, journalistic style. The articles engage directly with the experience of the occupation, whereas his ontological treatise remained, with the exception of some cursory references to war situations, largely abstracted from the social and political issues of the time. The core proposition of *L'Être et le néant* – that human beings are compelled to be free and should therefore assume responsibility for their action – remained a central theme in the articles, but was now rephrased in light of the experience of the occupation. From 1944 onwards Sartre managed to concretize his philosophical views and convey them in the context of recent social and political events.

In this chapter we shall read closely three of Sartre's essays which appeared between September 1944 and August 1945: 'La République du silence', 'Paris sous l'occupation' and 'Qu'est-ce qu'un collaborateur?' Drawing on some of the existentialist themes of *L'Être et le néant* such as freedom and bad faith, each article addresses a broad audience and reflects on the period of the German occupation. 'La République du silence' celebrates the heroics of the Resistance, whereas 'Paris sous l'occupation' conveys the complexity of everyday life under the occupation and 'Qu'est-ce qu'un collaborateur?' explores the psyche of those who collaborated with the enemy. The timing is important for our analysis, because the first two articles appeared very shortly after the liberation of Paris and the third essay in the midst of the trials of collaborators. During this period – between the autumn of 1944 and the summer of 1945 – Sartre's star rose steadily. It just precedes what de Beauvoir called the 'existentialist offensive': the autumn of 1945 when she, Sartre and existentialism caught the public imagination. However, the articles already reveal an adept writer who was in tune with the time, who articulated so vividly the trauma of the recent past, while presenting hope for the future.

'La République du silence'

Sartre's 'La République du silence' was published in September 1944 in one of the first 'free' issues of the formerly clandestine Resistance journal *Les Lettres françaises*.[15] It is a short, crisp essay, under four pages, but extremely rich in so many ways. The timing of the publication is important, just one month after the liberation of Paris. The experience of the occupation was still fresh in people's minds, which explains Sartre's emotive language and vocabulary of trauma, writing as he did about the humiliating and degrading conditions of the occupation and the immense 'cruelty of the enemy'.[16] It is under these extreme circumstances, he continued, that French citizens learned to recognize aspects of the human condition which they would otherwise ignore. Freedom is one such feature, and indeed most commentators focused on this aspect of Sartre's argument, citing the opening line: 'We have never been as free as under the occupation.'[17] Obviously, Sartre did not want to assert that people were somehow less free in a more democratic setting. Rather, his point was that the repression had made some people, including himself, conscious of their freedom and of the weight of their actions and, crucially, had made more conscious choices. After all, a single word could have massive consequences, leading to further arrests and executions. Even thinking in itself had become a more conscious act because the Nazi propaganda forced people to attend to their own thought processes in ways in which they had not beforehand.[18] In this article, Sartre used 'freedom', the central notion of his existentialist philosophy, in a distinctive fashion. Firstly, the notion of freedom had become less of an abstract philosophical entity than it had been previously; it was now central to the understanding of life under the occupation. This is indicative of how Sartre started to refashion his philosophy to shed light on recent experiences. Secondly, Sartre did not promote the notion of freedom in isolation but linked it to the two other Republican principles of equality and solidarity. He explains in the essay that, within the context of the extremity of the war, all people, from those high up in the hierarchy to those at the bottom, were in the same boat, having to protect and look after each other.[19] It is no surprise therefore that he talked about the Resistance as a 'Republic', embodying as it did, at least in his portrayal, the three pillars of the Republican tradition.

The title of 'La République du silence' also suggests another important theme: silence. We already learned about the significance of not speaking under the occupation and how clandestine Resistance publications attributed heroic status to it. Sartre built further on this theme in two ways: one passive and negative, the other active and negating. Firstly, he talked about the act of being silenced – something imposed on people. Indeed, Sartre provided a straightforward description of the German occupation with the censor ensuring French people were unable to speak out. It is, according to Sartre, this act of being silenced which makes everyone so conscious of the power of words.[20] Secondly, he wrote about silence as a form of assertion – as a heroic, though potentially fragile, resistance against the oppressor. For instance, he wrote about someone's agony of whether under torture he or she would be able to remain silent and not give in.[21] Here Sartre linked the act of silence to both solitude and solidarity. In the desperate conditions of a prison cell, for instance, each French Resistance fighter is alone when faced with the torturer, knowing that silence is his or her only weapon and knowing too that it might lead to his or her death. Nobody else can help the prisoner; he or she is left entirely on his or her own, but their silence can save the lives of many.[22]

This is precisely where the heroic nature of the Resistance comes into play: unlike soldiers who operate in broad daylight, each Resistance fighter was involved in clandestine operations in which solitude and solidarity were intertwined. When Sartre ended the essay with a description of the Resistance as a 'Republic of Silence and Night',[23] he was not just referring to the nocturnal activities of the Resistance (although this was an important feature), but the night as metaphor captured more broadly the covert nature of the operations and the silence that went with it. It should be clear, therefore, that the term 'La République du silence' refers to the Resistance, and indeed the whole text can be read as an ode to the Resistance. Sartre even talked about the 'elite of the real Resistance fighters' as opposed to other French people.[24] At another level, however, the text subtly obfuscates the distinction between the two groups in various ways. It moves back and forth between the torrid experience of the Resistance and the reality of everyday life for French individuals in general, as if the dilemmas and heroics of Resistance fighters were those of all French people. 'We' is used ambiguously, sometimes referring to the Resistance (which clearly includes Sartre himself) but at other times to the whole of French society.[25] The slippage is remarkable and the reader cannot help but get the impression that all French people must somehow have been part of the 'Republic of Silence and Night'. This Resistance brotherhood represents a yardstick for the present as much as hope for the future: indeed, the essay ends with Sartre's wish that the new Republic which French citizens are about to embark upon will incorporate the virtues of the 'Republic of Silence and Night'.

'Paris sous l'occupation'

If 'La République du silence' addressed a group of like-minded Resistance intellectuals, 'Paris sous l'occupation' targeted a different audience.[26] It was published in Aron's *France libre* on 15 November 1944, roughly three months after 'La République du silence'. *France libre* did not just cater for the French expat community in London. It also had a British audience and indeed the essay 'Paris sous l'occupation' was written as if addressing the British public – not the French abroad. Gone is the triumphant style of 'La République du silence', understandably so because Sartre was writing for a more sceptical audience which was very conscious of French duplicity during the war and certainly more resistant to the power of the Resistance myth. The essay overall has a more defensive tone, bordering on the apologetic, mainly depicting the tribulations and complexities of everyday experience in Paris rather than the heroics of the Resistance. Sartre explicitly stated in the opening paragraphs that he was addressing those in Britain who felt that the French might not have suffered as much hardship as the Brits did.[27] He then explained that he wanted to show those British sceptics they were wrong, that life under the occupation was horrific albeit in unexpected ways. He also admitted the difficulties in conveying this to a British public, and this is where he used references to the experience of collective trauma. Sartre argued that it was nearly impossible to explain the French experience to a British audience because the situation in both countries had been so different: whereas Britain experienced the war with pride and strength, France did so with desperation and shame.[28] He set himself to write about the differences not in physical suffering (which both nations had experienced, though in different ways) but rather in psychological pain (which, he argued, was more acute in the French case). Sartre paid particular attention to the swiftness of the defeat and the subsequent occupation which amounted to a national humiliation and a widespread sense of 'inferiority'. He talked about the contempt for the French by other nations, something of which, he argued, French people were very much aware.[29] Meanwhile, Vichy promoted the view that the French defeat was a just punishment for its decadence. This humiliation, according to him, led the 'best among us' to join the Resistance, knowing all too well that their actions were mainly symbolic and that the war would be won or lost by the Allied forces – not by the activities of the Resistance.[30]

The pain went further than that. Everyday life was a struggle. Drawing on his existentialist philosophy, Sartre held that with the uncertainty of the occupation French people had been devoid of a future, no longer able to develop projects. They had turned into objects, unable to go beyond themselves and project into the future.[31] People gradually adjusted to this situation. In so far as people had collective projects (and there was a *sense* of solidarity, Sartre insisted), the occupation made it impossible for them to be acted upon: the Germans had infiltrated French institutions and exploited French resources to such an extent that any activity on the part of the French to help rebuild French society would ultimately be to the advantage of the occupiers.[32] Every choice was problematic but choices had to be made. Meanwhile their hate for the occupying forces could only be of an abstract kind given their constant presence: extremely polite in daily exchanges, the French eventually got used to having German soldiers in their midst.[33] The enemy was invisible: the Germans made arrests only at night, with those arrested unable to return and tell their story.[34] While superficially the Germans acted 'correctly', the repeated bombings by Allied forces of French towns and trains made it difficult for French people to forge emotional ties with the British, especially as the assaults were inevitably accompanied by destruction and casualties.[35] The occupation also exacerbated existing tensions within French society: between the North and the South (they were cut off from each other and living in Paris was very different from living under Vichy), between cities and rural areas (some farmers were able to profit from the situation of scarcity), between the different social classes (the working classes were more likely to face hardship), and between those who fought in the First World War and those who fought in 1940.[36]

In this confusing context, Paris was no longer the vibrant city it once was. Paris was 'dead'; it had become a 'desert'. Many people had fled the city, and those who remained preferred to stay in and certainly not venture out of their neighbourhood. Many buildings were derelict or were reused by the occupiers. Various buildings and institutions were just a façade: the Louvre without paintings, the Parliament without parliamentarians, a school without pupils, etc. Because of the separation of North and South, Paris was now cut off from the provinces with which it used to be organically linked; it was no longer the natural centre of France. Comparing Paris with London, Sartre argued that London had remained the capital throughout the war even when it was bombed, whereas during the occupation Paris had been reduced to a mere symbol rather than a true capital – an idea of Paris, conceived by the occupiers.[37] This sense of emptiness seemed intensified at night. Alluding again to the significance of silence which was so prominent in 'La République du silence', Sartre argued that Paris was a 'no man's land' (Sartre's terminology) at night when the curfew was in place and the only noise was that of the soldiers' walking.[38] Silence here no longer held the heroic associations which it so clearly had in the earlier article. It was an eerie silence, associated with waiting and the fear of being arrested.

We mentioned earlier that there is very little of the celebratory tone of 'La République du silence' in this text. Yet, 'Paris sous l'occupation' still manages to hail the Resistance. Sartre made clear that while few rose to the occasion, some managed to do so and made up for the paralysis and indecision of the others. In the midst of the ambiguity and confusion of the occupation, it was indeed up to the 'very best among us' to join the Resistance.[39] If during this period France did not quite show its 'grandeur', the Resistance was *the* 'exception'. Resistance fighters were 'martyrs without hope' and their heroics did more than enough to compensate for the weaknesses of the other people. In sum, the Resistance embodied the French spirit and saved its honour. It is in this light that he argued that the French 'deserve respect' from their neighbours across the Channel.[40] The concluding paragraphs also allude to the possibilities for a liberated France, with French citizens now in charge of their own destiny again, but needing time to become accustomed to the new situation.[41]

'Qu'est-ce qu'un collaborateur?'

Published nine months later, Sartre's essay 'Qu'est-ce qu'un collabo-rateur?' also addresses a foreign audience.[42] The article appeared in

La République française in New York in August 1945. Compared to 'Paris sous l'occupation', the article no longer explores the complexities of life under occupation, nor is it as apologetic about collaboration during the war. The main aim of the article is to answer the question summed up in its title – what is a collaborator? Or, more precisely, how are collaborators different from other people. There is an interesting ambiguity in the text: while it is presented as a *general* socio-psychological theory of collaborators, the examples provided are all related to the recent period in France. While attempting to subtract the notion of collaborator from its specific historical context, the latter pops up repeatedly so that this piece could be read as an attempt to figure out what made French collaborators during the Second World War so distinct from other French people at that time. Sartre answered this question in two ways: firstly by identifying the social causes that make some people collaborators, and secondly by elaborating on their psychological traits. As we shall see, from both angles French collaborators are shown to be clearly separate from the core of French society and this distinctiveness and marginality account for their collaborationist tendencies.

The first part of the essay explores the social causes of collaboration and is clearly Durkheimian both in terms of explanation and vocabulary, though it remains impressionistic throughout and does not follow Durkheim's methodological principles strictly. The essay starts off with the observation that collaboration, like suicide, is a 'normal phenomenon', to be found in any society, and that roughly 2 per cent of the population collaborated, though no real evidence is provided for this figure. He also maintained that collaborationist attitudes could be found everywhere, but only under certain circumstances, such as occupation by a foreign invader, would they come to the surface. This is, of course, a tautology, and again the examples he provided remained unclear. Sartre even referred to those who mused about who within British society would have collaborated if Germany had successfully invaded, again implying that specific circumstances, rather than national features, make for the phenomenon.[43]

So important for our analysis is that right from the start Sartre asserted that French collaboration was limited to a small minority; and that collaboration as a phenomenon is not distinctly French but is universal, only becoming visible under extraordinary conditions. This early attempt to dissociate collaboration from French society continues throughout the essay and becomes the central tenet of his sociological explanation of this phenomenon. Collaboration, so he argued, is the product of social disintegration, and in that sense he likened collaboration to crime and suicide.[44] Sartre provided examples to support his case, mainly from the intellectual realm. In the political sphere French collaborators could be found among those who did not fit the major parties: extreme-right politicians such as Déat, Doriot and Marquet did not feel at home in or were expelled from the Socialist or Communist Parties. In the intellectual arena, collaborationist intellectuals such as Drieu la Rochelle and Ramon Fernandez tended to reject their bourgeois origins without establishing a link with the proletariat, whereas others such as Laubreaux had failed to make a successful career in journalism or literature. More broadly, collaborationist intellectuals, such as the 'royalists' of *l'Action française* or 'fascists' of *Je suis partout*, failed to accept the French Republican tradition, and were therefore, according to Sartre, outsiders in contemporary France.[45]

But in what sense would the lack of social integration make it more likely for people to become collaborators? Here again Sartre drew on a Durkheimain view for he argued that, without being properly integrated within their own society, people would hanker after a strong external force, hence the fascination with fascism. Underlying this view is the Durkheimian assumption that social integration and moral regulation make for a healthy society, and that, left to their own devices, people will be at a loss. Hence, according to Sartre, the paradox of 'right-wing anarchists', who are dissociated from society and disdainful of the rule of law, but who seek 'radical integration' which only a foreign authoritarian order can provide.[46] In the context of the trials, this essay rebuffs the way in which the French right had repeatedly portrayed the Resistance, and indeed the left in general, as antithetical to the values and integrity of the French nation. Whereas advocates for collaborationist intellectuals depicted them as true patriots who acted out of selfish love for the nation, this essay presented a sociologically tainted alternative and was in that sense a coherent riposte to the defence of Brasillach and others.

Subsequent historians of Vichy would reiterate the observation that on the whole collaborators had previously been on the margins of French society, but without necessarily taking up the Durkheim-inspired explanation which Sartre provided. For our purposes, however, what is interesting about Sartre's analysis is what it left out. While Sartre's narrative makes intuitive sense when accounting for the likes of Doriot and Drieu la Rochelle, it is quite remarkable for the way in which it ignores, to the extent of effacing, the many proponents of collaboration, such as Pétain, Laval, Maurras and Brasillach, who by all accounts were well integrated during the interbellum.

Not only does Sartre's sociological take on collaborators locate them outside the social fabric of the French Republic; it is, in his account, precisely their dissociation from the core of the French nation which has turned them into collaborators. Sartre's sociological account makes the recent collaboration 'un-French', a process that continues in this psychological treatment.

The second part of the essay elaborates on the psychology of the collaborator, and it is here that we find a further explanation for why those who are not integrated properly are more likely to be involved in collaboration. Not only do they hanker after an external force, but they also genuinely hate the country in which they have never fitted, and the occupation presents an opportunity to enact revenge for the many years, if not decades, of marginality which they had suffered. Collaboration is precisely this act of revenge, whereby the erstwhile misfits who revel in their unpopularity 'violate' this 'proud' country and force it into submission.[47] There are, besides hatred, further emotions and dispositions that characterize the collaborator: Sartre was at pains to show how they virulently oppose Enlightenment and Republican values and more generally are at odds with modern society. Collaborators refuse to respect the universal laws of the Republic and instead express loyalty only to specific entities: a leader, a party, a foreign country. Eager to obey this strong singular force, they have no core principles of their own and are willing to shift position depending on the instructions they receive from higher up. Not only did Sartre stress the anti-Republicanism of the collaboration, he also implied that the collaborators inhabited a pre-modern, feudal set-up: they relate to the occupier like a 'vassal' to his 'overlord', helping to execute his power without having any of their own.[48] Sartre paid particular attention to the nature of this relationship between the collaborator and occupier, resorting to sexual metaphors to describe it. Particularly telling in the context of Brasillach's trial in which homoerotic passages of his writings were used against him, Sartre described the collaborators as admiring the 'virility' and 'masculine values of the occupier' and resorting to the tactics of the 'weaker party' – that is, the 'woman' – to manipulate him.[49] Indeed, unable to exercise real power, collaborators use 'ruse' and 'seduction' to achieve small victories. Sartre went on to describe the cultural climate of collaboration as 'feminine' and a 'peculiar mixture of masochism and homosexuality'.[50] This gross stereotyping was not unusual at the time; we already commented earlier on how Resistance intellectuals employed the gender dichotomy to describe the distinction between the Resistance and collaboration. Against the

85

background of the trials, Sartre's portrayal of the homosexual climate of collaboration alluded to the several collaborationist writers who were known, or at least rumoured, to have had homosexual relations, some with Germans.

The second part of the essay also elaborates on how collaborators relate to the past, present and future, and it is here that the notion of responsibility props up more prominently, as Sartre elaborated on the Hegelian logic of history that underpins the collaborationist mindset. Drawing on his existentialist philosophy, he depicted collaborators as fugitives of the present, exhibiting bad faith and unwilling to recognize the genuine choices they have. For Sartre, the collaborator conflates what is with what ought to be by submitting himself to the 'reality' of the present. He promotes an 'ethics of virility', attributing a moral dimension to the contemporary constellation simply by virtue that it managed to force itself upon us.[51] The collaborator embraces a fallacious 'historicism' in which history is portrayed as a tale of progress, with the present as a necessary improvement on the past. He projects himself into the future and claims that, from the point of a distant future, the then-present state of affairs – with its collaboration – would make perfect sense and would be justified because by then the criteria by which we judge political events and decisions will be substantially different.[52] Armed with this perverse logic of historicism and 'realism', the collaborator evades the responsibilities of the present. By looking at the present from the perspective of a distant future, the present is portrayed as the (future) past and stripped of its intolerable features. Once portrayed as a past, the present becomes abstract and no longer something made and lived through. In a clear reference to Vichy, Sartre concluded that this way of representing the present – as a future past – enables us to forget a 'devastating defeat'.[53]

Like the other two essays, 'Qu'est-ce qu'un collaborateur?' finishes with hope for the future and an ode to the Resistance. He observed that the recent anti-Republican phase was far from a new phenomenon. As a democracy France has tolerated various opinions including those that are hostile to its Republican heritage, and this explains how ever since 1789 there have, in French history, been various counter-revolutionary moments. What France now needs is a new sense of unity, a coming together of different factions. What it also needs, however, is a politics of principles, one that does not subject itself to the brute facts like the 'pseudo-realism' of the collaboration, but one that has the courage to negate the reality of the present.[54] And tellingly Sartre ends with an example of the Resistance which was able to 'triumph' and which according to him was able to say 'no' to the facts when it looked as if people had to subject themselves to them.[55]

Concluding comments

Before moving on to the autumn of 1945 when Sartre suddenly became such a prominent public figure, it is worth recalling the central themes running through these three essays and establishing precisely how Sartre drew on his existentialist philosophy to articulate the experience of the war and make sense of the confusing episode of the occupation. What strikes the contemporary reader first and foremost is the celebration of the Resistance, which is portrayed as encapsulating the essence of France and providing guidance for the imminent political decisions which France was then facing. The three essays all applaud the Resistance, albeit in slightly different ways. The first article, 'La République du silence', is the most obvious as it can be seen in its entirety as an ode to the Resistance: the latter is described as *the* 'elite' which encapsulates the ideal of the French Republican tradition and functions as a blueprint for the Republic of tomorrow. Then there is the occasional slippage in the text which gives the impression that the Resistance embodied the French spirit altogether. More moderate in tone, 'Paris sous l'occupation' still praises the Resistance which 'the best among us' joined: it is presented as *the* 'exception', an instantiation of French grandeur in the midst of a barren moral landscape. Its heroic interventions saved French honour and they are the main, if not sole, reason why other nations should respect France. Likewise, 'Qu'est-ce qu'un collaborateur?' ends with a note on how the Resistance managed to stand up to what appeared inevitable, therefore becoming an example and guide for 'principled' political action.

Striking too, from a contemporary perspective, is Sartre's rich use of vocabulary to express the disorientation, distress and pain of living in France under the occupation. Especially the first two essays, published shortly after the liberation of Paris, testify to this trauma. 'La République du silence' uses vivid language to describe the dehumanizing conditions during the war: it describes the 'Nazi venom' which permeated people's minds and the 'cruelty' of the enemy, not to mention the 'atrocious' and 'unbearable' circumstances in which members of the Resistance found themselves, resulting in 'debasement' and 'solitude'. 'Paris sous l'occupation' elaborated on how difficult it was for Parisians constantly to live beside this enemy 'without a face' in a 'hollow' and 'dead' city devoid of its past traditions and detached from the rest of France. Paris had become a merely decorative entity, and Sartre compared it to a flowerpot which you put outside during the day. 'Dehumanized' and in a state of 'absolute debasement', the people's future was 'stolen' from them and they were reduced to mere 'objects'. Then further national 'disgrace' and 'humiliation' followed: France had to suffer the 'contempt' of its allies, resulting in an 'inferiority complex'. Published one year after the German capitulation in Paris, 'Qu'est-ce qu'un collaborateur?' no longer deals as explicitly with the pain and sorrow of French people under the occupation. It is a less moving text, more analytical in tone and exposition, but it still manages to convey the trauma of this war, especially when 'hatred' and revenge for France are portrayed as the primary motives for the outsiders to turn into genuine collaborators. It is their desire to 'enslave' and 'violate' France that prompted them to collaborate with Nazi Germany.

A third feature is the way in which Sartre managed to depict collaboration as antithetical to the essence of what France stood for. Using an ambiguous 'we', 'La République du silence' famously obscures the distinction between the Resistance and French society, giving the impression that the majority of the French were at least in spirit Resistance fighters. 'Paris sous l'occupation' tries to argue that the constraints made it very difficult for French people to act more forcefully than they did and that Nazi Germany had permeated France to such an extent that even the most patriotic acts would ultimately serve the enemy. The text uses other techniques to depict the period of the occupation as uncharacteristic for France: in Sartre's depiction Paris then had little in common with what the city used to be and likewise the Parisians had become a mere shadow of their former selves. Of the three texts, it is particularly 'Qu'est-ce qu'un collaborateur?' which disconnects the act of collaboration from the core of French society. Here Sartre is at his boldest, not only in portraying collaborators as marginal characters who were never properly part of French society, but also in arguing that it is precisely their marginal position in France which fuelled their resentment against their own country and led them to help the external aggressor against France. Further, while collaborationist intellectuals juxtaposed French specificity and history with the abstract principles of the Enlightenment, Sartre equated Republican values with the French tradition, thereby portraying those opposed to those principles as antithetical to the very essence of France. If 'La République du silence' is quintessentially *résistantialiste*, 'Qu'est-ce qu'un collaborateur?' supplements it with the counter-image of collaboration as essentially un-French. Crucially, this text leaves France untarnished, presenting a narrative that would enable sections of French society to draw a line underneath this difficult period and move forward.

'Moving forward' is indeed another theme that unites the three articles. While all three articles are 'historical' in so far as they reflect on the traumatic events of the recent past, each piece expresses its hope for a better future in which the French find unity and togetherness. These two themes – hope and solidarity – loom large in the concluding sentence of 'La République du silence', which expresses the wish that the forthcoming Republic will preserve the virtues and cohesion of the Resistance. The concluding sections of 'Paris sous l'occupation' develop an aligned position. Sartre explained how, in spite of the tensions and conflicts within French society during the occupation, a sense of solidarity still remained, albeit one which could not be acted upon. In contrast with this 'long dream of powerless unity', the French today are in charge of their destiny and can enact their 'desire for solidarity'. In the latter parts of 'Qu'est-ce qu'un collaborateur?', Sartre expressed the hope that the Resistance can inspire a new politics in which the future is no longer subjected to the bare facts of the present. In contrast with the 'pseudo-realism' of the collaborators, this ability to say 'no' to what appeared inevitable should be the basis for a reinvigorated progressive Republic. So, all three articles end with expressing hope for a future that would build on the heroics of the recent past but also learn from its grave failings.

All three articles draw on Sartre's existentialist philosophy to make sense of the recent past and articulate the experience of the occupation. But Sartre did it very subtly, using very little of his existentialist jargon. 'La République du silence' locates one of his central philosophical notions, freedom, at the centre of wartime experience. It boldly claims that the extraordinary circumstances of the occupation made French people, especially the members of the Resistance, acutely aware of their freedom and of the immense significance of the choices they made. So Sartre's depiction ties his philosophy to the Resistance – this sacred entity that represents a valiant France. 'Paris sous l'occupation' also draws on his philosophical framework, especially its distinction between human beings and objects. We learn that under the occupation people were reduced to 'things', no longer able to think ahead and make proper plans. Or in existentialist parlance, the individual had become a mere being-in-itself, no longer a being-for-itself. This explains why Sartre wrote about 'depersonalized' individuals. In a similar vein, 'Qu'est-ce qu'un collaborateur?' elaborates on the self and temporality, presenting the collaborationist mindset in terms of 'bad faith'. Indeed, the collaborator flees the responsibilities of the present by looking at it from the point of view of a distant future in which the current aggressor would be victorious and past values no longer hold. Here again, Sartre's existentialist vocabulary enables him to present a compelling narrative of Vichy and the German occupation.

The articles also indicate an interesting shift in the cultural landscape. In the two earlier articles, 'La République du silence' and 'Paris sous l'occupation', the notion of silence is very prominent and is linked to the bravery of the Resistance. We already mentioned how the Resistance celebrated the act of silence, which was associated not only with discretion and the strength of withholding information under pressure, but also with the decision not to write given the censorship. In both essays, this theme of silence is very prominent and there are three ways in which it is played out. Silence is first of all associated with the night and crucially with the dangers of being arrested by the Germans which tends to occur at night. It secondly refers to the act of being silenced, of not being able to speak out. And thirdly it is associated with the heroism of the Resistance, the withholding of information under torture and the related protection of others. What is particularly interesting, however, is the extent to which none of these issues appears in 'Qu'est-ce qu'un collaborateur?'. By then, the notion of silence no longer obtained quite the same resonance as it had done the previous autumn. Heroism was now no longer tied to the performativity of silence, but with its exact opposite: the act of speaking out and the responsibility for doing so. Soon Sartre would be at the vanguard of this revolution, which gave intellectuals and the act of writing an unprecedented centrality in French culture and politics. It is to this intellectual revolution, later referred to as the 'existentialist offensive', that we shall now turn.

— 4 —

THE AUTUMN OF 1945

In the previous chapter we have seen how Sartre's journalistic writings between mid-1944 and mid-1945 helped to articulate and make sense of the experience of the war, and also build further on some of the central themes of the trials of collaborationist intellectuals. It is during this period that Sartre's public profile rose steadily, though this ascent was nothing compared to his meteoric rise to prominence during the autumn of 1945. When Simone de Beauvoir retrospectively referred to this period as the 'existentialist offensive', she was not exaggerating. It was during September and October of 1945 that existentialism became the name of the game and Sartre a pivotal figure in the public realm.

Part of the explanation for this sudden interest in existentialism has to do with the numerous intellectual interventions – publications, plays or public lectures – by its main protagonists which caught the interest of the French media. It is important to note that, then as now, autumns are important in the intellectual cycle of France, associated as they are with the *rentrée*, the beginning of the start of the school and of the academic year. It tends to be in late summer or September that new novels are published, and in the autumn that prizes are being awarded and careers are made. The remarkable output of 'existentialist' plays and novels during the autumn of 1945 was central to the rising interest in the new philosophy. In September 1945 de Beauvoir published her second novel, *Le Sang des autres*, and the Théâtre des Carrefours staged her play *Les Bouches inutiles*. In the same month, Sartre published the first two volumes of *Les Chemins de la liberté*, *L'Âge de raison* and *Le Sursis*. However, two other events were also crucial. On 1 October Sartre, de Beauvoir and others published the first issue of their journal *Les Temps modernes*, which symbolized and concretized their positioning as engaged intellectuals. On 29 October Sartre gave his public lecture on *L'Existentialisme est un humanisme*, in which he explained, to a huge audience and a great number of journalists, the main tenets of his philosophy and defended it against its detractors. Within those two vital months an existentialist whirlwind had hit the Parisian intellectual landscape and had left very little untouched.

Les Chemins de la liberté and Le Sang des autres

The trilogy of novels of *Les Chemins de la liberté*, published between 1945 and 1949, explores the lives of a small number of characters against the socio-political landscape of France between the summer of 1938 and the summer of 1940. The first novel, *L'Âge de raison*, takes place in Paris during two days in the summer of 1938, and centres round the attempts of the main character, Mathieu Delarue, to persuade his girlfriend Marcelle to have an abortion and to find the necessary 4,000 French francs to fund this. The second novel, *Le Sursis*, is set between 23 and 30 September of the same year, the period just preceding the Munich Agreement. Drawing on new literary and cinematic techniques, *Le Sursis* moves rapidly from one scene to another, breaking with the notion of continuity. The last novel, *La Mort dans l'âme*, takes place in the summer of 1940, partly in New York, Paris, the battleground and then a German war camp. Whereas the first two novels came out in 1945, the third appeared four years later. A fourth volume, *La Dernière chance*, was never completed as Sartre's interests had, by then, moved away from the concerns that were central to his earlier work.

L'Âge de raison was written between the beginning of 1939 and the end of the summer of 1941; *Le Sursis* between 1942 and the end of 1944. So both volumes were, at the time of writing, reflections on the recent past and crucially on the shift in France from a period of peace to war and defeat. By the time of the publication the period to which the story referred was no longer a recent past but it dealt with the traumatic transition from the relative and deceptive calm of 1938 to the turmoil of 1940, a shift which most readers had witnessed first-hand and which the two volumes brought to life. Further, *Les Chemins de la liberté* was like a practical companion to *L'Être et le néant*, elucidating its main concepts but also giving them flesh. Both *L'Âge de raison* and *Le Sursis* addressed various philosophical themes that were central to *L'Être et le néant*, such as freedom, choice and bad faith, exemplifying them with the help of the central characters. The two volumes brought home the fact that Sartre's existentialism was not merely an abstract philosophy but relevant to contemporary experiences.

Nobody in *Les Chemins de la liberté* embodies these existentialist themes more than Mathieu, the central character. He is very much an alter ego of the author, not just because he is born in the same year and is a philosophy teacher, but also because he is beset by the same dilemmas that haunted Sartre during the period concerned and seems to evolve similarly. Like Sartre, Mathieu rejects bourgeois morals and commitments, and he is preoccupied with the pursuit of freedom even at the cost of the people around him. Hence his agony when faced with Marcelle's pregnancy and his determination to end it and to persuade her to agree to it and to make it her decision. His older brother Jacques, a wealthy lawyer of bourgeois disposition, reminds him that he has now attained the 'age of reason' and should come into the fold, offering him 10,000 francs to marry Marcelle; Mathieu refuses, more determined than ever to exert his agency and autonomy. Like Sartre, he is somehow unable to act, but eventually, towards the end of the trilogy, the onslaught of the war heralds the end of his apathy and the beginning of his political engagement. Like Sartre's intimate circle, Mathieu and his *entourage* are initially insulated from the outside world and show little interest in the political events until the latter force themselves upon them. Mathieu comes to realize that his earlier solipsistic pursuits of freedom were mere acts of bad faith; genuine freedom is only achieved through acts that embrace the freedom of others. Most of the other characters are inauthentic throughout; Daniel, for instance, is unwilling to accept his homosexuality and decides to marry Marcelle. Only Brunet and Gomez, committed Communists, seem to escape the spectre of bad faith.

The press reviews and critical commentaries at the time show that Sartre, through *Les Chemins de la liberté*, got his message across; the readers understood the link between his philosophy and the political context of the late 1930s and the early 1940s. Not all reviews were positive though, and the Catholic press in particular was critical. J.-W. Lapierre's review in *Témoignage chrétien*, characteristically entitled 'Le mal du siècle', was typical of the Catholic view that Sartre's existentialism was devoid of meaning, 'preaching a false freedom'. Lapierre deplored the obscenities and grotesqueness in the novel which seemed to attract young people and argued that it is difficult to identify with the main characters who are not 'normal people like us'.[1] Likewise, André Rousseaux, reviewing the same novel in

93

Le Figaro, was critical of the amoral universe that it promoted. He was scathing about the type of freedom that it implied, 'a freedom to abort', that is more generally 'directed against life' and 'towards destruction'. Sartre's society, so he continued, is a collection of 'a-social', 'egoistic' individuals without 'humanity' and 'love'.[2]

Yet, there is a telling passage in André Rousseaux's review where, in spite of all his reservations, he still acknowledged *Les Chemins de la liberté* as a 'Resistance and liberation novel'. Therefore, even one of Sartre's harsher critics interpreted the two volumes, which dealt with the period preceding the war, as commenting on and interwoven with the Resistance. Furthermore, Sartre's supporters identified a clear shift in his work towards a more constructive philosophical position. Whereas the earlier Sartre emphasized inaction, nausea and despair, the new Sartre talked about political engagement and responsibility. For instance, Armand Hoog, writing in *Carrefour*, argued that the two volumes of *Les Chemins de la liberté* were remarkably different from *La Nausée*.[3] Whereas the latter linked freedom to passivity, the former associated it with the responsibility to act. Hoog depicted an analogy between Sartre's trajectory and that of the nation. Whereas in the interbellum the French refused political engagement, this changed dramatically as a result of the political events of the late 1930s – the Spanish civil war, Nazism and the failed Munich Agreement. According to Hoog, Sartre showed why France had to 'wake up', and wake up it did.

De Beauvoir's literary creations during this period also contributed to the spread of the new philosophy, although her play *Les Bouches inutiles*, written during the war, was more explicitly feminist than existentialist. Set in a medieval town, Vaucelles in Flanders, the all-male town council, facing unprecedented scarcity, decides to sacrifice the 'useless mouths': women, children and the elderly. In comparison, her novel *Le Sang des autres* was clearly an existentialist tract, maybe even more didactic in tone than *Les Chemins de la liberté*. The book is set in France, before and during the Second World War. Drawing equally heavily on her personal experiences, the main characters of the novel, Jean and Hélène, play out the existentialist themes of freedom, choice and bad faith. Both Jean and Hélène, brought up in privileged households, realize that the war brings about their responsibility to act and to join the Resistance, contributing to freeing France from the occupying forces. Hélène's death only confirmed the dangers members of the Resistance faced. Not only are the heroics of the Resistance intertwined with key existentialist notions, but the novel also conveys the message that not standing up to the Germans amounts to accepting the occupation. This dictum, that not taking a stance is a choice too, had become a central theme in the existentialist rhetoric at the time and was brought to life here. With the two volumes of *Les Chemins de la liberté*, *Les Bouches inutiles* became the prototypical existentialist novel. In some respects, it was more powerful in diffusing the new philosophical doctrine than Sartre's *L'Âge de raison* and *Le Sursis* because it focused, not on the period preceding the Second World War, but on the actual occupation and the Resistance. It helped the public to articulate the trauma of the war while emphasizing the valiant nature of the Resistance.

The press reviews in the autumn of 1945 show that the clarity of *Le Sang des autres* paid off and that, even more than *Les Chemins de la liberté*, it conveyed to the reader how an existentialist outlook was essential for understanding the war. Emmanuel Clancier, reviewing the novel in *Gavroche*, put it in the context of the last couple of years, which according to him were unique in that French people had to make significant decisions. Once 'habits' and 'lies' were abandoned, French people were forced to reveal their 'secret mask' and 'make choices'. According to Clancier, de Beauvoir was one of the new authors to have emerged recently and who spoke so eloquently to these themes. For Clancier, Dostoyevsky's epigraph at the beginning of the novel sums up its central message but also conveys the historical significance of that message: it is indeed during the war that French people learned how '. . . everybody is responsible for everything towards everybody.'[4] If commentators picked up the existentialist themes of choice and political responsibility, they also understood the novel very much as conveying the dangers of inaction. André Rousseaux, in *Le Figaro*, for instance, mused about the perils of 'cowardice' during the occupation. The novel taught us that, in this context, not going into battle could do more harm and lead to more deaths than deciding to fight. Or in de Beauvoir's own words, 'I have learned in this war that the blood saved is as inexplicable as the blood spilled.'[5]

If de Beauvoir's *Le Sang des autres* was difficult to misread, the flipside was the accusation of a lack of subtlety. Clancier's only reservation about the book was its strong didactic flavour. The whole narrative seems geared towards the existentialist themes of freedom and choice, he complained. Nevertheless, her unequivocal messages meant that commentators now knew where she stood, and Jacques Le More's description of her as the 'star of existentialism' was typical of her newly discovered stature and label.[6] Her association with existentialist philosophy affected how commentators interpreted her other work: René Lalou, in *Gavroche*, described *Les Bouches inutiles* as a 'drama of engagement' in the same spirit as *Le Sang des autres*.[7] It also meant that her work came under critical scrutiny from Catholics, though they remained less negatively disposed towards her writings than towards Sartre's. Jean Sauvenay, in *Témoignage chrétien*, referred to her, alongside Sartre and Camus, as belonging to 'the school that is now in fashion'.[8] Striking a moral tone throughout the review, he criticized the passages in her novel about the absurdity of life and lack of direction, while praising her comments about the sanctity of life.

In sum, the rise of Sartre and existentialism was due in part to the didactic nature of the literary output in 1945, not just by him, but also by de Beauvoir. Not only did their novels, through their main characters, elucidate core existentialist concepts, exemplify them and make them come to life, they also showed the contemporary significance of the new philosophy. Indeed, the novels showed how existentialist philosophy was more than an abstract framework: it was able to make sense of recent events and experiences. As the reviews of their novels testify, readers at the time certainly made the link with the war and the occupation, not just in the case of *Le Sang des autres* but also in the less obvious case of *Les Chemins de la liberté*. The novels fitted into the cultural landscape of the immediate aftermath of the war: by condemning inaction as cowardly and by positing people's responsibility to choose and act politically, they celebrated the Resistance. With the novels also came a growing recognition that existentialism was a 'philosophy of the present' in two meanings of the word: a philosophy that was not only timely, but that engaged with the contemporary world. Of course, technically speaking, these novels, just like Sartre's earlier journalistic pieces, engaged with the recent past rather the present. It is the journal *Les Temps modernes* that will mark a decisive step towards a fully present-orientated philosophy, and it is to this journal that we will turn now.

Les Temps modernes

Sartre's rise owed considerably to the journal *Les Temps modernes* which provided him with an important platform for the diffusion of ideas. In this respect, politico-literary journals in general are significant because of their serial nature and because of their relatively wide and loyal readership. *Les Temps modernes* was particularly important because it was, at the time, in the minds of many associated with

Sartre and with existentialism, although, right from the start, other people were involved. Besides de Beauvoir and Sartre, the founding editorial team included a mix of people with multiple interests: philosopher and sociologist Raymond Aron, ethnologist and art critic Michel Leiris, philosopher Maurice Merleau-Ponty, journalist and historian Albert Ollivier and the novelist and critic Jean Paulhan. The mix of expertise in the group underscored the wide scope of the journal, addressing literature and philosophy as well as political issues. However, while each of these individuals was directly involved in *Les Temps modernes*, there is no doubt that Sartre was, from the outset, the main driving force behind the new journal and that he, more than anybody else, set the intellectual agenda. We shall analyse Sartre's careful positioning work, especially in his introductory piece to the journal, but first it is worth elaborating on the unique publishing situation at the time which provided a fertile ground for ventures of this kind.

The occupation and the purge had indeed created unprecedented opportunities for new journals. During the war various journals of leftish disposition had been banned, and they would take time to reappear if they did at all. In addition, by 1945 many collaborationist journals that had flourished during the war had been closed down. The upshot was a market for new politico-literary journals such as *Les Temps modernes*. Furthermore, by 1945, some of the upcoming authors, including Sartre, suddenly held positions of power *vis-à-vis* their publishers, mainly because of the *épuration*, which was meant to target editors and publishing houses as well as authors. If indeed many authors had written pro-fascist or anti-Semitic material, the publishing houses and editors that made this possible were held responsible too. This explains why a special Comité d'épuration de l'édition was set up with Sartre as a representative of the Comité national des ecrivains. As we learned in the previous chapter, in comparison with authors, publishing houses came off lightly: all major publishing houses managed to survive the purge except for Bernard Grasset. The main reason for this is that key members of the committee, like Aragon and Sartre, managed to protect their publishing houses and spoke out in their favour on several occasions.[9] This gave them a temporary, but decisive, position of strength towards their publishers. Sartre's interventions on Gallimard's behalf meant that it was easier for him subsequently to set his own intellectual agenda and persuade Gallimard to publish *Les Temps modernes*. Gallimard, on his part, had to change in order to survive. Championing a very different philosophical approach, associated with the Resistance, was the best way for a publishing house to shed its old associations and be rehabilitated.[10] Sponsoring authors with a wide public following was also a way to guarantee sales, and commercial survival, in the austere post-war economic context.[11] It is unlikely that Gallimard did not realize the unique market possibilities for an independent politico-literary monthly of progressive persuasion. There were two main left-wing journals but they had a marked profile with a different target audience: *Esprit* was clearly a Catholic review associated with Mounier's philosophy of personalism, while *Europe*, supposedly *the* CNE journal, had close ties to the Communist Party. There were, of course, a few new journals with independent status, such as *Poésie*, but they had a limited impact.

Then there was also the absence of *La Nouvelle Revue française*. Discredited by its wartime past, this erstwhile prestigious journal was now suspended, creating space for a new quality journal. It would not be until 1954 that Jean Paulhan, editor of the NRF between 1925 and 1940, re-established the journal, and even then he felt it necessary to rebrand the journal as *La Nouvelle Nouvelle Revue française* as a way of demarcating it from its previous incarnations. Notably, in 1945, the same Paulhan joined the editorial board of *Les Temps modernes*, bestowing intellectual prestige on the new journal. However, while the collapse of *La Nouvelle Revue française* had created a niche for *Les Temps modernes*, the latter was far from a replacement for the former. On the contrary, it positioned itself against *La Nouvelle Revue française* which had been associated with André Gide and Drieu la Rochelle's notions of art for art's sake and the autonomy of art. Not only had Drieu la Rochelle's stint as editor of *La Nouvelle Revue française* undermined the journal, but the separation of culture and politics had been one of the core tenets of the defence of collaborationist intellectuals. The use of the notion of art for art's sake to defend the likes of Maurras only contributed to its further demise within progressive intellectual circles. In contrast, *Les Temps modernes* built further on the arguments developed by the prosecution of collaborationist intellectuals, emphasizing the political responsibility of the author. There was, however, an important difference between the arguments by prosecuting lawyers and Sartre's position. The lawyers had explored the theme mainly negatively; collaborationist intellectuals were held responsible for the harm their writing had done. Sartre interpreted the same theme positively and made this the hallmark of the journal: its contributors have the responsibility to engage with the present. The name in itself – *Les Temps modernes* was named after Chaplin's film – emphasized the fact that the new journal dealt with issues of contemporary social and political relevance.

Needless to say, the name of the journal, however catchy, was not enough to position it. The positioning of *Les Temps modernes* was an ongoing achievement and the various articles that appeared over the next couple of years contributed to its profile. Of all the articles that appeared in the journal, however, it was Sartre's introduction to the first issue that was crucial in positioning it. Written as an intellectual pamphlet, it *explicitly* positioned the author and the other people associated with the project. It did so by developing a series of arguments and meta-arguments about the nature of writing and literature. It is important to analyse this text in more detail because it shows how Sartre used it as a platform to promote his views while navigating carefully the troubled waters of post-war France.

As editor of *Les Temps modernes*, Sartre wrote the extensive introduction, titled 'Présentation', to its first issue of 1 October 1945.[12] As we have already mentioned, the essay reads like an intellectual pamphlet, a bold proposition about what writing should be about. But the reader is also struck by an ambiguity. At one level, this introductory piece clearly explains the editorial line of *Les Temps modernes*, as one would expect from the editor of a newly established journal. In this sense, Sartre was writing on behalf of the journal and the text can be read as positioning the journal within the socio-political and intellectual field at the time. The repeated use of 'we' confirms this 'collective' positioning, and the reader gets a clear sense of what is to be expected from the journal. At another level, the essay very much states Sartre's views and draws on his philosophy. It locates him, rather than the other writers involved with the journal. The other editors and contributors are not mentioned by name, nor is there any reference to the other articles included in the first issue. Given the fanfare with which the journal was launched, this introduction provided Sartre with a unique platform to elaborate on his philosophical orientation about the role of the writer. Indeed, Sartre used this essay to elaborate on some key notions of his existentialist philosophy, rejecting attempts to define the individual in universalistic terms and promoting instead the view that individuals are always 'situated'. That is, the individual is always faced with a situation in which he or she is compelled to make choices, and not taking a stand is also a choice. Further, Sartre used this preface to elaborate on people's freedom, even if it is the case, as he admitted, that their choices are constrained.[13]

This piece became known, rightly so, for promoting so clearly the notion of the engaged intellectual.[14] Closer scrutiny of the text shows this notion to have different facets. Firstly, the introduction mentions the *contemporary* focus of the journal: Sartre clarified that the contributions to *Les Temps modernes* would address the social and political issues of the day.[15] As we mentioned earlier, the title of the journal already revealed a commitment to engage with contemporary concerns. In line with his notion of bad faith, Sartre juxtaposed the focus of the journal on social issues of contemporary significance with the individualistic preoccupation with posthumous recognition. Indeed, reminiscent of his critique of collaborators who superimpose a 'certain' future onto the present,[16] Sartre saw this preoccupation with an elusive future as a failure to embrace the present.[17] Secondly, engaged intellectuals do not just comment on the present; they also take a clear *position* while retaining their independence. Indeed, Sartre promised that the articles in the journal will not be neutral – they will take sides – but the contributors will remain independent from political parties.[18] Taking a position requires 'passion',[19] hence Sartre's antagonism towards apathy: he contrasted his agenda with Balzac's 'indifference' towards the political events of 1848 and Flaubert's 'lack of understanding' towards the French Commune.[20]

Thirdly, the notion of the engaged intellectual implies a desire to bring about *change*. Sartre wrote about changing the social conditions of individuals as well as the conception they have about themselves.[21] There is a certain ambiguity here. While Sartre suggested that the act of writing in itself is significant enough to bring about change, there is also the underlying assumption in this text that change requires more than just writing and that intellectuals have an obligation to complement their writing with more overtly political activities. Fourthly, Sartre emphasized the notion of *responsibility*. He linked this notion, which was a central component of his existentialist philosophy, to the act of writing. Like any other act, writing entails effects for which writers are responsible and can be held accountable. Note the extent to which the notion of responsibility is stretched in that ultimately people can also be held accountable for unintended and unforeseen effects of their writings. This implies that the writer should consider the possible meanings a text might acquire further down the line – a responsibility, that is, to foresee and think ahead. Conversely, Sartre insisted that writers can also be held accountable for not speaking out – for not intervening – when it mattered.

The background of the occupation and the trials of collaborationist intellectuals still loom large in this essay. While Sartre referred to other historical contexts in which writers had intervened or had not done so, the experience of the war remained the most prominent point of reference. In this context, Sartre compared the engaged intellectuals of *Les Temps modernes* with iconic figures of the past: just as Voltaire felt it was his responsibility to intervene in the trial of Calas, Zola his responsibility to speak out in the Dreyfus case and Gide his to intervene in the Congo, the occupation taught Sartre's generation that it was their responsibility to act politically.[22] When he wrote that writers ought to be aware of the fact that they are wage-earners and cannot pretend to be ignorant of the effects of their writings, he made it absolutely clear that he was referring to the trials of collaborationist intellectuals. 'Today, things have gone so far that some writers, blamed or punished for selling their craft to the Germans, ask in astonishment: "so this writing commits us, does it?"'[23]

There is also a clear difference with the Resistance discourse only one year earlier. We mentioned in the previous chapters the extent to which Resistance intellectuals, including Sartre, associated the notion of silence with the heroism of nocturnal Resistance activities and of not giving in under torture. By the autumn of 1945, this very specific association, tied to the period of the occupation, no longer had the same resonance, even for those intellectuals who had been involved in the Resistance and had written for clandestine newspapers. Instead silence was increasingly seen as a cowardly act – a failure to speak out and not take fully the responsibility which is bestowed upon us. In an ironic twist, intellectuals like Sartre decided that they had a responsibility to speak out and intervene in social and political matters of their time precisely at the moment when it had become safe again to do so. Very few of the French intellectuals who promoted the notion of the engaged intellectual in the autumn of 1945 had during the occupation – when it really mattered and when literally the future of the country was at stake – enacted anything remotely similar to what they were now vigorously advocating. It is possibly this earlier failure or inability to practise what was now being preached that might explain the fervour with which this new creed of the engaged intellectual was introduced. And it is possibly the collective silence of France under the occupation that might explain at least partly why so many people were receptive to this idea of political commitment and responsibility, as if the cult of the engaged intellectual would exorcise the ghost of a shameful past.

Besides the introductory piece, in 1945 Sartre wrote two other pieces for *Les Temps modernes*: 'La Nationalisation de la littérature' and 'Portrait de l'antisémite'. 'Portrait de l'antisémite' was published in December as the first part of *Réflexions sur la question juive*; we shall discuss it at length in the next chapter. For now, we pay attention to 'La Nationalisation de la littérature', which appeared in *Les*

Temps modernes on 1 November, during the famous existentialist autumn.[24] Notably, like Sartre's contribution to the October issue, this essay is the leading article of the November issue. Both tone and content could easily give the impression that it is a follow-up from the preface: with the exception of one passage, Sartre still used the first person plural pronoun, and throughout the essay he pontificated on the state and status of literature in France in 1945. There is, however, a clear difference with the preface: 'La Nationalisation de la littérature' is less prescriptive. It describes recent trends in how contemporary critics read literature and in how society treats its literary figures. It shows the difference between the 1930s and 1945. Still, the essay adopts a moral tone, deploring the current state of play, and urging critics and writers to resist the temptations that have recently come to the surface.

Which shifts did Sartre identify? Whereas in the 1930s critics showed little interest in literature and literary figures had received little recognition, intellectuals have since the end of the war undergone a remarkable change of fortunes. Even very young writers are now being celebrated as national treasures, as icons of French cultural heritage, and this based on only one or two novels.[25] When Sartre coined the term 'nationalization of literature' and used it in the title of the essay, he was referring precisely to how intellectuals had become appropriated and domesticated by the French nation and had been portrayed by critics as personifying the strength and soul of the nation.[26] Intellectuals might then even act as French ambassadors, conveying to a foreign public how glorious or brilliant French people are. There is a biographical dimension to the latter claim as Sartre, together with some other writers, had gone to the United States in a semi-ambassadorial role in early 1945, where they were regularly paraded and presented as Resistance heroes. The broader claim that intellectuals were at risk of becoming national treasures was probably also based on his recent personal experiences in France given the increasing attention that was given to him in the French press. There is possibly a competitive element to the piece when Sartre, now already 40, warned against the recent tendency to consecrate young writers who still had so much to prove.[27] This was understandable, Sartre insisted, given that so many older writers had their fingers burned during the war; it was deplorable, nevertheless, because a writer's whole *oeuvre* would need to be read before judging his or her worth.

What explanations did Sartre provide for this nationalization of literature? Here the text becomes interesting because Sartre acknowledged the devastating effects of the war for national pride. Sartre pointed out that France had gradually been losing its central role in world politics and no longer had much military or strategic power. The war experience had been especially humiliating for France and had brought home its insignificance on the world stage, leaving literature as its only world-class achievement.[28] Whereas other nations could celebrate their military prowess, France had only its writers and novels, hence the need to glorify them and to turn them into national assets. In the process, however, writers are being mummified and every novel is treated as another 'ism' or as a sign of future recognition.[29] This is problematic, not least because it is impossible to foresee what meaning or importance particular texts or authors will acquire in the distant future. For Sartre, it is important for writers to be vigilant and to resist this tendency to turn them into monuments. It is also crucial that they resist treating their writing as a future relic and that they act in the present, fully responsible for that present.[30] Here we have the reappearance again of one of Sartre's *bêtes noires*: the focus on the distant future as a way of avoiding the responsibilities towards the present.

Compared to Sartre's journalistic writings of 1944 and early 1945, this text is no longer triumphalist about France and the Resistance. On the contrary, it explicitly acknowledges the trauma and humiliation of the defeat of 1940 and the general sense of France's decline, which culminated in the widespread need among French citizens today to seek national heroes. The essay is remarkably reflexive, recognizing how the specific conditions at the end of the war had turned intellectuals into national treasures, ready for internal consumption or for external propaganda purposes. Although throughout the text Sartre mentioned his own treatment by critics only once, it would have been difficult at the time to read the essay without making the association between Sartre's central argument and his own recently acquired celebrity status. Sartre argued persuasively that the special context at the end of the war had made possible the rise to prominence of a new group of writers, though in a format which potentially curtailed his own project of a committed intellectual. Importantly, this essay shows that Sartre in the autumn of 1945 already felt recognized and established enough so as to critically reflect on the dangers of a celebrity status. At the helm of *Les Temps modernes*, arguably the most vibrant politico-literary journal at the time, he was secure enough, and felt entitled, to comment sarcastically on the hollow world of contemporary Parisian critics. Sartre would, of course, remain concerned about the dangers of symbolic and institutional recognition for the rest of his life, culminating famously and most dramatically in his refusal of the Nobel Prize for Literature in 1964.

L'Existentialisme est un humanisme

While the 'Présentation' provided a short, written statement of the agenda of Les Temps modernes, L'Existentialisme est un humanisme was initially a lecture which Sartre gave in Paris on 29 October 1945 and which only one year later found its way into print.[31] The talk was organized by the Club maintenant, a literary organization which was set up shortly after the liberation by Jacques Calmy and Marc Beigbeder. Sartre's lecture was an instant hit: publicized widely across Paris and attended by journalists of the main newspapers, the hall was overcrowded and Sartre encountered a highly enthusiastic audience. Subsequently the press reported positively about Sartre's project and his oratory abilities. Although the little booklet, based on the lecture and published by Nagel in 1946, became a bestseller and helped the dissemination of Sartre's ideas well beyond France, it was the talk itself that first made a huge impact in France and cemented the view of Sartre as a charismatic figure, able to talk with great authority and without notes. The theatricality of the occasion – a one-off lecture to a large audience rather just a written text – contributed to Sartre's aura and his reputation as an authoritative public intellectual. Boris Vian's depiction, in L'Écume des jours, of the mass hysteria surrounding a lecture by the fictional character Jean-Sol Partre was a thinly disguised mockery of Sartre's lecture, the buzz around it in Paris and the huge appeal he had at the time.

The massive crowds at the lecture and the resulting chaos meant that the exchange with the discussant Pierre Naville had to be postponed and eventually took place in private quarters, but the lively debate between the two interlocutors was included in the book. Naville was a good choice for Sartre, whether simply fortuitous or calculated. Naville was a Marxist but no longer a member of the Communist Party. In his youth he had been an active member, but was expelled from the party in the late 1920s because of his Trotskyist leanings. By October 1945 he had already dissociated himself from hard-line Trotskyism and positioned himself as a left-leaning intellectual with sympathies towards the French Socialist Party. The exchange with Naville, therefore, provided an opportunity for Sartre to engage with a critic who in spite of his Marxist leanings had shown himself to be opposed to a doctrinaire reading of Marx and who was open

104

to alternative perspectives. Crucially he was independent from the Communist Party, which had been orchestrating a vicious campaign against Sartre for a while. This did not stop him, during the debate, from accusing existentialists for pseudo-engagement and for courting old-fashioned liberal principles. Nor did it stop him propagating Marxism as the ultimate intellectual and political yardstick against which existentialism needs to be judged. But his critique was altogether mild in comparison to the harsh criticisms Sartre would have faced from intellectuals closer to the Communist Party.

From the vantage point of today, it might seem obvious that Sartre would use the term 'existentialism' in this lecture, but it was actually one of the first times he had publicly acknowledged this label. The term was relatively new, coined by Gabriel Marcel as late as 1943.[32] Journalists had been using the term 'existentialism' to refer to Sartre's philosophy, but he himself had resisted calling his own philosophy as such. Only two months earlier, he had explicitly refused the term 'existentialism' at a conference in Brussels, claiming he did not know what it stood for and that his philosophy was a 'philosophy of existence'.[33] There was probably a good reason why he had been reluctant to adopt the term 'existentialism': it was used regularly as a catch-all concept with pejorative connotations. Sartre gave a telling anecdote at the beginning of his lecture about a woman who, having let slip an unfortunate expression, apologized by saying '. . . she might becoming an existentialist'! But if hitherto Sartre had wanted to distance himself from a concept with such obvious negative meaning, he had now become media-savvy enough to identify himself with it. If most journalists were using it and if it had become common currency, then why not embrace it and make it one's own? This is precisely what Sartre did in this lecture.

The little book itself, a *verbatim* transcription of the lecture, has often been seen as a neat and accessible summary of Sartre's position. Many people present at the talk probably appreciated its clarity and succinctness. Compared to the density of *L'Être et le néant*, the lecture managed to introduce and clarify his existentialist themes with remarkable simplicity, while also providing examples which seemed relevant to the French at the time. In the discussion with Pierre Naville, included in the text, Sartre defended his vulgarization, arguing that public engagement requires an element of simplification; although deplorable, it was a price worth paying.[34] Subsequently, Sartre would regret the publication on the grounds that it simplified complex ideas. He would blame the book for helping to reduce his thought to sound bites and for contributing to various misunderstandings as to what existentialism stood for. The lecture certainly became known for some of its dicta. This included the famous 'existence precedes essence',[35] subsequently understood to mean that there is nothing intrinsic in what it is to be a human being that compels us to act in a particular way.

Right from the outset, however, Sartre explained in the lecture that his concerns were not merely to elucidate his existentialism but to defend it against criticisms from different corners.[36] By now, Sartre had become a prominent figure, especially since the publication of the first two volumes of *Les Chemins de la liberté* and the launch of *Les Temps modernes*, and he had become the target of various attacks,[37] not least from the more popular press which found his philosophy negative and degenerate. His work also came under scrutiny from intellectuals, with some of his former allies in the Resistance becoming his harshest critics. Left-wing Christians, including those around *Esprit*, felt uneasy with the perceived nihilism of Sartre's existentialism.[38] Even an abstract play like *Huis clos* was seen as depicting the degrading aspects of human life. Christian existentialists also distanced themselves from Sartre, disapproving not just of his atheism but also of the atomized and fleeting lifestyle that he was supposedly promoting.[39]

The most ferocious and relentless attacks on Sartre came from Communist intellectuals. They criticized him in various ways. They emphasized the link with Heidegger and the latter's chequered past during the Third Reich. They pointed out that Sartre's work was 'bourgeois', too preoccupied with the individual, promoting an unbridled 'subjectivism' and ignoring structural forces.[40] Or it was typically 'petit-bourgeois', reflecting the despair and lack of hope of a declining class. The work was too 'speculative', a rebranded 'metaphysics'. Relatedly, it promoted an 'abstract individualism', a quietism in disguise: why would people wish to pursue freedom if, for Sartre, they are always free anyway? In addition, members of the Communist Party also tried to tarnish Sartre's reputation. They questioned the motives behind his existentialism, emphasizing the commercial gains from his sudden public status. Or they spread unsubstantiated rumours about his activities during the war: Sartre had supposedly provided the Germans with information about the Resistance in exchange for his release.[41] These attacks were relentless and the Communists had a very good reason for this: their hostility disguised – or, in some respects, emphasized – their unease with a rival movement which, though mainly cultural, was seen, by them, to make it more difficult for the party to recruit among the young.

Existentialism was a rival movement. In December 1944, Sartre had already replied to their criticisms in the Communist weekly *Action*, leading to a ferocious counterattack in the same journal by Lefebvre. Sartre used *L'Existentialisme est un humanisme* as an opportunity to put the record straight.[42]

The title of the talk, *L'Existentialisme est un humanisme*, is intimately connected with these criticisms. Sartre's humanism underscored his rejection of the criticism by both communist intellectuals and progressive Christians that his philosophy was too individualistic. Indeed, early on in the talk Sartre pointed out that choosing one's own course of action has consequences for all – for the 'entire humanity' as a matter of fact. He gave the example of people who, by starting a family, are not only making a choice for themselves and their partner, but actually promote a particular monogamous pattern affecting all of us.[43] In other words, to make a choice is to promote a value, which ultimately applies to everybody. Further, Sartre was particularly keen to demonstrate that existentialism was a positive philosophy, not the 'ugly', 'sombre' doctrine critics had made it out to be.[44] Especially *La Nausée* was regarded as an anti-humanist novel. The title of the lecture already revealed Sartre's intent to counter these criticisms, and indeed early on he stated that '. . . existentialism is a doctrine which makes human life possible.'[45]

This background – the repeated allegation that his philosophy is negative – makes intelligible Sartre's return, towards the end of the book, to the issue of 'humanism'. He distinguished between 'classical' and 'existential humanism'. Whereas the former takes the individual as the ultimate goal and value, the latter sees the individual as always unfinished, always in the process of trying to go beyond him or herself.[46] As such, Sartre managed to depict his earlier anti-humanism, notably in *La Nausée*, as directed against classical humanism, while presenting his philosophy as an altogether positive enterprise. Throughout this lecture, Sartre emphasized that various existentialist notions, which are *prima facie* negative, are actually life-affirming: for instance, he pointed out that 'anxiety' and 'abandonment' do not lead to despair and inaction, but are the prerequisite for commitment and responsible action.[47] Likewise, he defended himself against critics who argued that the characters in his novels and plays tend to be invariably weak or cowardly. Sartre's reply, as spelled out in this lecture, is that there is, for existentialists, nothing intrinsic to these people to act in the way in which they do. Existentialism, according to his reading, is a 'positive' philosophy: as there are no evil or weak dispositions as such, individuals are entirely responsible for what

107

they do and even those people who have acted poorly in the past can change course at any time.[48]

Sartre made an effort to demonstrate the usefulness of his existentialist philosophy with the help of hypothetical and real examples. Some of these examples addressed the occupation and the war. These applications allowed Sartre to accomplish three things. Firstly, they enabled him to provide a vivid and lucid explanation of the key concepts of his philosophy. Although undoubtedly losing some of its complexity and depth, his philosophy was now made accessible to a larger public. Secondly, consistent with his preface to Les Temps modernes, Sartre showed the contemporary relevance of his existentialist philosophy. The lecture presented this philosophy as not merely an abstract framework but as properly engaged with recent events. Thirdly, a couple of examples provided by Sartre resonated with the public, providing a vocabulary that articulated and made sense of the wartime experience and the traumas it entailed. In particular, Sartre's terminology enabled him to explore the kind of decisions and dilemmas which French citizens had faced between 1940 and 1944. For instance, in order to explain the term 'abandonment' ('délaissement') and to illustrate that individuals are 'condemned to be free', Sartre talked about a former student who, during the war, had to choose between looking after his mother and fighting the Nazis, and who came to realize that no *a priori* principles could help him make that decision.[49] This, together with other examples, shows that individuals cannot help but make choices for themselves and have to bear that responsibility.

The lecture was meant to be an explanation of existentialism to a broad audience, but it was in many respects Sartre's selective reading of his own unique version of existentialism. While throughout the talk he purported to summarize the views of atheist existentialism and used the royal 'we', he actually presented his own philosophy, but now rebranded for contemporary consumption. Gone is the complex engagement with Heidegger, Husserl and Hegel, which characterized L'Être et le néant. In this new account, the notions of freedom and choice reign supreme: people are compelled to be free and they cannot escape having to make choices. They may, of course, exhibit bad faith, denying that they have any other options than the ones which are supposedly imposed on them, but choice always comes into play even when forgoing it. What distinguishes people from natural objects or tools is that the former are open-ended. There is nothing fixed in what they are – there is no human essence. Whereas scissors are made to operate like scissors and it would be difficult to conceive

108

of them or use them in any other way, there is nothing intrinsic in us to act in the way we do. This means that each individual can always move beyond what he or she is, or, in Sartre's existentialist parlance, be a being-for-itself rather than a being-in-itself. The absence of any *a priori* criteria to guide our choice creates existential anxiety, but this anxiety is a positive feature – an acknowledgement on the part of the individual of his or her intrinsic freedom.

In *L'Existentialisme est un humanisme*, Sartre simplified the ideas developed more fully in *L'Être et le néant*. By doing so he also altered them to fit the new socio-political context. For instance, *L'Être et le néant* presented a bleaker picture of human relations embedded in an ongoing conflict, whereby individuals are trying to deny each other's freedom by turning them into objects. In the lecture, there is less scope for this complexity, with Sartre recommending that people recognize their freedom and pursue that of others. In *L'Être et le néant* Sartre articulated the self in terms of a perpetual struggle between the being-in-itself and the being-for-itself. Sartre acknowledged that bad faith can manifest itself not only when individuals deny their freedom but also when they fail to recognize their facticity or being-in-itself. In the lecture, it is the being-for-itself that is emphasized as leading to authenticity.

Concluding comments

Sartre's rise in the autumn of 1945 was partly due to a broader, powerful network in which he had managed to occupy a leading role. Sartre's network consisted of strong ties,[50] not just because Sartre had frequent contact with the individuals of his network, but also because these relationships were characterized by emotional intensity and intimacy. Sartre's relationships were never merely professional and the friendships ran deep. Sartre had known several of the people for a long time, and some were his former university friends at the École normale. Others, like Camus, he had met more recently, but even there the bond was strong. Institutionally, the network centred round Gallimard, and the network included various writers who published with this French publishing house. Among this group of writers, Sartre, de Beauvoir and Camus were the most visible exponents of what was now known as existentialism, but other connections of Sartre also played a part in his rise. *Les Temps modernes* drew, *inter alia*, on the authority and experience of Paulhan, as well as on the emerging talents of Merleau-Ponty and Aron. Few of these connections were devoted to the existentialist cause, but they did subscribe to some broad themes which became the hallmark of Sartre's project, in particular the notion that literary endeavours should speak to the present constellation. Of all the people who were part of Sartre's circle, de Beauvoir's literary products around this time contributed directly to the rising popularity of existentialism and to a growing sense that, as a philosophy, it spoke to recent experiences and current concerns. The case of de Beauvoir shows this network to have many tentacles, using different media to reach its audiences. By the autumn of 1945, she, like Sartre, had written plays, novels and journalistic pieces. Both Sartre and Beauvoir's novels and plays were visibly connected to the newly emerging philosophy, with the various situations depicted as instantiations of existentialist themes and concepts. The didactic nature of these literary products made the new philosophy easily digestible and helped its diffusion; it also meant that by the end of 1945 Sartre's existentialism provided a coherent vocabulary through which educated people could see and articulate the trauma of the war and the occupation.

Drawing on the broader intellectual debates around the trials of collaborators, Sartre continued, throughout 1945, to reflect on writers' responsibility for their writings. In the process, he stretched the notion of responsibility, regarding people as responsible even for the unintended and unanticipated effects of their actions. In the course of 1945, however, Sartre also started to employ the notion of responsibility differently, steering it in the direction of his newly found vocation for the intellectual. The concept of responsibility, then, had become the central core of his new literary agenda, now virtually devoid of the earlier legal connotations of the term. Now referring less to how people retrospectively can be accountable for the negative effects of their past actions, Sartre increasingly saw 'responsibility' as a pressing need to use literary interventions as political tools for dealing with contemporary social and political issues. Whereas the intellectual debates surrounding the trials had reflected on the dangers of certain types of literary involvement in the realm of politics, Sartre's vision of the committed intellectual emphasized how pernicious intellectuals' withdrawal from politics could be. Whereas previously left-wing writers had been preoccupied with identifying whether a particular political involvement amounted to treason and what type of punishment was appropriate for it, Sartre and his entourage were keen to identify very different culprits: those who fail to engage and take a stance when it really mattered. Gone, therefore, is the much earlier mythical status attributed to silence, and it is now

110

replaced with the new heroics of speaking out. Yet, there remained continuity in a variety of ways between the earlier discussions surrounding the trials of collaborators and Sartre's bold proposal for intellectuals. Among the most striking continuities was the central role allocated to intellectuals within society – they seem to eclipse any other group or profession – and the underlying assumption that their writings had a crucial impact on the course of events. Sartre's new vision, here still in an embryonic form, would be fully developed in his *Qu'est-ce que la littérature?*

With this notion of responsibility, Sartre was clearly in the process of repositioning himself. His conservative critics still continued to portray him as a degenerative and negative influence, but his supporters now pointed out that his recent work constituted a neat break with his pre-war writings: while the latter depicted a bleak, amoral landscape in which despair and nausea reigned, his recent writings presented a more constructive philosophy of life which embraced humanity and promoted solidarity. His advocates were right, especially considering the tone and content of his contributions to *Les Temps modernes* and his *L'Existentialisme est un humanisme*. Once read through the prism of these texts, even the two volumes of *Les Chemins de la liberté* did not sound quite as desolate as they might otherwise have done. In his subsequent autobiographical reflections, Sartre himself would reinforce this view and make the discontinuity thesis a centrepiece of his own story about himself, arguing that the war had been a watershed moment for him which had altered his whole outlook. In the autumn of 1945, Sartre did not explicitly raise the issue of discontinuity with his earlier work, but his writings very much implied it. Sartre's own insistence on associating himself with humanism helped this repositioning and so did his new intellectual agenda of the committed intellectual. This was still early days, but within the next couple of years Sartre would further develop the notion of engaged literature, not just theoretically through *Qu'est-ce que la littérature?* but also in practice through *Réflexions sur la question juive.*

— 5 —

SARTRE'S COMMITTED LITERATURE IN THEORY AND PRACTICE

If the autumn of 1945 had been decisive in forging Sartre's public profile, Sartre used the next couple of years to consolidate and strengthen his position intellectually by further developing his notion of engaged literature in two complimentary ways. Firstly, he published *Qu'est-ce que la littérature?*, which integrated the notion of the committed intellectual within a broader theory of (and historical perspective on) literature. Secondly, he wrote *Réflexions sur la question juive* which became known as the first systematic work of applied existentialism. Whereas the former developed a coherent theoretical framework, the latter showed how this intellectual project worked in practice when analysing a sensitive social and political issue. This chapter will explore how these two works further cemented his position as a leading critic, and it will focus in particular on his *Réflexions sur la question juive* given its significance at the time.

From the previous chapter, it should be clear that by the time Sartre published the first essays of *Réflexions sur la question juive* and *Qu'est-ce que la littérature?* – respectively the end of 1945 and early 1946 – he was in the process of becoming a major public figure. To make sense of these two pivotal books, however, we need to clarify what *type* of public intellectual Sartre was during this period. Based on what we have learned so far, we are able to depict more precisely the nature of Sartre's positioning within the intellectual and cultural landscape of mid-1940s France. Two interrelated but analytically distinct features stand out: Sartre presented himself firstly as an authoritative public intellectual and secondly as an intellectual in the French Dreyfusard tradition. It is important to explore both notions briefly before analysing the two texts.

Authoritative public intellectuals not only possess high cultural capital but also exhibit charisma and character.[1] Although they might be formally educated in a high-status discipline like philosophy, they tend to be generalists whose interventions have a strong moral component and who thrive on taking an outsider position. They are quite different from *professional* public intellectuals who draw on their expertise and on the authority derived from this expertise to speak out about socially and politically relevant issues. In the 1970s, Michel Foucault, for instance, acted predominantly as a professional public intellectual when the publication of *Surveiller et punir* was accompanied by his involvement in the Groupe d'information sur les prisons.[2] So, in the 1990s, did Pierre Bourdieu when his sociological research into the effects of the erosion of the welfare state formed a social scientific platform for his increasing political involvement in the fight against neo-liberalism.[3] In contrast, authoritative public intellectuals, like Sartre, are generalists; they might be formally educated in a certain discipline but they rely on their vast cultural resources and charisma to speak out about a wide range of topics well beyond their area of expertise. In the cultural and intellectual climate of 1940s France it was still possible for authoritative public intellectuals to thrive; it was only in the course of the 1950s and 1960s that the social sciences took centre stage and became fully professionalized and institutionalized.[4] For example, sociology and political science were institutionally weak and lacked public visibility shortly after the war. Therefore, there was space within the cultural landscape at the time for what appears, from a contemporary angle, to be an amateurish and unmethodical analysis of social and political issues. While *Les Temps modernes* set out to study contemporary topics of social and political significance, none of the initial contributors was trained in the social sciences.[5] The journal was a politico-literary journal and Sartre's contributions had a strong literary flavour.

Then there is the Dreyfusard dimension. By the mid 1940s Sartre presented himself as a politically engaged intellectual in the Dreyfusard tradition, in contrast with the period before the war during which Sartre's political involvement had been minimal.[6] Dreyfusards at the end of the nineteenth century not only spoke out in support of Dreyfus, but in the process defended progressive Republican principles against conservative critics and expressed their scepticism of the judiciary, political and military establishment. In what follows we refer to Dreyfusard intellectuals, more generally, as writers who use their authority within their field to speak out about current political issues, who position themselves clearly to the left of the political spectrum and who are suspicious of the state and authority.

Three features in particular characterize Sartre as a public intellectual in the Dreyfusard tradition. Firstly, we have learned in the previous chapter how by 1945 Sartre set out to engage with issues of *contemporary* social and political relevance. In contrast with Gide's notion of art for art's sake, Sartre emphasized that writers had a responsibility to tackle social and political issues of the day, as can be inferred from the remit of the journal *Les Temps modernes*.[7] Secondly, although Sartre's political agenda remained nebulous during this period, he was sympathetic towards *progressive* political agendas, siding with the political causes of the working class and promoting a more just and meritocratic society. This was different from the period before the war when he was generally apolitical. Throughout the 1940s he became increasingly political and gradually adopted a more militant position and vocabulary. Thirdly, consistent with his position before the war, Sartre located himself as an *independent* public voice: that is, he was keen to emphasize his independence not only from the government but from any political party.[8] Although in the mid-1940s he was broadly sympathetic towards the political causes of the left-leaning political parties including the French Communist Party, he emphasized his autonomy. It is only between 1952 and 1956 that he would become more aligned with the Communist Party, but even then he kept his independence and never became a member.[9]

Theory of literature

Let us look at the theory first. As we discussed earlier, Sartre introduced the notion of *littérature engagée* for the first time in his essay on 'New writing in France' in the July 1945 issue of *Vogue,* and he developed it further in the 'Présentation' of the first issue of *Les Temps modernes* on 1 October 1945.[10] But it was in *Qu'est-ce que la littérature?*[11] that he fully explored this theme and developed the most bold and controversial expression of his proposal for engaged writing. The book came out in 1948 as *Situations II*, but was a compilation of articles which had appeared earlier in *Les Temps modernes*. It is structured around three simple questions, which are intimately related to each other: what is writing, why write, and for whom does one write? There is also a long fourth essay about the role of the writer in 1947. In spite of the neat structure, each essay inevitably deals with all four issues, and the fact that each chapter was initially published separately might explain an element of repetition throughout the book. Also, for those who were familiar with

Sartre's position on the committed intellectual, *Qu'est-ce que la litté-rature?* did not bring anything substantially different from what they already knew. Rather, it further developed the ideas and located them within a broader historical context stretching back to the seventeenth century.

When Sartre did introduce a new idea, it was in answer to the first question (what is writing?). This is the most contentious part of the book, as Sartre tried to make a case that prose was unique among artistic activities. Although the introductory pages of the text dwell on the difference between writing and artistic activities like painting and music, it is the distinction between prose and poetry that forms the centrepiece of this essay. Sartre's argument is straightforward to the point of simplicity: whereas poets are preoccupied with the inner dynamics of language and see language as an end in itself, those involved with prose conceive of language as a tool to bring about change. Prose, then, ties in with Sartre's notion of the committed author whose mission it is to 'reveal' the world so that people can no longer claim to be ignorant or innocent.[12] Controversially, Sartre used this argument to attack those preoccupied with form: concerns of style should never take precedence over the revelatory task of prose-writing. Sartre's belittling of poetry was possibly even more contentious at the time given the prominent role that communist poets had played in the Resistance (something Sartre briefly mentioned, yet failed to elaborate properly).[13] Sartre also dismissed those who failed to speak up and use their rhetorical skills to intervene. We already mentioned earlier how after the war the notion of silence had lost its heroic connotations and had become associated with cowardice. Sartre, in *Qu'est-ce que la littérature?*, went further. Silence, in his view, is a conscious act of refusal, but one that fails because it ends up being another signifier which demands justification. 'This silence is a moment of language; being silent is not being dumb; it is to refuse to speak, and therefore to keep on speaking. Thus, if a writer has chosen to remain silent on any aspect whatever of the world . . . one has the right to ask him . . . "Why have you spoken on this rather than that, and – since you speak in order to bring about change – why do you want to change this rather than that?"'[14]

In the second essay, dealing with the question why one should write, Sartre spent a long time exploring the relationship between writer and reader. A text has no definite significance until it is read; it contains so many 'voids' or 'silences' that need to be interpreted. Any written piece is therefore an 'appeal' for the 'generosity' of the reader which, exercising his or her freedom, attributes meaning to the text. In return, the reader has to trust the author and accept his or her generosity. It is possible, therefore, to speak of a 'pact of generosity' between author and reader.[15] Sartre infers from this an idea which he had already expressed in embryonic form in a clandestine publication in *Les Lettres françaises* in April 1944.[16] From the pact of generosity it follows, according to him, that the written text should not be used to justify injustice or oppression because that would contradict the principles of generosity and freedom which are so intertwined with the process of writing and reading. Writing in favour of a fascist regime, for instance, would be what we now call a 'performative contradiction'[17] because the very act of writing presupposes the freedom which is being argued against. In the clandestine publication Sartre did not mention any names but it should have been clear to his readers that he had Drieu la Rochelle in mind. In *Qu'est-ce que la littérature?* Sartre explicitly invoked the example of Drieu la Rochelle, whose writings, during his stint as editor of *La Nouvelle Revue française*, invoked no reaction because nobody was free to reply as they wished. 'He had demanded the enslavement of others, but in his crazy mind he must have imagined that it was voluntary, that it was still free. It came; the man in him congratulated himself mightily; but the writer could not bear it. While this was going on, others, happily, were in the majority, and understood that the freedom of writing implies the freedom of the citizen. One does not write for slaves. The art of prose is bound up with the only regime in which prose has meaning, democracy.'[18] Sartre's theory of literature, therefore, managed to put the intellectual – more precisely the *prosateur* – at the centre of the mythology of the Resistance because the writer's profession, according to his theory, presupposes and relies on democratic principles, which in the minds of the people at the time, were central to the fight against Nazi Germany. Collaborationist writers, in this view, not only betrayed their nation, but also their trade, employing the latter to deny its own lifeblood. Looking forward to the future, the theory, propounded here, clearly attributed a privileged position to the writer of prose in the political struggle for progressive ideals, but also acknowledged that, in some circumstances, writing might not be enough and that other forms of action, even armed resistance, might be called for.[19]

The subsequent essays, 'For whom does one write?' and 'Situation of the writer in 1947', depict an historical exploration of the conditions of the writer, from the Middle Ages to the present day. In both essays, Sartre also explored a prevailing tension within this project of the committed intellectual. On the one hand, an intellectual is

116

always situated. He or she is brought up in a particular background, with specific values and concerns, addressing a particular audience with which he or she shares a culture and understanding. On the other hand, the intellectual will be referring to universal values which transcend the present.[20] Sartre also mused on the state of literature in a future, classless society, arguing that his utopia of a 'concrete universality' could only be achieved under these conditions of equality. Sartre's vocabulary and the themes towards the end of the third essay reveal a growing engagement with Marxism.[21]

In both essays, Sartre was particularly interested in the ambivalent and complex relations between the writer and the bourgeoisie. His sweeping historical sketch starts with the Middle Ages, but quickly moves on to the eighteenth century when writers managed for the first time to use their skills to challenge the dominant order, helping to undermine the *Ancien régime* and aristocratic privileges.[22] Their appeal for freedom and equality suited the emerging bourgeoisie, but soon the latter would seek further ideological justification for their economic activities, with some writers happily providing it. The nineteenth century not only saw the increasing power of the bourgeoisie, but also a growing preoccupation of writers with 'psychological laws'. Of course, psychological determinism was not entirely new, but the total lack of emancipatory zeal was. While seventeenth-century forms of literature might also have been reduced to psychology, they nevertheless implied an 'appeal for freedom'. This was no longer the case in the bourgeois literature of the nineteenth century which, in reflecting the utilitarian logic of the dominant classes, oozed complacency and inertia and was in many respects the antithesis of the committed literature which Sartre advocated.[23] The recent war situation made Sartre's generation of writers aware of how pernicious an apolitical bourgeois stance can be; it brought home the necessity of a literature of engagement. This form of literature prides itself on clarity of expression, clearly distinct from the obscurity of 'poetic prose'.[24]

In 'Situation of the writer in 1947', a rather long-winded and at times repetitive essay, Sartre drew, among other things, a juxtaposition between the experience of the Second World War and that of the Great War. In contrast with the First World War, the Second World War made people aware of the political significance of writing, the real difference it can make and the responsibilities it entails. But there are also structural differences: more people are now educated so there is a growing public. Engaged writers, like Sartre himself, should no longer write solely for a bourgeois public, but should address the workers who are, politically, their natural allies and who are increasingly receptive to them. To reach them, there is no need for writers to vulgarize what they want to convey. Instead, it might be effective to use 'mass media' such as newspapers, radio and cinema to reach the masses, though Sartre added that the book remains the 'noblest', 'the most ancient of forms'.[25]

In *Qu'est-ce que la littérature?* Sartre continued to position himself as an authoritative public intellectual. Firstly, in this text he took a strong moral stance in that he spoke out against a wide range of injustices and oppressions, from the British involvement in Palestine to the wrongs of Stalinism. Further, he also developed a meta-theory that spelled out the need for a moral dimension to writing: faced with the war, writers could no longer avoid their responsibility. 'It is hoped that all literature will become moral . . .'[26] Similar to Isaiah Berlin's critique of Marxism, Sartre argued that members of the Communist Party contradicted themselves by promoting the notion of morality and subscribing to economic determinism.[27] Morality assumes the possibility that individuals can make a difference, something which crude versions of historical materialism deny. In other words, not only did Sartre intervene with the moral vigour which characterizes the authoritative intellectual, but his second-order reflections put morality centre stage, providing meta-theoretical justification for his moral stance. Secondly, he spoke out with great moral authority about a plethora of social and political issues, ranging from art history to foreign policy. Throughout the text, Sartre exhibited broad knowledge in philosophy, history and literature, without displaying the methodological rigour and precision which characterizes the writings of the specialist. The historical excursions, for instance, include broad generalizations about the conditions of writers in various centuries, with little empirical evidence provided and no references to the specialist writings on the subject covered. Moreover, the text puts literature and the prose-writer centre stage, even when addressing issues which require expertise or at least acquaintance with social and political analysis. His various questions about writing are answered in relation to literary works. As we shall see later on, Sartre's focus on the prose-writer will be consistent with his literary take on anti-Semitism.

Qu'est-ce que la littérature? also positioned Sartre clearly within the Dreyfusard tradition. Firstly, he wrote about how he and his contemporaries, faced with an uncertain future and some faced with torture, were forced to become aware of the responsibilities of the present. For Sartre, this contemporary focus goes hand in hand with recognition

118

of the utilitarian function of language. Writers should consciously use words to bring about change, and it is this consciousness that distinguishes proper engagement from simple involvement.[28] The responsibility to engage with the present also requires clarity of exposition. 'The function of a writer is to call a spade a spade. (. . .) In many cases modern literature is a cancer of words. (. . .) There is nothing more deplorable than the literary practice which, I believe, is called poetic prose and which consists of using words for the obscure harmonics (. . .) and which are made up of vague meanings . . .'[29] Secondly, Sartre further developed his progressive political stance, now using Marxist vocabulary and a revolutionary rhetoric. He elaborated on the need for solidarity with the 'proletariat' to bring about a 'classless society' and a 'socialist revolution'.[30] He then went to link the future of literature with 'the coming of a socialist Europe'.[31] Thirdly, he also insisted that writing should remain autonomous from external forces, whether from political parties or government institutions, and that in particular an overly close link with the French Communist Party would be problematic. 'If it should be asked whether the writer, in order to reach the masses, should offer his services to the Communist Party, I answer no. The politics of Stalinist Communism is incompatible in France with the honest practice of the literary craft.'[32] As Sartre explained himself in the text, his insistence on autonomy *vis-à-vis* the French Communist Party was partly related to the latter's unconditional allegiance to the Soviet Union and its aggressive tactics towards writers who did not toe the party line, but it also reflected his broader theoretical stance that writers should remain both critical and independent. Whereas in *L'Existentialisme est un humanisme* Sartre still struck a conciliatory tone towards Communist critiques, Sartre was now adopting a more assertive line as he had become increasingly exasperated with the barrage of criticisms from intransigent critics.

Building further on previous writings such as the 'Préface' to the first edition of *Les Temps modernes*, Sartre's *Qu'est-ce que la littérature?* presented a coherent meta-theory that would accompany, support and justify his recently discovered persona of the engaged intellectual. It amounts to a solid historical and philosophical framework that puts the writer, especially the prose-writer, at the vanguard of progressive politics. There seems to be an unspoken assumption that literature is particularly well suited for this purpose. Indeed, there is sometimes a slippage in the book whereby writing of any significance is equated with the writing of literature. Of course, the type of clarity and political effectiveness which he sought could not always be achieved through literature (or indeed theatre) without compromising

119

it, and he himself had increasingly been using other means of communication, such as journalism and political commentary, to get his message across. *Réflexions sur la question juive*, to which I will now turn, is a prime example of the type of engaged writing which he had been advocating in *Qu'est-ce que la littérature?*, and, as we shall see, it would be more apt to call it a critical commentary rather than literature, although it contains many literary references.

Anti-Semitism

The main message of his 'Préface' and *Qu'est-ce que la littérature?* was that writing needs to side with the oppressed and reveal contemporary injustices. *Réflexions sur la question juive*,[33] an analysis of anti-Semitism and the position of Jews, was thus an obvious counterpart to this theoretical treatise. In France it was heralded as a fine example of 'applied existentialism'. Like *Qu'est-ce que la littérature?*, chapters of this work had appeared beforehand in *Les Temps modernes*, but its publication as a book, together with the numerous translations, brought it to the attention of a wider audience. Each of the four chapters of the book discusses the psychological traits of a type – the anti-Semite, the democrat, the inauthentic Jew and the authentic Jew. It is the first chapter – the depiction of the anti-Semite – which was widely regarded as perceptive and powerful.

Jean-Paul Sartre's *Réflexions sur la question juive*[34] has been a controversial text since it was published. Sartre was, of course, not a stranger to controversy, but by the mid-1940s his critics had come from specific groups: they were either people associated with the French Communist Party or with the extreme right. *Réflexions sur la question juive* was unusual in that it also attracted criticisms from his 'allies' – that is, from progressive intellectuals and, crucially, from sections of the Jewish community itself of which the text was meant to be supportive. Initially French Jewish intellectuals were positively disposed towards *Réflexions sur la question juive*[35] and its vivid depiction of anti-Semitism (a large part of the book is devoted to this phenomenon), but later Sartre was criticized for his stereotypical portrayal of the Jewish people and for the problematic distinction between the 'authentic' and the 'inauthentic Jew'.[36] The English translation, which came out two years later with the less provocative title *Anti-Semite and Jew*,[37] received even harsher criticisms than the original publication.[38]

Réflexions sur la question juive was published by Paul Morihien in 1946, but the first part, entitled 'Portrait de l'antisémite', was published in the journal *Les Temps modernes* in December 1945. There is no evidence as to when precisely he wrote the text but the large bulk of it must have been in the latter stages of 1944.[39] We will focus on Sartre's positioning within the French context because both 'Portrait de l'antisémite' and the larger *Réflexions sur la question juive* were written in French and were addressing a French public and French concerns. Although there is some value in reading the text in the context of Sartre's 1945 trip to America[40] – notably in the way in which Sartre occasionally compares the situation of Jews in Europe and black people in America – the French context is undoubtedly more important.[41]

Sartre as an authoritative intellectual

As explained above, by the mid-1940s, Sartre was positioning himself as a public intellectual, in particular an *authoritative* public intellectual. That is, he drew on high cultural capital and spoke with great moral authority about a wide range of issues without necessarily possessing expertise in any of them. This accounts partly for why, again from today's perspective, *Réflexions sur la question juive* is such an unusual text in that it sets out to analyse social and political phenomena – anti-Semitism and the position of Jews in modern society – without remotely investigating it empirically as social scientists would do. It also partly explains why the English version of the book received a particularly hostile reception in the United States where the professionalization and visibility of the social sciences were more advanced, and indeed the relative popularity and methodological rigour of *The Authoritarian Personality*[42] – which came out two years after *Anti-Semite and Jew* and dealt with aligned phenomena – is testimony to the different status which the social sciences had acquired there and the extent to which they had managed to carve out a niche protected from philosophy and the humanities. By the mid-1960s, the professionalization of social sciences had become consequential in France too, so much so that Sartre eventually acknowledged that, as a 'phenomenological description', his *Réflexions sur la question juive* had failed to incorporate historical and economic research.[43]

Two issues require further analysis: firstly the position of literature in Sartre's text, and secondly his relationship to the social sciences and in particular sociology. Starting with the former, Sartre's *Réflexions sur la question juive* is clearly a quasi-literary and impressionistic account of a social phenomenon. Sartre did not attempt to provide a comprehensive historical account of the issues involved, nor did he rely on a systematic sociological analysis, whether through surveys or properly conducted in-depth interviews. Sartre acknowledged subsequently that his knowledge of Jewish culture and history was extremely limited and that he did not carry out any further research.[44] His research was in his own words 'phenomenological', referring to sporadic interviews which he conducted with Jewish friends, most of whom were integrated and secular intellectuals, and with people of anti-Semitic disposition.[45] His depiction of the authentic Jew was probably based on his friend Raymond Aron.[46] In many respects, Sartre positioned himself as a literary writer rather than a social scientist. As Michael Walzer[47] points out, the four ideal types in the book – the anti-Semite, the democrat, the inauthentic Jew and the authentic Jew – appear like characters in a play, and Sartre devoted more attention to their psychological dispositions and complexities than to the sociological dimensions of their being.

Besides the people he interviewed, Sartre referred extensively to literary writers and literary works. Some of the literary works referred to go beyond the French context. For instance, his theory of the anti-Semitic psyche drew on the depiction of the Jewess not only in Drieu la Rochelle's *Gilles* but also in Sir Walter Scott's *Ivanhoe*.[48] Likewise, he used Kafka's *The Trial* to convey that the public achievements of the Jews in society today, especially the rewards and honours bestowed on them, do not protect them against persecution but actually hide their true vulnerability.[49] But most of his literary references were French and often involved contemporaries of Sartre. For instance, when he defended French Jews against the anti-Semitic view that they can never be properly French, he chose as examples Jewish literary figures like the poet André Suarès and the philosopher and novelist Julien Benda.[50] More significantly, Sartre's description of the anti-Semite was based to a large extent on his impressions of the lives and works of French literary writers like Louis-Ferdinand Céline, Charles Maurras and Edouard Drumont.[51]

These literary references in *Réflexions sur la question juive* should be seen in the context of the Second World War and its aftermath. As explained in chapters 1 and 2, between 1940 and 1944 Resistance and pro-Nazi writers had been involved in vitriolic exchanges, with the former writing in clandestine publications and the latter in charge of high-profile journals like the *Nouvelle revue française*.[52] Most of the collaborationist authors like Brasillach were explicitly anti-Semitic. Sartre wrote the large bulk of *Réflexions sur la question juive* when the trials of the collaborationist writers were under way. Sartre's portrayal of the anti-Semite drew heavily on the views expressed in their writings, so the text can be seen as Sartre's commentary on the views, motives and personalities of the collaborationist writers, thereby contributing to their verdict and implicitly approving of the *épuration*. But Sartre stood out in the way in which he highlighted the anti-Semitic dimensions of collaborationist writings; these were largely ignored in the heated discussions at the time. As we have seen in chapter 2, the prosecution of collaborationist authors generally ignored the anti-Semitism of the authors on trial, focusing instead on whether or not collaborationist writers committed treason or the lesser crime of 'national indignity.'[53] In this sense, *Réflexions sur la question juive* was an important corrective to the *épuration* which largely ignored crimes against humanity.[54] Although Sartre did not mention the trials explicitly, they loomed large in the text, especially when he started off with a scathing attack against the depiction of anti-Semitism as a mere opinion.[55] At the trials, lawyers defending collaborationist authors argued precisely that: anti-Semitism was an opinion, which, like any other, ought to be respected. Hence Sartre's sardonic line that in '. . . the name of democratic institutions, in the name of freedom of expression, the anti-Semite asserts the right to preach the anti-Semite crusade everywhere'.[56]

What about the role of the social sciences? After all, they are particularly well placed to analyse the phenomenon of anti-Semitism. In the context of Sartre's numerous literary references, it is not entirely surprising that he was dismissive of social scientific approaches that study anti-Semitism as '. . . the result of external causes . . .' and that, according to him, '. . . are prone to neglect the personality of the anti-Semite . . . They succeed in revealing a strictly objective situation that determines an equally objective current of opinion, and this they call anti-Semitism, for which they draw up charts and determine the variations . . . (and which) appears to be . . . an impersonal and social phenomenon which can be expressed by figures and averages, one which is conditioned by economic, historical, and political constants.'[57] Sartre's preference for a literary genre ties in with both his particular methodological take on the subject and his general philosophical position. From the viewpoint of his philosophy of existence, to account for anti-Semitism in terms of external factors is to ignore that it is ultimately a 'free' and 'total choice'.[58] Further, to account for the history of the Jews in terms of 'historical facts' or 'social facts' is to ignore the extent to which the anti-Semite depiction of the Jew creates the Jew. It is this 'idea of the Jew' which affects history – not the 'historical fact' that supposedly determines the idea.[59] Sartre identified a vicious circle whereby, throughout history, the Jewish people have had to react and adjust to various forms of anti-Semitism, with these behavioural adaptations fuelling more anti-Semitism.[60] Put simply, Sartre thought that the anti-Semite creates the Jew, and subsequent critical commentaries focused on this dictum.

Sartre's literary stance also made him more susceptible to anti-Semitic stereotypes or at least remarkably ill-equipped to combat or refute them effectively. This is particularly striking in a passage early on in the text where he wanted to unpick the repeated allegation against Jews that they have acted in a cowardly way in war situations, especially as soldiers. Sartre seemed unaware that there was empirical research available at the time that refuted this claim.[61] Given this apparent lack of knowledge, one would then have expected him to point out that there is no empirical evidence available to support this portrayal. Interestingly, Sartre reasoned quite differently and argued that '. . . if people believe there is proof that the number of Jewish soldiers in 1914 was lower than it should have been, it is because someone had the curiosity to consult the statistics.'[62] So instead of questioning the empirical assertion, Sartre implicitly assumed that the statistics *can* be interpreted as confirmation of the fact that, at the beginning of the First World War, the proportion of Jews among the soldiers was smaller than the proportion of Jews in the general male population. This explains why he continued his peculiar reasoning with a defeatist attitude towards historical research according to which '. . . the information that history gives on the role of Israel depends essentially on the conception one has of history . . .'[63] He thereby not only belittled the validity of historical and social scientific data and overstated the power of interpretation, but he also regarded historical and social research as potentially pernicious in that they can be used to fuel and justify anti-Semitic beliefs. Rather than forming the basis for a critique of racist attitudes, they can be complicit in them. Needless to say, this position also made it difficult for Sartre to denounce anti-Semitic views because any appeal, in this fight against anti-Semitism, to historical or social scientific data could, according to his own perspective, be challenged. Devoid of social scientific criteria, it is not surprising that, as Suleiman[64] points out, Sartre ended up reiterating anti-Semitic views himself, such as when he wrote that he will '. . . not deny that there is a Jewish race . . .',[65] or when he described Jews as 'critical',[66] 'rational',[67] exhibiting 'lack of tact'[68] and having a 'special relationship to money'.[69]

This is not to say that Sartre always shied away from sociological reasoning. But when he invoked a sociological logic, his argumentation faltered. Theoretically, he combined Durkheim's views about the transition from mechanical to organic solidarity[70] with Tarde and Le Bon's theory of crowd behaviour,[71] blissfully unaware of the methodological incompatibility of the two perspectives.[72] Empirically, Sartre's sociological claims were generally crude, contained little evidence, and often overstated the case. This is particularly striking when he discussed the relationship between social stratification and anti-Semitism, depicting the latter as an overwhelmingly middle-class or lower- middle-class phenomenon.[73] Without presenting any evidence, he asserted that '. . . many anti-Semites – the majority, perhaps – belong to the lower middle class of the towns; they are functionaries, office workers, small businessmen, who possess nothing'.[74] This is followed by the unequivocal statement that '. . . we find scarcely any anti-Semitism among workers'.[75] The first of the two assertions, even in its vagueness, reflects his earlier contempt for the middle classes and provides a supposedly 'empirical' basis for his psychological account of the anti-Semite. However, social research fails to corroborate this alleged correlation and refutes the second quote, namely the proposition that the working classes tend to be immune to anti-Semitism.[76] Sartre's cavalier attitude towards the study of social facts and the opportunism with which he referred to those facts when it suited him are indicative of his self-positioning as an authoritative public intellectual – that is, a generalist, steeped in philosophy and the humanities and willing to speak out about social and political phenomena without methodical investigation.

Sartre as a Dreyfusard intellectual

We mentioned earlier that Sartre positioned himself as an intellectual in the Dreyfusard tradition. It is now worth disentangling this in the context of *Réflexions sur la question juive*. We will firstly show how Sartre positioned himself as politically *engaged*; that is, developing a progressive political stance, while sceptical and independent of authority. We will subsequently discuss how Sartre, through his analysis of anti-Semitism and the 'Jewish question', managed to demonstrate the *contemporary* significance of existentialism. Thirdly, it will become clear that Sartre, in line with the Dreyfusard tradition, was sympathetic to the Enlightenment, although his commitment to Enlightenment principles remained a qualified one.

Let us start with the issue of political commitment. Building on his earlier writings, the notion of *littérature engagée* underscored *Qu'est-ce que la littérature?* which emphasized the significance of political engagement and commitment, and which located the author

125

and existentialism as generally sympathetic towards the political causes of the communists while retaining its autonomy from party-political influences. This political engagement, combined with an insistence on the writer's autonomy, had been the hallmark of Sartre's public persona since the end of the war. However, it primarily remained a philosophical stance until the publication of *Réflexions sur la question juive*. With this book, analysing as it did the problem of a persecuted minority, Sartre put his theory of engagement into practice. In this text Sartre was also clear about his political position. As in *Qu'est-ce que la littérature?* he employed Marxist notions either explicitly (class struggle) or implicitly (false consciousness), for instance, when he asserted that anti-Semitism is a '. . . mythical bourgeois representation of the class struggle, and (. . .) it could not exist in a classless society'.[77] He drew the analogy between the predicament of the working class and that of the Jews: the Jews, too, needed to become aware of their societal condition and mutual interests, organize themselves and rise up. Crucially, Sartre found the solution in a 'socialist revolution' because anti-Semitism would, according to him, be absent in a classless society with collective ownership of the means of production. Bad faith and envy, characteristic of the declining middle class, would be eradicated. Once the classless society is established, authentic Jews would be ready to assimilate because the assimilation would be a proper one.[78] As in *Qu'est-ce que la littérature?*, Sartre kept his autonomous stance, stopping short of committing himself to any political party that might bring about the classless structure in which Jews would thrive. He was not opposed to political mobilization and organization, and he even praised the recently reconstituted 'Jewish League against anti-Semitism'[79] but he wished to position himself as autonomous *vis-à-vis* any political party.

More generally, Sartre's Dreyfusard stance tied in with his recurrent references to principles of meritocracy, for instance, when he provided the example of someone who failed to enter an elite university and who resented the Jews who manage to pass the *concours* and blamed them for his own failure. Throughout the text, Sartre depicted the anti-Semite as belonging to the 'lower middle class' or, as he calls it, 'petty bourgeoisie'[80] and in general those who fail to be successful in systems based on meritocracy. Anti-Semitism is a 'poor man's snobbery',[81] allowing struggling sections of society to feel better about themselves by portraying Jews as intrinsically inferior. The anti-Semite sees himself belonging to an elite based on birth. 'By treating the Jew as an inferior and pernicious being, I affirm at the same time that I belong to the elite. This elite, in contrast to those of modern times which are based on merit or labour, closely resembles an aristocracy of birth. There is nothing I have to do to merit my superiority, and neither can I lose it. It is given once and for all. It is a *thing*.'[82]

Even more central to the Dreyfusard notion of the intellectuals is their continuous intervention in contemporary society. Hence Sartre's applied existentialism, which was central to his attempt to position his existentialist philosophy as having contemporary significance. Parallel to Sartre's rejection of art for art's sake and his political take on literature and drama, he insisted that philosophy should not just be an abstract, timeless construction, but intertwined with and relevant to the social and political issues of today. His philosophy underscored his plays and novels which tied in with and reflected on current topics. Sartre's *L'Existentialisme est un humanisme* introduced the key existentialist notions to a wider public and showed its wide applicability especially to war situations that still resonated with the public at the time.[83] But *Réflexions sur la question juive* was at least equally central to his effort to demonstrate the relevance of existentialism today; it was in many ways his first 'committed work'.[84] Drawing heavily on the existentialist vocabulary of *L'Être et le néant* and related texts, the significance of *Réflexions sur la question juive* lies in the way in which the text applies those philosophical notions systematically to a socio-political phenomenon with contemporary significance. This certainly did not get unnoticed at the time. After its publication the distinguished philosopher Emmanuel Lévinas was particularly impressed by how *Réflexions sur la question juive* employed existentialist arguments to attack anti-Semitism and that, in the process, it showed the vitality and contemporary relevance of existentialist philosophy, '. . . bring(ing) back the Jewish question from the outmoded discourses where it is often broached to the very summits where the twentieth century's true, terrible, and gripping history is taking place'.[85]

Indeed, existentialist concepts like choice, authenticity, inauthenticity and bad faith provided the conceptual framework for Sartre's main arguments throughout the text. Sartrean notions of freedom and choice permeate the book, in particular in the portrayal of the anti-Semite and the authentic Jew. Examples abound. Sartre invoked the notion of being '. . . in a situation . . . as a universal structure in which the individual has . . . to *choose oneself* . . .'.[86] There are no essential features to Jews, but the distinctiveness of their situation – created by the anti-Semite – at least partly accounts for who they are today.[87] The anti-Semite '. . . has *chosen* to live on the plane of passion . . .

127

and hatred'.[88] Whereas historically anti-Semitism created the Jew, Jewish authenticity '. . . consists in *choosing* oneself as a Jew'.[89] Likewise, the concept of bad faith and related notions underpinned his discussions. For instance, the distinction between being-in-itself and the being-for-itself underscored Sartre's view that the anti-Semite is '. . . attracted by the durability of a stone . . .'[90] and does not wish to change: he '. . . seeks only what he has already found . . . (and) becomes only what he already was'.[91] Just like Sartre's earlier depiction of Lucien Fleurier in his short story 'L'enfance d'un chef' which appeared in the collection *Le Mur* in 1939, *Réflexions sur la question juive* portrayed the anti-Semite as someone who exhibits bad faith by fleeing contingency and groundlessness, trying to find fixity in culture, history or the *patrie*.[92] The notion of 'bad faith' also underscored the controversial distinction between the 'inauthentic' and the 'authentic' Jew. The former refers, in Sartrean parlance, to those Jewish people who seek to integrate at all costs – to assimilate and become fully part of French society. This inauthentic Jew exhibits 'bad faith' by choosing an 'avenue of flight', becoming 'detached from himself' and concealing the truth about himself, that truth being that he will still be regarded and treated as a Jew. In contrast, the authentic Jew refuses to integrate at all costs. He is conscious of his condition, '. . . makes himself a Jew . . .'[93] and only wishes to integrate with his tradition and customs intact.[94]

It is worth mentioning that Sartre departed slightly from the archetypal Dreyfusard notion of the intellectual in so far as he exhibited an ambivalent attitude towards the Enlightenment. On the one hand, throughout *Réflexions sur la question juive* Sartre promoted Enlightenment principles and depicted anti-Semitism in juxtaposition to Enlightenment values. Anti-Semites were seen as distrustful of abstract reasoning and experience: '. . . they wish to lead the kind of life wherein reasoning and research play only a subordinate role . . .'[95] Anti-Semitism was repeatedly described as primarily a 'passion'[96] in opposition to reasoning. When Sartre described anti-Semites as exhibiting bad faith he explained that this is because they '. . . seek not to persuade by sound argument but to intimidate and disconcert'.[97] So they stand for 'irrationalism', 'tradition', 'intuition', 'sentiment', the 'particular', the 'past' and the 'concrete' and oppose the Jew because of his association with 'critical rationalism', 'intelligence', 'universalism', the 'present' and the 'abstract'.[98] The anti-Semite is incapable of operating in and grasping modernity in all its complexity, and he is nostalgic for an undifferentiated 'primitive community'.[99]

On the other hand, Sartre expressed reservations about the

merits of Enlightenment philosophy. He had already done so in *L'Existentialisme est un humanisme* in which he rejected univer-salism.[100] In *Réflexions sur la question juive* he went further, questioning the Enlightenment both philosophically and politically. Philosophically, he continued along the same vein as *L'Existentialisme est un humanisme* in rejecting the essentialism of the Enlightenment, preferring instead to talk about people as 'being in a situation'. Contrary to the view that people have a 'nature' in common, Sartre suggested they share a 'condition' or 'basic human situation'. By this, he referred to an abstract set of constraints common to all situations: all individuals are born in a world already inhabited by other people, most need to work to survive and all will eventually die.[101] Politically, Sartre posited that Enlightenment principles might contribute to the precarious conditions of the Jewish people. This is particularly telling in the passages where he depicted the character of the democrat whose naïve Enlightenment belief in universal rights, justice and assimilation inadvertently undermines, rather than contributes to, the emancipa-tion of the Jews.[102] For Heidegger modern 'man' is condemned to a life of inauthenticity, and Sartre's inauthentic Jew cuts an equally pathetic figure, desperately trying to assimilate in a society that deep down rejects him or her, in the process losing his or her identity.[103] In short, Sartre departed here from the quintessential Dreyfusard notion of the intellectual who speaks out in the name of universal rights or justice. Sartre argued that this Enlightenment pursuit, insensitive as it is to Jewish culture, would end up eradicating it.[104]

Sartre's forgetting

Drawing on the general outlook of existentialist philosophy and explicitly referring to its key notions, *Réflexions sur la question juive* was meant to be an exercise in 'applied existentialism'. As mentioned before, applied existentialism utilized the philosophy to tackle current social and political issues, and Sartre regarded anti-Semitism as a significant social phenomenon with contemporary relevance. He was one of the few to do so at the time, and although the publication of the whole text with a larger publisher would have enhanced its dissemination, the publication of the first part, which dealt with the anti-Semite, in one of the first issues of *Les Temps modernes* certainly helped to cement the issue of anti-Semitism as a relevant political issue. The significance and originality of Sartre's text comes to the fore when put in the socio-political context of de Gaulle's concerted attempts to reunite a fractured society. At the time, there was little political appetite in Gaullist circles – and indeed on the left – to delve into the issue of anti-Semitism given its divisive qualities and French involvement.[105] This general reluctance to 'revisit' the potentially explosive issue of anti-Semitism might also partly account for Gallimard's lack of interest in publishing the book.[106]

But the very same socio-political climate might also explain some of the peculiar aspects of the text. *Réflexions sur la question juive* treaded carefully through the political minefield of the post-war era. The text did this both by the theoretical claims that were being made and by the type of issues or events that were explored or left out. To start with the theoretical component, consistent with Sartre's earlier portrayal of the archetypal collaborator as someone who lives on the margins of society (and is therefore in search of an authoritarian force from outside),[107] Sartre held that anti-Semitism flourishes when integrative forces are weak and declines when society finds a renewed common purpose.[108] At his most eclectic, Sartre combined the theory of crowd behaviour with Durkheim's evolutionary theory to argue that under conditions of diminished solidarity the anti-Semite cuts an isolated figure and precisely because of his atomized state becomes susceptible to the overpowering and destructive force of the crowd.[109] Not only did Sartre's account exclude a proper investigation of the culture and institutions of French society or the role of the state, he portrayed anti-Semitism as antithetical to a properly functioning French society; it only surfaces and will only resurface in periods of anomie when solidarity is on the wane. Sartre's argument, in conjunction with de Gaulle's unifying efforts, portrayed anti-Semitism not just as a hankering for a mythical past but also as potentially a thing of the past itself if, as he hastily pointed out, the divisions between the classes are finally eroded.

Moving on to the more 'descriptive' dimension of Sartre's navigation skills, while dealing with a highly sensitive issue in which the French were heavily implicated, the text still managed to avoid opening some of the darker pages of recent French history. Sartre's account was abstract and, crucially, contained hardly any references to the Holocaust and none to Vichy's active involvement in the deportation of the Jews. These omissions were in line with Sartre's journalistic writings of 1944 and 1945 which colluded with de Gaulle in depicting a cohesive and defiant French nation and in developing a *résistantialiste* account of history according to which a significant number of the French were Resistance fighters and few were genuine collaborators.[110] This is particularly striking in 'La République du silence'[111] which praised the activities of the French Resistance and then equated their heroics to those of the French people.[112] Equally revealing was Sartre's 'Qu'est-ce qu'un collaborateur' in which collaborators were portrayed as not properly integrated, living on the margins of society and in search of a strong social force from the outside.[113]

Réflexions sur la question juive concentrated on the emotional state, views and rationalizations of anti-Semites, not on the atrocities that took place. As Traverso[114] pointed out, the Holocaust was surprisingly marginal in Sartre's argument. In so far as Sartre mentioned anti-Semitic *actions*, the text tended to ignore what the French actually did to the Jews. He discussed anti-Semitic actions in abstract terms or tended to provide examples from outside of France: for instance, the 'butchery of Lublin'[115] or the killing of Jews by the Gestapo.[116] There were a few exceptions to this rule. For instance, Sartre came close to recognizing the French involvement in the persecution and deportation of the Jews when he depicted the '. . . democrat (who) . . . during the occupation was . . . indignant at the anti-Semitic persecutions . . .'[117] but Sartre remained vague about who the persecutors were. The reference to the 'occupation' – not to Vichy or to the French officials who appeared very willing to follow German orders – seemed to suggest that the Germans were the sole persecutors. Sartre came closer towards acknowledging French responsibility for the atrocities committed against the Jews when he wrote that '. . . in 1940 . . . the Pétain government . . . initiated anti-Semitic measurements . . .'[118] However, not only did the reference to 'measurements' remain mild and fail to do full justice for what took place, the acknowledgement was then followed by the statement that '. . . today those Jews whom the *Germans* did not deport or murder are coming back to their homes . . .',[119] thereby suggesting that the deportations were exclusively a German responsibility. Towards the end of the book, Sartre wrote about the responsibility which 'we' all share but it remains unclear to whom 'we' refers, and even here he was only willing to admit '. . . our *involuntary* complicity with the anti-Semites'.[120] In short, while Sartre was one of the first to systematically analyse anti-Semitism and to bring it to the fore at this time, there is no doubt that he consciously or unconsciously curtailed his applied existentialism in accordance with the political sensitivities of the day, stopping short of writing openly of the French treatment of the Jews and their involvement in their deportation to the concentration camps.

There is another omission in the text, one which concerns Sartre directly and which is intimately related to his silence about the French involvement. While in other publications in this period Sartre positioned himself as an engaged writer and virulently condemned authors who did nothing to halt the injustice and atrocities of their time, it is worth qualifying this 'heroic' stance with two observations. Firstly, Sartre propagated this position precisely when the political context had become safer again and when taking a political stance had (at least for a while) become more of a symbolic act than one which made a 'real' difference. Secondly, at crucial points during the war he himself had not spoken out when it really mattered: he had remained silent at the sight of the mistreatment and deportation of the Jews.[121] In that sense his sarcastic comments about the democrat were particularly misplaced (at least the democrat had the courage to speak out when the lives of the Jews were at stake), but the 'we' towards the end of the book could possibly include Sartre himself and this was the closest he came to expressing his 'guilt' ('guilt' from the perspective of his own theory of responsibility of the writer, that is). Be that as it may, Sartre carefully left out any reference to his own inaction from the narrative of *Réflexions sur la question juive*, something which was made possible by the abstract tone of the text and of course by his neglect of the French context. Admitting to those failings would have made it particularly difficult for him to position himself as an *intellectuel engagé* or to maintain that position.

Concluding comments

We have seen how both *Qu'est-ce que la littérature?* and *Réflexions sur la question juive* enabled Sartre to position himself as an authoritative public intellectual – a generalist with a strong moral voice, commenting on a wide range of issues without methodical analysis – and as a politically committed writer with a progressive and autonomous stance. Both *Qu'est-ce que la littérature?* and *Réflexions sur la question juive* attribute immense importance to literary figures: the former does this by ignoring other types of intellectual activities and the latter by taking a distinctly literary and impressionistic stance on the phenomenon of anti-Semitism. While *Qu'est-ce que la littérature?* provided the theoretical backbone of his intellectual programme, *Réflexions sur la question juive* demonstrated its applicability to a significant and sensitive topic. As the first systematic piece of *applied* existentialism, *Réflexions sur la question juive* was indeed important, demonstrating as it did that the notion of engaged literature was not just a theoretical posture. In his text, Sartre also navigated carefully around the sensitivities surrounding the traumatic experiences of the war, implicitly confirming the official narrative of the French involvement in the war and protecting the narratives underlying his own self-presentation. In this sense, *Réflexions sur la question juive* continued Sartre's delicate balancing act which started with his journalistic pieces in 1944, commenting thoughtfully on the trauma of the war while treading carefully so as not to upset the way in which the majority of the French might have liked to see themselves portrayed through this whole episode.

Both texts show that the erstwhile apolitical Sartre was now increasingly willing to adopt a quasi-Marxist vocabulary and had started to phrase his notion of engaged literature in those terms. In the aftermath of the war, socialist and communist currents swept through France, changing people's sensitivities and general outlook both in politics and in culture. Sartre was clearly responding to this, merging his existentialist concerns with vague Marxist notions. Whereas Sartre had explicitly tackled communist critics of his work in *L'Existentialisme est un humanisme*, Sartre now appeared less defensive, happy to use Marxist jargon and more or less embracing a Marxist outlook. Yet, throughout both texts, Sartre's use of Marxism remained sporadic. Furthermore, during this period Sartre's use of Marxist terminology did not run very deep. Initially trained in phenomenology and as a novelist and dramaturge more attentive to individual motives and idiosyncrasies than social structures, Marxist reasoning was alien to Sartre and his references to class come across as rather contrived. Sartre's knowledge of Marx remained limited and it would not be until the 1950s that he started to study Marx's writings properly and would make a concerted effort to integrate existentialism and Marxism.

If *Qu'est-ce que la littérature?* and *Réflexions sur la question juive* further established Sartre as a public intellectual, his other activities during this period complemented the books. Consistent with his recommendations in *Qu'est-ce que la littérature?*, he started making effective use of other media, not just plays but also the radio. It is during these activities that he became more provocative, reaching a broader audience and also becoming the target of the tabloid press. His provocative stance was already apparent in his 1946 piece *Morts sans sépulture* which included torture scenes, but it became particularly prominent in his radio appearances. Indeed, in the autumn of 1947 the editorial members of *Les Temps modernes* were able to broadcast on the state-controlled French radio.[122] Applying the notion of the engaged intellectual, this show, called 'Tribune des *Temps modernes*', addressed social and political themes that were relevant at the time. These included 'Gaullism', 'communism and anti-communism', 'liberalism and socialism' and 'the crisis of socialism'. Nine programmes were made; six were broadcast. Eventually the government intervened and the remaining three were censored. The programmes tended to mix analytical arguments with slapdash and anecdotal comments. The most famous (or infamous, depending on one's perspective) broadcast was the first one, which dealt with de Gaulle and Gaullism. The Gaullist RPF (Rassemblement du peuple français) was becoming an important political force at the time, and the team reflected on the possible dangers of concentrating so much power in one person. This broadcast was heavily criticized because it included personal attacks on de Gaulle, comparing him to Hitler.

These radio appearances also demonstrated the practical difficulties for Sartre in positioning himself as autonomous *vis-à-vis* external forces. The radio was state-owned and the Ramadier government had given permission to the broadcasts. Many commentators at the time noted how the broadcasts, critical as they were of both the PCF (Parti communiste français) and the RPF, served the interests of the Ramadier government, which by the second part of 1947 no longer included members of the PCF.[123] Sartre remained insistent that the radio broadcasts were an expression of autonomous intellectual activity, and he thought the subsequent censor by the Schuman government confirmed this autonomy. Others counter-argued that Sartre's intentions were irrelevant in that the programmes, however well intended, had clearly been beneficial to the government that was then in charge. The furore around the radio broadcasts showed the limitations of the notion of the autonomous, committed intellectual. His theory of literature, as spelled out in *Qu'est-ce que la littérature?*, focuses on the moral compass of the single intellectual, and tends to ignore how, even with the best of intentions, intellectual interventions can become a means to other people's ends.

— 6 —

RISE AND DEMISE:
A SYNTHESIS

We will now pull together the threads of the arguments presented in the previous chapters, providing a multifaceted explanation for the rise of Sartre and existentialism in the mid-1940s. Indeed, as we have seen, many factors helped to contribute to this phenomenon, and it is important now to distinguish these different aspects but also to analyse more closely how they came together and interacted. None of the factors was decisive, but their confluence was crucial. It made for a unique historical setting in which Sartre appeared particularly adept at resonating with his public, rearticulating his philosophy in ways which expressed the recent trauma of the war as well as the hope for the future. This enabled him to remain a pivotal public figure until well into the 1950s. Once that setting changed, we will argue, Sartre's popularity and that of existentialism decreased. And change it did. Many societal shifts occurred, which made Sartre and existentialism less relevant. One such shift, as we shall see, was the rise of the social sciences. Another was structuralism.

The rise: a synthesis

What is the unique context in which Sartre and existentialism came to the fore and which accounts for the latter? Which factors were important? Let us summarize the main points that have emerged from the previous chapters.

Intellectual vacancies

Firstly, it was a socio-historical setting in which, to put it bluntly, there were plenty of intellectual vacancies. By this we mean that, in the mid-1940s in France, there was unusual scope for new intellectual figures and intellectual movements. Why was this the case? The experience of the war had undermined the legitimacy of a substantial part of the intellectual establishment, either because of the wartime activities of some well-known writers or because their ideas no longer resonated with the public. The former concerned the collaboration of some writers with Nazi Germany or Vichy, whereas the latter referred to changing notions of what writing was or should be about.

What had some writers done to undermine their credibility? Towards the end of the war, a significant number of writers were regarded as being compromised either because they had written openly in support of fascism and Vichy or because they had appeared ambiguous or at least not clear enough in their condemnation of Nazi occupation or Vichy. Most formerly occupied countries prosecuted collaborators, but France was unique in targeting its collaborationist intellectuals. As can be inferred from Resistance novels like Vercors' *Le Silence de la mer*, some sections of the Resistance portrayed French literature at the core of national identity and Germany as intent on destroying it. In this light, collaborationist literature was the ultimate betrayal.

The purge took two forms. One was a naming and shaming exercise orchestrated from within the writers' profession. This had started early on in the war: articles appeared in *Les Lettres françaises*, the clandestine Resistance literary journal, in which various authors were criticized, for instance, for attending the International Writers' Congress in Weimar (Brasillach), writing pro-Nazi material (Chardonne, Céline, Montherlant) or for publishing in collaborationist outlets (Colette, Giono) or simply for studying the German language (Gide). More importantly, at the end of the war, the communist-dominated Comité national des écrivains (CNE) compiled a 'blacklist' of 165 authors which included explicit fascist sympathizers like Robert Brasillach, Louis-Ferdinand Céline and Pierre-Eugène Drieu la Rochelle, but also a large number of authors who are not as easily classifiable but whose inclusion on the list meant nevertheless that their careers were blighted, if not destroyed.

Besides the naming and shaming, the purge of intellecuals also took a judicial form. The temporary French government under Charles de Gaulle prosecuted some of the most explicit fascist authors, with

Maurras' and Brasillach's trials among the most well-known *procès d'épuration*. The sentences were severe, especially in the earlier trials where the defendants were often accused of treason: several writers were sentenced to death, though some were commuted to life sentences. With time, sentences became more lenient, with national indignity rather than treason becoming the main accusation. However, even with a light sentence, a writer's career would be tainted.

What is striking about the French case is not the number or intensity of pro-fascist writings, nor the lack of pity for those responsible, but the collective effort, determination and considerable organization that brought about the end of numerous literary and intellectual careers (and indeed in some cases lives). The 'purge' did not go unchallenged at the time, and it would not take long for a consensus to emerge within France that the *épuration* had been a problematic period in its history. However, by then the purge had wiped out the careers and futures of many individuals, not just of openly fascist authors (like Brasillach, Céline, Drieu la Rochelle and Maurras) but also of those with a more moderate or ambiguous disposition (for instance, Henry de Montherlant, Paul Morand, Jacques Chardonne). The discrediting of a large section of the old guard created what Hewitt rightly calls a 'cultural power vacuum'[1] and therefore possibilities upon which writers associated with the Resistance such as Sartre would seize. Indeed some of those Resistance writers had also been involved in the act of administering disgrace. Of course, some of the discredited people were later rehabilitated – for instance, Chardonne and Morand became prominent members of the *Hussards*, an anti-existentialist and anti-Gaullist movement[2] – but not during the period we are considering here.

However, the *épuration* had its most dramatic effect on the post-war cultural landscape in France not by denouncing or imprisoning writers, but in more subtle ways: by changing the notion of what writing should be about. The experience of the war made certain intellectual positions or genres no longer tenable or at least less attractive, even if the people representing them had not been associated with Vichy. For instance, the close connection between the Catholic Church and Vichy made it difficult for conservative Catholics to keep afloat within the new intellectual scene, while progressive Catholics, centred round the journal *Esprit* and the philosophy of personalism, capitalized on their Resistance credentials and kept a high profile. Most importantly, the notion of *l'art pour l'art* might have found resonance among some circles in the 1930s, but by the mid-1940s it appeared like a relic from a bygone era. Against the background of the war, it became less plausible to think of literature and writing as divorced from the political. Writers were now seen as having social and political responsibility. Several articles published during the war in *Les Lettres françaises* had already criticized attempts to separate art from politics. Against this distinction, which was denigrated as a fascist ploy, literature and language were described as 'instruments' and 'ways of acting'.[3] In the highly publicized trials of Maurras and Brasillach, the defence maintained the separation of art from politics while the prosecution underscored the political significance of writing. In Sartre's parlance, not to act politically was regarded as having significant political ramifications because writers are always *en situation*. Not only had it become unacceptable for writers to think of art for art's sake, but realist or naturalist notions of literature were now also regarded with suspicion: impartiality and objectivity were no longer seen as plausible aims. In sum, not only were some writers sidelined because of their perceived or actual collaboration; some genres or intellectual positions, which had been significant before the war, were now regarded as irrelevant, problematic or possibly pernicious.

Within this new climate, three intellectual positions would flourish: existentialism, Marxism and finally progressive Catholicism (especially the doctrine of personalism). Authors within the three camps would not only acquire authority because of their Resistance activities, but would also stress the immense political responsibility of the author. In a lecture in New York, in January 1945, Sartre introduced Camus, Cassou and Leiris as the new generation in opposition to the old guard of Gide, Giraudoux and Anouilh. The writers of this new generation lived through the war and in the process became aware of how writing is an act with significant consequences.[4] In this context, *Les Temps modernes*, Sartre's flagship launched in the autumn of 1945, was in direct opposition to *La Nouvelle Revue française* which had been associated with notions of art for art's sake. The name of the journal – after Chaplin's film – positioned it as addressing issues of contemporary social and political relevance. In his editorial to the first issue of *Les Temps modernes*, Sartre denounced the theoreticians of both *l'art pour l'art* and *réalisme*, showing that those views of literature shared a cowardly lack of political commitment.

Publishing

Intellectual ideas spread mainly through publications. Whether through books, magazines or articles, publishing is central to the rise of intellectual movements. For such movements to be successful, authors have to be well connected to the main publishers and need to have sufficient freedom and power to be able to write what they want to write. Until the mid-twentieth century the publishing industry in France was dominated by a number of relatively small publishers whose proprietors, such as Gaston Gallimard, would establish close connections with their main authors.[5] Often, prospective authors would be introduced by established authors whom they knew through mutual membership of elite institutions like the École normale. This is how, for instance, Sartre managed to publish *La Nausée* and the collection *Le Mur* in the 1930s.[6] Both the novel and the short stories gave him a limited public profile while his more technical philosophical writings during the 1930s were well respected by a specialized audience but did not enhance his public status.[7] Tellingly, *L'Être et le néant*, published in 1943, only received four reviews in the two years after its publication, but at least six-fold that number in the subsequent two years – that is, *after* he achieved a public profile.[8]

By 1945, some of the upcoming authors, including Sartre, suddenly held unprecedented positions of power *vis-à-vis* their publishers, mainly because of the *épuration*, which was meant to target editors and publishing houses as well as authors. If indeed many authors had written pro-fascist or anti-Semitic material, the publishing houses and editors that made this possible were held responsible too. This explains why a special Comité d'épuration de l'édition was set up with Sartre as a representative of the CNE. However, in comparison with authors, publishing houses got off lightly: all major publishing houses managed to survive the purge except for Bernard Grasset. Key members of the committee, like Aragon and Sartre, managed to protect their publishing houses and spoke out in their favour on several occasions. Gallimard was arguably as guilty as Grasset, and Sartre's interventions on his behalf meant that it was easier for him subsequently to set his own intellectual agenda and persuade Gallimard to publish *Les Temps modernes*. Gallimard had to change in order to survive. Championing a very different philosophical approach, associated with the Resistance, was the best way for a publishing house to shed its old associations and thereby to rehabilitate itself. Sponsoring authors with a wide public following was also a way to guarantee sales, and commercial survival, in the austere post-war economic context: public popularity as well as intellectual credibility could ensure that academic ideas would achieve circulation in book form, and successful engagement with the public helped intellectuals like Sartre sell their ideas to publishers.

Besides books, magazines and journals are crucial to the spread of new movements. Their serial nature and wide readership help to diffuse new ideas, especially in the French context where educated people have a considerable appetite for high-brow journals.[9] The launch of new magazines or journals becomes particularly effective when rival ones have been discontinued or discredited. This was the case in France at the end of the war. Some political and literary weeklies, like *La Gerbe*, *Je suis partout* and *Gringoire*, had been so obviously connected to the fascist cause that there was no place for them at the end of the war. However, several prominent literary journals had also been compromised, not least the highly prestigious *La Nouvelle Revue française*, which during the war had been edited by the anti-Semitic Nazi supporter Drieu la Rochelle with the full support of Otto Abetz, the German ambassador. In this unique context, there was space for new magazines like *Les Temps modernes*, launched as a monthly in October 1945 by Raymond Aron, de Beauvoir, Maurice Merleau-Ponty and Sartre and, initially at least, connected with, if not dedicated to, the new school of existentialist philosophy.

Finally, newspapers also play an important role in the dissemination of ideas. Critics who write for newspapers can count on a large readership and in some circumstances can influence the success of literary careers. From 1943 until 1947, Albert Camus was the editor of the Communist-leaning *Combat*, initially founded in 1942 as a Lyon-based Resistance paper. Its Resistance credentials gave *Combat* considerable authority after the war, when it became an influential Paris-based newspaper in its own right. In 1945 *Combat* sold between 150,000 and 200,000 copies per day, giving Camus – and indeed Sartre, who wrote for the newspaper – a platform to promote existentialist notions and to defend them especially against attacks by communists.[10] *Combat* promoted a progressive political agenda but was clearly independent of the French Communist Party; the latter controlled *L'Humanité*, a rival to *Combat*. The contributions by Camus and Sartre to *Combat*, and indeed to other newspapers and journals, show them as both intellectuals and critics; that is, they are both creative writers and commentators on each other's work. As we shall discuss in the next section, it is as a journalist for *Combat* that Sartre visited the United States in 1945, thereby enhancing his public profile both in France and abroad.

Public performances

The spread of a philosophy or doctrine within the broader public not only depends on publishing opportunities but also on the other media. In the middle of the 1940s the radio was an important medium. The broadcasting of intellectual tracts on national radio stations was a regular occurrence, providing legitimacy to their intellectual content and an implicit endorsement of the authors. Writers associated with existentialism benefited from this state consecration, whether it came from the French or the British. The BBC famously broadcast Camus' first non-clandestine editorial for *Combat*. Given the significance of the BBC for the French during the war (amidst Vichy and pro-Nazi propaganda, it was the only Resistance voice on air), this was a notable seal of approval. Probably less well known in Anglo-Saxon circles is the extent to which the French national radio contributed to the consecration of some of its writers. For instance, the Radiodiffusion nationale broadcast Sartre's article 'La République du silence', shortly after it had appeared in the first non-clandestine issue of *Les Lettres françaises*. French national radio did for Sartre what the BBC had done for Camus: not only were significantly more people now exposed to the text, it provided credibility and Resistance kudos to the author.

Even more important than the broadcasts of the texts were the public performances by Sartre himself. His contemporaries often commented on how charismatic Sartre was as a speaker – able to communicate clearly and succinctly without notes. His ability to captivate an audience became legendary after his famous lecture, entitled *L'Existentialisme est un humanisme*, held in Paris in October 1945. In his novel *L'Écume des jours*, Boris Vian parodied this lecture, depicting a talk by a fictitious character, Jean-Sol Partre, where the audience got '... worked up and showed its admiration for (Partre) by repeated shouts and acclamations after every word he said.' For all the irony of Vian's parodic example, it was not far from the truth: the actual lecture by Sartre was apparently an electric performance which was widely discussed in the media. However, when trying to assess the significance of this talk at the time, Sartre's ability to navigate the complex cultural setting at the end of the war was probably more important than his oratory skills and overall charisma. Indeed, in the talk he deftly addressed the criticisms which had been levelled at him from both Catholic and Communist circles, while aligning himself with the humanist consensus which prevailed in the immediate postwar era. His exchange with the Marxist critic, Naville, enabled him

141

to show his affinities with a progressive political agenda. In the talk, Sartre managed to play down the German origins of his existentialism – Heidegger was only mentioned once – and emphasized the contemporary significance of his philosophy. The wide advertisement of the talk across Paris and the subsequent reports in the major newspapers contributed to its mythology and to the broader sense that he was a man on the rise.

Although we are focusing on Sartre's existentialism in France, it is worth mentioning that during this period, Sartre's public appearances were not limited to his home country as he spent two long spells in the United States. As early as January 1945, Sartre, together with six other French journalists, left for the US for a five-month trip, sponsored by the US Office of War Information and approved by the French government. The French journalists played a semi-promotional role for both France and the US, presenting a favourable picture of France to an American audience while reporting back home about their American experiences. Sartre was presented to the American public, not just as an intellectual, but also as having considerable Resistance credentials. In 1946, Sartre went on a lecturing tour in the US, speaking at several prominent East Coast universities, and receiving considerable attention from the American press. The American interest in Sartre helped to fuel further the feeling back home that Sartre was becoming a significant figure.

The prominence of existentialism derived partly from Sartre's use of the media. As we have seen in the previous chapter, Sartre was very conscious of the opportunities radio, television and journalism offered, actively pursued those media-avenues and consciously wrote in a format that fitted these new media. It is worth putting Sartre's engagement with the new media in the context of Debray's well-known distinction between the era of the academic (1880–1930), the period of publishing (1920–1960) and finally the age of the media-intellectual (from 1968 onwards).[11] Interestingly, in Debray's nostalgic depiction of a bygone era, Sartre, the quintessential writer whose fortune was once intertwined with that of the publisher Gallimard, epitomised the second stage, whereas the Nouveaux philosophes such as Bernard-Henri Lévy and Glucksmann represent the third phase and are his obvious target. The previous chapters have shown this depiction of Sartre to be only partly correct. In the period between 1944 and 1947, Sartre already exhibited features of the media-intellectual long before this type became prominent. In 1947 Sartre and his colleagues of *Les Temps modernes* managed to persuade the French government to allow them to broadcast a number of sessions on issues of contemporary political relevance. Although the government eventually pulled the plug on the programme because of its incendiary content, the series had given Sartre a unique platform to reach a broader audience and engage with the politics of the day. With those radio performances, Sartre positioned himself no longer as merely a philosopher or a literary figure, but very much as a political commentator. From here it would be a small step to embracing his new role as an activist, and indeed, it would not take long before Sartre would redefine himself as such.

Cultural trauma and the role of the intellectual

The notion of cultural trauma can be used to describe a situation where particular events force large sections of a given society to reconsider their societal history in a very different, and often negative, light, identifying and reassessing central presuppositions which they previously held. Sociologists have used the term to account for how a number of phenomena, ranging from the Holocaust and Watergate to slavery, have threatened the social fabric of society, leading to a 'trauma process' through which society, or at least a significant section of it, has to grapple with the nature of the disruption, its causes and effects and its general significance.[12] 'Carrier groups' play a dominant role in this trauma process, helping people articulate and come to terms with the traumatic experiences, and intellectuals can often be found among those carrier groups.[13] From 1944 onwards, French existentialist writers were such a carrier group in at least three ways. Firstly, they helped to rebuild the nation by presenting a cohesive picture of France; secondly, existentialist vocabulary more generally enabled sections of French society to describe and assimilate the complexity of the war experience; and thirdly, the notion of responsibility in particular can be seen as a corollary of the *épuration*.

(a) The French experience of the war was particularly traumatic in a variety of ways. Not only was the military defeat, and the speed of it, devastating to morale, but so were the occupation and the Vichy regime, characterized by widespread inaction of many French people and active collaboration of the French authorities with the occupiers. Furthermore, national pride was dented by the way in which Pétain depicted German victory as a rightful punishment for French sins.[14] Towards the end of the war, various attempts had to be made at rebuilding French pride and repairing and reunifying the nation; and the transmission of what Maurice Halbwachs termed 'collective memory' played a central role in this.[15] This collective reconstruction of recent history overplayed the extent of French Resistance and downplayed the collaboration as an activity of the few. Different parts of the political spectrum would embrace this *résistantialisme*, a compelling reconstruction of history, according to which most French people actively fought the occupier but were betrayed by sections of the political class. De Gaulle's speeches of the mid-1940s were quintessentially *résistantialiste*, elaborating on the heroics of the French fight against the German occupation and portraying a unified picture of a defiant nation. Communists would also subscribe to this picture: given their central role in the Resistance, the *résistantialiste* account of history implied that the French Communist Party embodied the will of the French nation. This helped the party to achieve a central role within the post-war political landscape and to gain electorally. It is only at a later stage – in the 1960s – that *résistantialisme* would be questioned. In 1945 it was the dominant narrative.[16]

During this period, intellectuals were highly regarded: the poet Paul Valéry would receive a state funeral in August 1945. As in the Third Republic, they were remarkably intertwined with state power. For example, the novelist André Malraux would become the Minister of Information and the sociologist Aron his *directeur de cabinet*. Intellectuals would play a central role in the rebuilding of the nation, and indeed Sartre's and Camus' journalistic writings towards the end of the war seemed to combine with de Gaulle in presenting a more cohesive picture of French society, occasionally conflating the position of the Resistance with that of the French in general.[17] This is particularly striking in Sartre's famous piece 'La République du silence', which appeared in the first non-clandestine issue of *Les Lettres françaises* in September 1944, and in which he not only portrays in lyrical terms a heroic picture of the Resistance but also seems to extend those heroics to all Frenchmen. Initially published in December 1944 in Aron's *La France libre* and addressing a foreign audience, 'Paris sous l'occupation' presents an equally positive image of the French nation, but the essay adopts a distinctly defensive tone. It points out the complexities of living under the occupation whereby, in Sartre's portrayal, all French citizens suffered and had to accommodate but few were authentic collaborators. 'Qu'est-ce qu'un collaborateur?' which appeared in the New York-based *La République française* in September 1945, continues this line by presenting collaborators as marginal characters and collaboration as the product of social disintegration, thereby dissociating collaboration from the core of French national identity.

So, contrary to the widespread view of Sartre as undermining the

144

myths of society, these journalistic writings of the end of the war show a different side to him, as someone who not only explained to the outside world the difficult role in which the French people found themselves, but who also promoted a picture of a cohesive and defiant France that resisted the occupier, if only mentally. However, the distinctive role which intellectuals took on during this period created a tension: if intellectuals were meant to be pivotal forces in the rebuilding of the nation, would this not put in danger their creative output and independence? By the autumn of 1945, Sartre would already be conscious of the dangers of being so closely connected to the workings of the state apparatus. In his essay 'La Nationalisation de la littérature', he lamented this recent *monumentalisation* or *panthéonisation* whereby the literati and their cultural products were seen as ambassadors and national assets, and he called on intellectuals to be vigilant and to make sure that they keep their own voice. He emphasized that, after the humiliating experiences of the war, people were looking for heroic figures, and intellectuals had to be wary of being complicit in this collective act of mystification. In this context, Sartre fell short of confronting his earlier *résistantialiste* views (as expressed in the three articles 'La République du silence', 'Paris sous l'occupation' and 'Qu'est-ce qu'un collaborateur?'), but his own adjustments to the reprinted editions of those articles in *Situations III* in 1949[18] indicate that by that point Sartre had already become aware of his own complicity in presenting a unified picture of France.[19]

(b)   There were more subtle ways in which Sartre's philosophical positions would enable French society, or at least a significant part of it, to assimilate and come to terms with the traumatic experience of the war. In comparison with Sartre's pre-war philosophical publications which addressed technical issues central to phenomenology, his later vocabulary of existentialism – with the key notions of existence, freedom, responsibility and bad faith – were closely tied to the specific dilemmas of the French war experience and the possible choices they entailed, as many of the examples provided in *L'Être et le néant* and subsequent publications testify. Sartre's famous dictum that existence precedes essence means that, unlike material objects, people have no fixed meaning or essence, and are fundamentally free to choose,[20] even in circumstances which are *prima facie* constraining, like the war situation in France. As Roquentin, the disaffected historian in *La Nausée*, found out, the experience of freedom provokes existential anguish, and therefore people often use various devices to avoid facing freedom. Bad faith is such a device at people's disposal, allowing them to mislead themselves into believing that they have no choice when they do.[21] From this perspective, when some people during the war decided that they could not join the Resistance because it was too dangerous to do so they exhibited bad faith because no danger, however great, can take away the fundamental freedom that people do have. For Sartre, it follows that people are merely the sum total of their actions – nothing more or less.[22] For instance, it does not make sense for individuals to say that deep down they were courageous but that the conditions, which they faced, made them weak and cowardly. It is plainly nonsensical for people to argue that they were in essence Resistance fighters but that circumstances made it impossible for them to act upon this.

However harsh the existentialists' verdict on people's actions may be, existentialist philosophy enables people to make a clean break with the past. It achieves this by offering an archetypal example of what G. H. Mead called a 'philosophy of the present'.[23] Towards the end of his life, Mead coined this term, consciously playing on its double meaning. Firstly, in line with the pragmatist outlook, Mead argued that his philosophy was not merely an abstract system but had a contemporary relevance. Secondly, rejecting the determinism implied in causal-mechanical and teleological views, he attributed particular significance to the present at the expense of the past and future: it is in the present that the past and future are continually reconstructed. Likewise, Sartre's line of argument is a philosophy of the present in both meanings of the term. Not only is it meant to be a philosophy *for* the present, but it too treats the present as an ongoing locus for new beginnings. However cowardly people might have acted in the past, there is, from an existentialist viewpoint, nothing intrinsic to them that would compel them to continue along this path. This means that while existentialist philosophy enabled sections of French society to assimilate the war experience, it also enabled them, individually at least, to draw a line under this whole episode. Not only can people break free from their past, they can also do so without being treated as mere puppets in a grand course of history. Nor should anyone be sacrificed in the name of a utopia; we make history here and now.[24]

(c)   The intensity of the *procès d'épuration* gives some indication of the cultural trauma that had engulfed the French nation, with the spectre of responsibility looming particularly large. The trials, including in particular Brasillach's, reminded people of the importance of writing and of the extent to which writers ought to be held responsible for the possible consequences of what they write. In this context, it is worth mentioning that the case for the prosecution

146

of Brasillach was twofold: it was argued firstly that his undoubted literary talent gave him more responsibility than ordinary mortals for what he had written, and secondly that some of his writings could be interpreted as denouncing individuals or spurring people on to kill. This was also significant for how writers on the side of the Resistance were perceived. If collaborationist writings were so pernicious that they deserved to be punished with great severity, it is because writing was regarded as particularly important and influential writers endowed with immense responsibility. But then, equally, those like Sartre and Camus who wrote for clandestine Resistance publications ought to be seen in a heroic light. From this perspective, the trial of Brasillach was not merely a condemnation of collaborationist writings and writers but also an implicit celebration of all those who risked their lives writing for clandestine newspapers. While the notion of engagement had a long pedigree in French intellectual history and was central to the doctrine of personalism in the 1930s and 1940s,[25] the trials enhanced and legitimized the image of the *intellectuel engagé*, willing to take risks and act in the face of adversity. It is worth remembering that intellectuals themselves were behind the purge of collaborationist intellectuals, and indeed Resistance intellectuals were to gain from this purge, presenting their activities in a heroic light.[26]

The *épuration* also helped to stretch the notion of responsibility. This notion loomed particularly large in Brasillach's trial: Brasillach repeatedly argued that he too had taken responsibility when it mattered, while the prosecution managed to turn this against him.[27] Neither Sartre nor de Beauvoir was willing to sign the petition to seek clemency for Brasillach on the grounds that he should take full responsibility for his actions.[28] Camus signed after agonizing over it and only because he was opposed to the death penalty in principle, not because he questioned the gravity of Brasillach's actions or his responsibility.[29] As this case shows, writers who had written pro-Nazi or anti-Semitic material were not just held responsible for writing against the Resistance or the Jewish people, but also for inciting hatred and ultimately for the killings that might result from this. It is during this period that Sartre and his fellow-existentialists made the notion of responsibility one of the cornerstones of their philosophy; and the context of the purge accounts for why this intellectual move struck a chord with a larger audience.[30] It also goes some way towards explaining why Sartre and his followers insisted that writers – and indeed people in general – are responsible for *all* consequences of their actions, including those which are unanticipated, thereby putting the burden on all to make an effort to think ahead.[31] Against this background, it makes sense to argue, as Sartre and others did, that people can never escape their responsibility and that declining to take a position – as so many people had done during the war – is *de facto* to take an endorsing stance. Finally, it is against this background that Sartre would apply the notion of responsibility to those areas not traditionally associated with it. Any literature becomes a political act, hence the blurring of the distinction between literature and journalism because the former has as much political power as the latter. Therefore, Sartre's plays have a distinctly didactic flavour, depicting politically charged situations in which choices have to be made. They are not just meant to entertain us; they are not meant simply to exude artistic sophistication or profound psychological insight; they are meant to force the audience to take a stance.

Further comments

This book has explained why existentialism, and in particular Sartre's version of it, rose from obscurity to prominence in the mid-1940s. Taking a different stance from those of Boschetti and Collins who both assume the relative autonomy of the intellectual sphere,[32] our reassessment of French post-war intellectual and social history shows the extent to which the specific socio-political context at the time at least partly accounts for the sudden rise in popularity of French existentialism. This is neither to deny the significance of Sartre's writing and oratory skills, nor his unusual ability to combine different genres and write philosophy, novels and plays while presenting them as a coherent project. Nor is it necessarily a rebuttal of the sociological arguments of Bourdieu[33] and Boschetti that, with his background (his maternal grandfather's education, followed by the École normale), Sartre had the right connections, confidence and ability to become a 'total intellectual' and assert his dominance in the post-war intellectual arena. However, none of these sociological-*cum*-biographical features – whether it would be Sartre's 'brilliance', his '*habitus*', his 'social and cultural capital' or his 'network' – suffices in itself to explain the enormous popularity of existentialist philosophy between 1944 and 1947.

We should not forget that, by early 1944, Sartre was approaching middle age – he was nearly forty years old – and was little known outside the small elite circle of Parisian intellectuals. Within two years he would become an international celebrity. While some of the sociological factors that Boschetti and Collins identify – in particular

148

Sartre's network and his cultural advantages – go some way towards accounting for the positive reception of his work within specialist circles well before 1944, they do not explain why existentialist ideas suddenly engulfed the public intellectual domain in the mid-1940s. The distinctiveness of the argument presented in this book lies in the way in which it connects the wider socio-political context at the end of the war with the emerging intellectual fashion. However compelling his philosophy as an intellectual enterprise, Sartre's rise to public recognition at that time relied at least in part on the way in which his intellectual approach helped sections of French society assimilate and come to terms with the traumatic recent past, while conceiving of the present as a potential discontinuity with the past. The purge of intellectuals and the discrediting of hitherto dominant ideas created an unprecedented space for new intellectual movements, and Sartre's key concepts, such as the writer's responsibility, were both constitutive of and a reflection of the climate surrounding the *épuration*. Partly because of the existing circumstances, Sartre and his fellow-existentialists were unusually well connected to the gatekeepers – such as publishers and critics – who control the flow from the intra- to the public-intellectual arena.

These times were unusual, but not unique: similar conditions arose in the US after the 1950s purge of 'crypto-communists', and in Eastern Europe after the revolutions of 1989. As in the 1940s in France, shifts in the American socio-political context of the 1950s were accompanied by changes in intellectual production, but this time also within universities. Indeed, McCarthyism had a profound effect on the American intellectual sphere with the expulsion of communist-inclined academics. There is also evidence that it contributed to the downgrading of Continental philosophy in favour of 'politically neutral' analytical philosophy, at least within academic institutions.[34] Likewise, the transition from state communism to liberal democracy in countries like Poland, the Czech Republic or Hungary was accompanied by a shake-up of the intellectual elites and of their relationship to Marxism and to power. Within this new context of 'anti-politics', neoclassical economics and neoliberal values flourished. The market was celebrated; and Marxism was portrayed as out of date and pernicious, even by the reconstituted socialist parties that quickly regained power in most of the region.[35] Just as in the 1940s in France, those two cases feature historical moments that give rise to a sudden hiatus in the intellectual elite, into which new movements are propelled by force of circumstance as well as intellectual force.

The fall

We have seen so far how Sartre reformulated his existentialism in the light of the experience of the Second World War. He did so by emphasizing the need for intellectuals to speak up and engage with current social and political issues. Prior to 1944 he developed an ontological framework that demonstrated the irreducible freedom of the individual, but it was only with the end of the war that existentialism as a philosophical doctrine became explicitly linked to the notion of the engaged intellectual. However, while Sartre's reformulation of his own existentialist philosophy fitted very well the immediate post-war climate and enabled sections of French society to come to terms with Vichy and the occupation, its emphasis on the engaged intellectual would ultimately conflict with and undermine the efforts needed to propagate and further develop existentialism. Getting involved with present concerns, as Sartre argued intellectuals should do, does not require elaborate philosophical work. If anything, continuous social and political engagement by intellectuals, when executed properly, takes a lot of time and energy and tends to overshadow more theoretical concerns. Philosophy tends to get in the way of the practical politics of the day. So Sartre's reformulation of his own existentialist philosophy, shifting from ontology to contemporary engagement, ultimately meant that less weight was attached to the philosophical underpinning itself. Sartre's trajectory in the late 1940s testifies to this, as very soon he became involved with pressing political issues, to a certain extent at the expense of in-depth theoretical concerns.

His appetite for political action was indeed remarkable. In 1948, he helped to set up a political party, the Rassemblement démocratique révolutionnaire (RDR), situated on the left but independent of the Soviet Union. While the RDR lasted only one year, Sartre's political interventions in relation to the Cold War continued this 'third way', denouncing Stalinism without siding with the US, and eventually culminating in his involvement in the peace movement. In the early 1950s he came closer to the Communists, in the process breaking up with Camus in a hostile public exchange in *Les Temps modernes* over Camus' *L'Homme révolté*. The latter had denounced the totalitarianism of the Soviet Union whereas Sartre was increasingly willing to accept that compromises had to be made in the pursuit of equality. Between 1952 and 1956, Sartre went further and publicly declared himself a 'fellow-traveller' of the French Communist Party, visiting the USSR, a closeness which would come to an abrupt end with the Russian invasion of Hungary. During the late 1950s Sartre became increasingly involved in the Algerian fight for independence, symbolized by his signing of the Manifesto of the 121 in support of the independence movement, and eventually leading to two assassination attempts on his life by the Organisation de l'armée secrète. In the 1950s and then 1960s he strongly opposed the war in Indochina, subsequently the Vietnam war, taking for instance a prominent position in the Russell Tribunal. In the 1960s and early 1970s he sided with the student movement and promoted Maoist publications, continuing his political involvement until failing health made it no longer possible.

In other words, from the late 1940s onwards Sartre reinvented himself to large extent as a political activist, fighting various causes. This metamorphosis was perfectly in tune with the philosophical position stated in the 'Préface' and in *Qu'est-ce que la littérature?*. While he remained prolific and retained his prominent status as a public intellectual, his existentialist philosophy inevitably lost significance. The term 'existentialism', which had been coined by Gabriel Marcel as late as 1943, had gained wide currency but was now used more broadly to refer to a wide range of cultural phenomena, ranging from the bohemian lifestyle of the Left Bank to an ill-defined feeling of anxiety and unease. This is not to say that there were after 1947 no further developments in existentialist philosophy: de Beauvoir's *Le Deuxième sexe* drew partly on existentialist notions to develop a unique feminist tract, and Sartre's own *Critique de la raison dialectique* attempted to integrate Marxism and existentialism. But the heyday of existentialist philosophy was over. Even those causes to which Sartre leant his support and which initially borrowed an existentialist outlook, acquired a political momentum of their own which eventually surpassed his philosophy. This is not least the case for the anti-colonial movements, which Sartre endorsed for instance with prefaces to both Fanon's *Les Damnés de la terre*[36] and Memmi's *Portrait du colonisé, précédé de Portrait du colonisateur*,[37] but which in the course of time found more inspiration in distinctly sociological theories such as Marxism. Sartre's existentialism provided insight into some of the psychological dynamics of colonization, in particular the way in which colonial culture and its 'superiority' is internalized by the colonized. Political activists, however, would inevitably be more drawn to theories that accounted for colonization sociologically and historically. There were some exceptions, but well outside the French colonial context, notably the South African black consciousness movement which was inspired by Fanon and Sartre, and which had real political momentum until the brutal murders of Steve Biko and Rick Turner at the hands of the Apartheid police.

It should also be noted that in the late 1940s and early 1950s Sartre's politics led to the break-up of three friendships which had been intertwined with his existentialist philosophy. One was a dramatic and public fall-out with Camus, ostensibly over a negative review of his book *L'Homme révolté* in *Les Temps modernes*, but also revealing their different backgrounds and diverging political orientations. Camus did not share Sartre's privileged *parcours*, a lack to which Sartre was implicitly referring when he described Camus' philosophy as 'second hand' and a lack which might also have explained Camus' wounded pride throughout the exchange. These sociological factors should not take away from the content of the dispute: whereas Sartre was willing to accept sacrifices for the sake of the greater socialist good, Camus was alarmed by the notion of a violent revolution and he was particularly agitated by the continuous human right infringements in the Soviet Union. Similar political differences led to the break-up with Merleau-Ponty and Raymond Aron, both more painful separations in some respects because Sartre had enjoyed a deep friendship with both of them going back to their time together at the École normale. Publicly, the split with Camus meant that French existentialism was now less seen as a united front. The break-up with Merleau-Ponty, however, was probably more important to Sartre as his engagement with phenomenology had been central to his project and Merleau-Ponty would become instrumental in the spread of structuralism (which, as we will discuss, was a rival and incompatible strand). He advised his students to look beyond existentialism and phenomenology and find out about psychoanalysis and linguistics, and he was crucial in resurrecting Saussure and promoting Lévi-Strauss within French circles.[38] In particular, Merleau-Ponty's *Signes*, a collection of essays published in 1960, acknowledged the significance of both structuralism and the social sciences. Likewise, the split with Aron was significant too. In the early 1930s, it had been Aron, on his return from Germany, who introduced Sartre and de Beauvoir to Husserl's phenomenology so he had been in some respects at the origins of Sartre's philosophical project. In the mid-1940s, after returning from London, he had been at Sartre's side with the launch of *Les Temps modernes*. But within a couple of years he had moved to the centre right, feeling increasingly uncomfortable with Sartre's politics, and by the mid-1950s, the two had moved so far apart from each other that his *L'Opium des intellectuels* could be read as an anti-Sartrean tract, elaborating as it did on the dangers of engaged philosophy. As we mentioned before, Aron was instrumental in promoting and institutionalizing sociology, which would further undermine the credibility of Sartre, the humanist and generalist *par excellence*.

Indeed, Sartre's existentialism, as a doctrine, was clearly located within the humanities. It was a philosophy with extensions into literature and theatre and of course also into politico-literary journalism, a uniquely French genre particularly prominent in the 1940s. As we have seen in the previous chapter, Sartre's applied existentialism, although it tackled social and political issues, drew largely on literature and philosophy and relied very little on social research. Existentialism, therefore, suited an intellectual climate in which the humanities, in particular philosophy and literature, occupied a dominant position at the expense of the social sciences. This was the case in the mid-1940s in France: the social sciences were poorly professionalized, not very much institutionalized and they had little presence in the public sphere. From the 1950s onwards the intellectual landscape changed dramatically, with the social sciences rapidly gaining ground and autonomy. Within academic circles, philosophy lost some of its symbolic power to the emerging social science institutions – for instance, Raymond Aron's Sociology Department at the Sorbonne, and various centres within the École pratique des hautes études.[39] For the first time, it became possible to study the social sciences, in particular sociology, at both undergraduate and postgraduate level without first having studied philosophy. This professionalization and institutionalization of the social sciences eventually had repercussions for the credibility of different types of public engagement and for the role of the humanities in the public realm. By the 1960s, reflecting on a social phenomenon, as Sartre had done in the case of anti-Semitism, required social science expertise and methodology. Not only did it become more difficult to make pronouncements about social and political issues without a solid basis in the social sciences, but humanistic types of philosophy such as existentialism became increasingly less tenable.

Instead, new intellectual currents suited the emerging social sciences much better. The most obvious example was structuralism – a doctrine or method that aims to uncover relatively stable, latent structures underneath the surface level – which proved to be a better fit for sociology and anthropology in a variety of ways. Structuralism was never a purely philosophical doctrine in the way in which existentialism had been. Its origins and development had been intertwined with various academic disciplines other than philosophy, in particular linguistics, sociology and anthropology. Once structuralism got a foothold through *inter alia* Lévi-Strauss' use of Jakobson, it became

153

possible for intellectuals to reassess Saussure's *Cours de linguistique générale* and Durkheim's *Formes élémentaires de la vie religieuse* and treat them as precursors of the new creed. At a later stage, structuralism was even seen as providing a new reading of Marx and Freud, rejuvenating two dominant social theories at the time. This suggests another 'advantage' of structuralism over existentialism: the former was compatible with a variety of major intellectual currents, whereas the latter was at odds with many. Indeed, Sartre not only struggled to make his philosophy gel with Marxism, but had explicitly taken exception to psychoanalysis and its notion of the unconscious.

Leaving aside Marx and Freud, some versions of structuralism were regarded to be compatible with contemporary mainstream social science. It is telling that in his autobiographical *Tristes tropiques* Lévi-Strauss explicitly contrasted the 'metaphysics' of existentialism and phenomenology, which he deplored, with the social sciences, which he admired and represented.[40] Rather than 'proving' philosophically, as Sartre had done, the notion of freedom which supposedly manifested itself even in the most 'un-free' situations, structuralism explored how, in various empirical situations, societal forces curtailed agency. Structuralism professed to provide an objective and scientific methodology for the uncovering of 'real' underlying structures. So it positioned itself as a scientific method that would enable researchers to unmask the social realm and reveal underlying structures largely unknown to the people affected by them. Once structuralism developed into post-structuralism, the scientific pretence disappeared, but this did not take place until the 1970s and even then remained altogether a minority development in the social sciences. More prominent in the social sciences, from the 1970s onwards, was Bourdieu's genetic structuralism, which deviated from the original structuralist template in various ways, but still presented itself as a scientific endeavour for the debunking of lay perceptions, similar to the structuralism it sought to replace.

In the aftermath of the Second World War the Communist Party occupied a prominent role in French politics. It had accumulated a considerable amount of kudos from its central position in the Resistance, leading, in the short term, to electoral success and, more durably, a significant role in the public sphere. Parallels could be found within the intellectual realm, with Marxist philosophy and social theory now in the ascendancy. Initially relatively ignorant about Marx, from the late 1940s Sartre started to engage with his writings, eventually attempting to integrate Marxism and existentialism. His *Critique de la raison dialectique*, published in 1960, was the culmination of this intellectual project, incorporating agency and creativity into a historical narrative of class struggle. However, few followed Sartre in this intellectual endeavour and, crucially, few committed Marxists did. In the course of the 1960s, French Marxist scholars, such as Louis Althusser and Nicos Poulantzas, found inspiration in a structuralist reading of Marx. Structuralist Marxists tended to portray Marx's intellectual biography as a justification of their structuralist position. In this view, the 'young Marx' of the *Economic and Philosophical Manuscripts* was still influenced by Hegel and wedded to a humanist position, whereas the 'mature Marx' of *Das Kapital* finally embraced a scientific structuralist account of the capitalist economy. While not all French Marxists were committed structuralists, there was not much appetite in France for humanist Marxism and certainly less than in the US where for instance Fromm and Marcuse gained a considerable following. The incompatibility of existentialism and Marxism within the French context made it very difficult for existentialism to retain its prominent role, especially given the significant presence of Marxism at the time. The elective affinity between structuralism and French Marxism helped both to eclipse existentialism.

There is a final factor that contributed to Sartre's waning influence. We mentioned earlier, in the context of Debray's typology of intellectuals, that Sartre was a media intellectual *avant la lettre*, how he had embraced the emerging media long before other intellectuals had done. Moving away from the aftermath of the war, it is worth pointing out that Debray identified the late 1960s as all-important: it is, according to him, then that the media started encroaching upon intellectual life in unprecedented fashion. While it remains debatable whether 1968 presented such a watershed as Debray suggested, he was of course right to draw our attention to the increasing role of the media in intellectual life in the course of the second half of the twentieth century.[41] It certainly had repercussions for the Sartre phenomenon. The rise of radio and television which had initially helped Sartre's ascendancy would eventually assist others in gaining public prominence. Once these media became more established and once other intellectuals became more aware of their significance for obtaining and maintaining a public profile, Sartre faced stiffer competition. Other people, who were especially adept at dealing with the visual media, came to the forefront. Sartre's own relationship with those media had not always been without problems in any case: his foray into film, for instance, had been fraught with difficulties, with Sartre apparently unable to adapt to its requirements. Although he had been

155

committed to adapting to the new conditions, he seemed unwilling in practice to adjust to the restrictions in format.

If Sartre's influence faded from the 1970s onwards, just as existentialism had done earlier, he has still remained a significant presence in France in two ways. First and foremost, some intellectuals emulated his notion of the engaged intellectual, as a writer who is not only media-savvy but also continuously politically active. The archetypal example remains Bernard Henri-Lévy, in the French media referred to as BHL, who initially accused Sartre, together with many other French intellectuals, of being impervious to the monstrosities committed in the name of Marxism, but whose subsequent sympathetic biography of Sartre marked a turning point and whose relentless media performances and political interventions, notably over Syria, are self-consciously Sartrean in style.[42] For many others, Sartre remained primarily a negative reference point. Initially written around the time of *Qu'est-ce que la littérature?*, Barthes' *Le Degré zéro de l'écriture* was structured similarly to Sartre's text and was very much a response to its subject-centred take on writing.[43] Lévi-Strauss' *La Pensée sauvage* contrasted the human sciences and structuralism with Sartre's project: whereas the latter attributes primacy to the subject and history, the former dissolves the subject and promotes synchronic analysis.[44] In their collective work *Lire le Capital*, Althusser and his collaborators rejected a humanist reading of Marx, presenting a thinly disguised critique of Sartre's attempt to integrate existentialism and Marxism.[45] In his semi-autobiographical text, *Esquisse pour une auto-analyse*, Bourdieu explained how early on he defined himself in opposition to the notion of the 'total intellectual' which Sartre represented.[46] Similarly, in various essays and interviews, Foucault contrasted himself with Sartre and his model of the generalist-intellectual; Foucault's 'specific intellectual' draws on his or her expertise to intervene in local struggles.[47]

If these intellectuals deviated from Sartre, it is telling that they often did so explicitly and that Sartre was a foil. The fact that different intellectuals, some with truly diverging projects, all felt obliged to refer to Sartre, albeit often negatively, is indicative of his enduring significance in France throughout the second half of the twentieth century. Even today Sartre is still part of the French collective imagination about the role of the intellectual in society. I already mentioned BHL's fascination with Sartre, but he is certainly not the only one. Sartre still frequently pops up on France Culture, the French radio station devoted to intellectual and cultural matters. In the last three years, for instance, France Culture aired his play *Les Mouches*, plus

156

five other major programmes *solely* devoted to him.[48] Both Sartre's persona and *oeuvre* are still regularly discussed and revisited on the literary pages of *Le Monde*, *Libération* and *Le Figaro*, sometimes, of course, prompted by sensationalist publications, including supposedly revelatory pseudo-biographies about his liaisons, but often by the appearance of new, weighty academic works. Cohen-Solal's latest book, *Une Renaissance sartrienne*, is a recent example of the latter, and indeed widely discussed.[49]

We mentioned *Une Renaissance sartrienne*, not just because its coverage in the French press is indicative of the interest in Sartre, but also because Cohen-Solal points out in the book that the ongoing fascination with Sartre goes well beyond France. She is right. Especially in the United States, seven decades after his first trip across the Atlantic, he is still remembered and celebrated as an iconic intellectual. What Cohen-Solal possibly ignores is that this American interest within the US is set within clearly defined parameters. Sartre is often taught as part of the curriculum of undergraduate education in the humanities. He is portrayed as a mythical figure, politically radical, an independent mind and not afraid to explore the darker side of human existence – all features likely to appeal to young students. Yet, if Sartre is part of the normal staple of a liberal arts education in the US, he is conspicuous in his absence from the core curriculum of most graduate work in philosophy. Even those US graduate programmes that pay attention to the history of philosophy tend to omit Sartre.

This picture is more or less representative of how Sartre is perceived outside the French-speaking world. It is indeed as the epitome of the authoritative public intellectual that Sartre is remembered and revered by many today, somehow a symbol of a bygone era when charismatic, free-floating thinkers were able to put their stamp on the world. In some countries, like England, there is a tendency to overplay the prevalence of this type of intellectual in France and portray it as a uniquely French phenomenon. Here, Sartre is again used as mythical foil against which, for instance, the English cultural landscape inevitably appears as wanting. Intellectual historians have gone some way towards correcting this picture, demonstrating that English intellectuals have been involved in similar forms of public engagement throughout the nineteenth and twentieth century.[50] It is precisely the fact that this type of public intellectual is no longer quite as feasible today as it was in the mid-twentieth century that explains why this romantic image still has such a hold over people and why Sartre's public prominence is so often used as a yardstick.

EXPLAINING INTELLECTUALS:
A PROPOSAL

Throughout the previous chapters we have tried to provide a comprehensive and historically sensitive explanation for the phenomenon of Sartre, his sudden rise as an authoritative public intellectual (and that of existentialism) in the context of the mid-1940s in France. The multi-level explanation that was provided draws on a broader sociological theory of intellectuals. This theory has so far remained largely implicit; only occasionally have we delved into some of the theoretical underpinning of the arguments. In contrast, this chapter will provide a more explicit articulation of the underlying theory. The theory proposed is applicable to intellectuals more broadly – not just public intellectuals like Sartre – and we will exemplify the theory by revisiting empirical material from the previous chapters and also through new cases. The theory which we wish to propose centres round positioning, but also involves networks and conflict.

Deficiencies of existing accounts

The strength of the theory which we propose will become evident in relation to, and in contrast with, current assumptions in the research on intellectuals. Whether conducted in literary studies, intellectual history or sociology, we can identify five recurring problems in this research which our theory attempts to overcome. These are an empiricist bias, a motivational bias, a structural fallacy, an authenticity bias and a stability bias. We will be providing mainly examples from the sociology of intellectuals, but similar biases can also be found in the other disciplines studying intellectuals.

Let us first address the empiricist bias, referring to the way in which studies of intellectuals are often insufficiently theorized. One tends to associate the lack of an explicit theoretical underpinning more with intellectual history than with sociology of intellectuals as the former is supposed to be more preoccupied with deciphering the context and depicting the intellectual moves within it than with broader theoretical considerations as such. However, even more sociologically inclined authors do not always elaborate on their theoretical stance, possibly leading to confusion as to what precisely is being explained. Take, for instance, Charles Camic's influential account of Parsons' earlier writings. In two seminal articles,[1] Camic shows that the institutional context in which Parsons worked – Harvard social sciences, where his career was dependent on senior economists who were ill-disposed towards institutionalism – goes a long way towards explaining why Parsons chose to ally himself with (at that point) relatively unknown European thinkers and not with institutionalists such as Veblen in spite of the obvious affinities between his work and the latter. Camic is right to draw attention to the significance of the intellectual prejudices and power relations at Harvard for understanding Parsons' work, but there remains a lack of clarity as to the precise nature of Camic's intellectual enterprise. Throughout the articles Camic seems to oscillate between two types of reasoning. The dominant mode is a causal explanation, accounting for what caused Parsons to opt for the type of intellectual interventions that he made. Occasionally, though, Camic shifts gear and spells out the effects of Parsons' interventions for his career and tenure at Harvard. Indeed, the young Parsons managed to acquire a competitive advantage at Harvard because of the extent to which both the content and sources of his intellectual production were compatible with the views of senior academics in a position of power. The reason for the lack of clarity in Camic's project lies, we think, in its under-theorization: while Camic's analysis has proven particularly useful in accounting for some of Parsons' idiosyncratic moves, notably his choices of intellectual allies, Camic's empirical research is in need of some theoretical scaffolding if it is to prove robust and above all clearer as to its precise remit. Camic presents a fruitful research programme with clear methodological guidelines but it lacks a broader theoretical agenda that would enable it to guide and make sense of the research conducted. Positioning theory, we will argue, will provide this theoretical framework.

There is secondly the motivational bias. By this we are referring to some of the problems with research programmes that attempt systematically to uncover the motivations or intentions behind intellectual interventions. Take, for instance, the Cambridge school of intellectual history. Exploring the 'linguistic' or 'ideological context' in which intellectual interventions take place, this approach has been particularly useful as a corrective to the type of intellectual exercise that postulates perennial questions or conceives of a past text in terms of concerns that were alien to the cultural landscape at the time when it was conceived.[2] The theory proposed here is in line with Pocock and Skinner's view that it is vital to study the 'intellectual milieu'[3] of the authors concerned and to conceive of writing in performative terms. It does not share, however, their attempt at '. . . decoding the complex intention on the part of the author'[4] because the reconstruction of the intent or purpose underlying intellectual interventions often lacks the necessary empirical basis, ending up as a more speculative endeavour than Skinner dares to admit.[5] Whereas in practice members of this school (in its original, Skinnerian mode) tend to take the meaning of an intellectual intervention within a given context to be synonymous with the intent behind it, we prefer to hold onto the distinction between the purpose behind an intellectual intervention and its effect. So rather than speculating on what certain intellectuals through their interventions intend to achieve, we shall see that positioning theory provides the conceptual tools to investigate how they and their products might acquire institutional or symbolic (dis)advantages within the cultural and political arenas in which they find themselves or in which those texts or ideas are appropriated. Further, like their predecessors in the intellectual history which they rightly criticize for a lack of historical sensitivity, the Cambridge school too takes for granted the canon in political philosophy, ignoring its historical formation. In contrast, the theory suggested here opens up conceptual space for the exploration of the social mechanisms through which some intellectuals come to prominence and others do not and, related, certain texts acquire classical status and others do not.

The motivational bias also underscores sociological research. Take, for instance, again Camic's study of the young Parsons within the Harvard context. Trying to provide clarity as to the motivations behind Parsons' early work, Camic warns the reader that '. . . Parsons's concern with the solid reputational standing of Marshall, Pareto, Durkheim, and Weber, against a backdrop where the institutionalists were in ill-repute (. . .) does not mean that his selection of the four European thinkers was an instrumentalist maneuver that set aside content factors in an effort to cater to the opinions of the local crowd'.[6] Further elaborating on this point, Camic's argument shifts: he asserts that Parsons did not make a one-off decision to opt for the European theorists over institutionalists after weighing their reputations. The decision process was more subtle; it '... crystallized gradually in the course of the 1930s ... while he was part of a well-signposted intellectual network that warned him of the defectiveness and uselessness of some lines of relevant work while announcing the greatness, brilliance, and fruitfulness of other lines.'[7] The latter seems to suggest that Parsons *unconsciously* picked up on various signs, and in response to Alexander and Sciortino's critique,[8] Camic and Gross' subsequent comments reiterate this theory of unconscious adaptation.[9] However, there is not sufficient evidence to support this theory. While Camic is right that it is unlikely that Parsons made a one-off decision at some point and then stuck to this throughout, it does not follow that Parsons did not operate instrumentally. For all we know, he might well have made repeated calculations throughout his career. With this example, we are not trying to argue in favour of an instrumentalist perspective, but want to give some indication of how difficult it is, in all but a few occasions, to speculate about the motivations behind intellectual choices.

There is thirdly the structural fallacy, by which we are referring to attempts to explain individual decisions by sociological determinants. It is worth recalling that when Durkheim,[10] in his *Règles de la méthode sociologique (Rules of Sociological Method),* advocated that social facts ought to be explained and predicted by other social facts, he was fully aware that this sociological explanation did not extend to individual facts. For example, while he thought that levels of societal integration and regulations explain and predict suicide patterns, he realized that they do not account effectively for an individual suicide.[11] The structural fallacy is a common trait of intellectual biographies, whereby a particular aspect of the social background is invoked to explain an individual trajectory. As Stefan Collini points out, even the most subtle and even-handed critics, such as Perry Anderson, tend to invoke sociological variables in this manner, as if someone's class background predisposes them towards this or that stance.[12] Some sociologically trained biographers, however, do not seem to pay heed either to Durkheim's distinction between social facts and individual instances. For instance, in his intellectual biography of the American pragmatist philosopher Richard Rorty, Neil Gross brings in sociological variables to account for Rorty's individual choices. So the reader is told that '... Rorty's social background predisposed him to be antagonistic to logical positivism and sympathetic to the project of metaphysics.'[13] Arguments of this kind risk conflating sociological and individual explanations. Gross might well be correct to argue that the 'first generation of intellectual aspirants', like Rorty's parents, were more likely to be disdainful towards the anti-intellectualism of the 'new rigour', but this is not an effective explanation for Richard Rorty's subsequent intellectual trajectory given the richness of an individual's biography and the multitude of influences at work. There is a similar slippage in Pierre Bourdieu's otherwise sophisticated account of Heidegger[14] when he argues that the latter's petty bourgeois background explained the anti-cosmopolitan and anti-modernism of his outlook and his predilection for a '*völkisch language*'. Just like Gross whom he inspired, Bourdieu erroneously takes a sociological explanation of social facts for a sociological account of individual action.

There is fourthly the authenticity bias. We are referring to those studies of intellectuals that assume that intellectuals have a clear sense of their identity and values, with these self-notions guiding their work and the choices they make. Again, the authenticity bias is integral to a particular genre of intellectual biography that attributes particular significance to the author's self-description as a guide for understanding the various intellectual moves that he or she made. The very same bias is present in Gross' notion of the intellectual self-concept. According to this notion, intellectuals tell stories about themselves to themselves and to others, and those stories, which tend to be typological, shape their creative output.[15] In what follows we dissent from this view. We do not think it is fruitful to conceive of intellectuals as pursuing authentic projects that correspond to their views about their identity and values.[16] Whether within the academy or outside it, intellectuals operate within competitive arenas, struggling over symbolic and institutional recognition and scarce financial resources. It makes a lot of sense, therefore, to recognize the extent to which their interventions – whether through books, articles or speeches – are an integral part of this power struggle rather than an expression of some deeper self. By emphasizing how intellectual production and the struggles over scarce resources are intertwined, we take it as essential to establish a critical distance *vis-à-vis* the way in which most intellectuals portray themselves to their audience. Indeed, as Bourdieu pointed out, as one of the components of what he coined the 'scholastic fallacy',[17] intellectuals have a tendency to depict their own intellectual trajectory as untainted by these material, symbolic and institutional constraints. For instance, there are remarkably few intellectual autobiographies that acknowledge the full extent to which considerations of this kind interfered with the intellectual choices that were made. This is because autobiographies too – just like other intellectual products – position their authors, their allies and opponents.

There is finally the stability bias; that is, the assumption that early formation makes for fixity of somebody's subsequent intellectual trajectory. While both the notions of self-concept and *habitus* have some currency, they cannot, in themselves, account sufficiently for the changes that take place in intellectuals' views and assertions over a lifetime. Both the notion of self-concept and *habitus* imply fixity within the project and output of an intellectual. Authors who subscribe to this view assume that once the self-concept or *habitus* of the intellectual has been formed (something which develops at a relatively early stage), it tends to perpetuate itself, guiding his or her intellectual work for decades to come and manifesting itself in his or her *oeuvre*. For instance, Gross holds that the intellectual self-concept '. . . once established may exert a powerful effect on her or his future thought'.[18] Again, the researcher might well make the mistake here of identifying with how the intellectual sees him- or herself, and with how he or she wants to be seen and remembered. While there is some currency in the general idea that an individual's formative years have a considerable effect later on, it still does not do proper justice to the complexity of his or her trajectory. Indeed, it is rare for intellectuals to stick to a single self-concept or coherent project throughout their lives; they sometimes reinvent themselves, articulating new outlooks and taking on new positions. Gross' own biography of Rorty underlines our case: while he elaborates on how from an early stage onwards Rorty saw himself as a progressive pragmatist, Gross' own analysis shows how Rorty presented himself quite differently while establishing his academic career in philosophy. Positioning theory is able to capture shifts of this kind. Of course, Bourdieu and Gross are right in so far as intellectuals' orientations remain *relatively* stable – they do not change their stance constantly – but we hope, with positioning theory, to provide a more convincing explanation.

Performativity

Positioning theory has its origins in speech-act theory, and it is worth contextualizing this philosophical perspective. Following Wittgenstein, speech-act theorists pay attention to how words, rather than representing or mirroring the external world, *accomplish* things. By the early 1960s, Austin, for instance, was intrigued by 'performative utterances'; these are utterances which are neither true nor false, but which nevertheless *do* something.[19] Promises, compliments or threats are examples of such utterances. At the time, Austin's interest in performativity put clear blue water between his philosophy and that of the logical positivist tradition: the latter took propositions as depicting the external realm (and therefore either true or false), whereas Austin was keen to explore their performative aspects. Through the second half of the twentieth century, fewer and fewer philosophers thought it fruitful to conceive of language as copying the external world. Many philosophers and theorists, belonging to otherwise different intellectual orientations, became committed to the idea that language is an act which, like any act, *does* something. This has had significant pay-offs, for instance, reshaping critical theory along communicative lines (Habermas) or even redefining philosophy altogether (Rorty). We do not, however, want to revisit these developments; there is a vast literature that does precisely that. Rather, we want to explore here the relevance of this performative turn for the theorizing of intellectuals.[20]

When accounting for the intellectual realm, a performative perspective explores what intellectual interventions *do* and *achieve* rather than what they represent. This might be *prima facie* counterintuitive. Indeed, we tend to think of intellectual tracts as somehow representational: we see them as reflecting on the world (or reflecting on the representations of others) rather than acting on it. In contrast to other interventions – say, policy briefings, music performances or military actions – intellectual interventions seem to have a more passive ring to them. The tendency to conceive of intellectual interventions as such tends to be greater when intellectuals seem to operate in a semi-autonomous realm, more or less separate from, say, the world of politics or economics. So we tend to think of a journal article in a highly specialized academic journal as representing something, whether through words, models or equations. We tend not to see it as something active, partly because it does not seem to have a visible, immediate impact on the external world.

The basic intuition underlying our theoretical perspective is that even this esoteric journal article *does* something. The article might not have obvious direct repercussions for the broader world, but it nevertheless does a wide range of things, for the author, for the authors cited, for the discipline, and so forth. The key notion that captures this activity is 'positioning'. This indicates the process by which certain features are attributed to an individual or a group or some other entity. Initially introduced in the context of military strategies, marketing experts have used the concept of position to indicate how the right kind of representation of a product, company or brand can fill a previously untapped niche in the market.[21] More recently, social psychologists have introduced the same notion to describe how in everyday conversation individuals ascribe characteristics to themselves, as well as to the other participants in the interaction.[22] Whereas positioning in the case of the military or marketing is often a deliberate act – the product of calculations – this is not necessarily the case in everyday conversation where an individual might be unaware of the illocutionary force of his or her utterances. Yet, positioning theory also acknowledges the ability of individuals to alter how they represent themselves and how they locate others. Whereas explanations in terms of rules and roles denote stability, positioning theory acknowledges fluidity – the ongoing changes in how people identify themselves and position others.[23]

Positioning theorists have traditionally focused on the analysis of face-to-face interactions,[24] but more recently the theory has also been employed for analysing other types of interaction, for instance international relations and politics.[25] Interestingly, very few positioning theorists have explored the intellectual realm, and those who did tended to focus on the natural sciences and engineering.[26] Their work showed some affinities with the 'rhetorical turn' in science studies, and indeed Bruno Latour,[27] while not associated with positioning theory as such, used the same term 'positioning' to denote the set of rhetorical devices by which research results are presented. The theory we propose differs from the previous positioning theory in a variety of ways. In terms of subject matter, we will be analysing intellectuals in general – not just academics – and with a particular focus on the humanities and social sciences – not the natural sciences. More substantially, we hope to provide a richer account of the mechanisms through which positioning takes place. We will need to avoid the individualistic bias that has beset positioning theory hitherto: it will prove essential to locate positioning within its social setting and it will also become clear that it is in many respects a collective endeavour. Finally, we will pay attention to the upshot of positioning for both the status and recognition of the intellectuals and for the diffusion of the ideas articulated.

Positioning

Our starting position rests on a simple idea: intellectual interventions, whether through writing or speaking, always involve positioning. By intellectual intervention we are referring to any contribution to the intellectual realm, whether it is in the form of a book, an article, a blog, a speech or indeed part of any of these (say, a passage or a sentence). The basic intuition underlying our theory is that any such intervention locates the author(s) or speaker(s) within the intellectual field or within a broader socio-political or artistic arena while also situating other intellectuals, possibly depicting them as allies in a similar venture, predecessors of a similar orientation or alternatively as intellectual opponents. According to this perspective, then, any intellectual move brings about two types of effects. The first type is the positioning itself: for instance, as we have seen, Sartre's preface to the first edition of *Les Temps modernes* located him (and any person directly associated with the journal) as an engaged intellectual and on the left of the political spectrum. The author or speaker does not necessarily embark on the intervention to bring about this positioning. As a matter of fact, he or she might not even be aware of the positioning altogether. This first type of effect – the positioning – manifests itself in so far as his or her contemporaries operating in the same cultural context would be able to recognize it and probably did identify it as such. For instance, familiar as they were with the French context and the experience of the war, readers of the first issue of *Les Temps modernes* would have been able to identify Sartre's positioning, and most definitely did so. A historian or literary critic will be sufficiently acquainted with the historical context at play and will therefore be able to ascertain how contemporaries of the author or speaker would have assigned a particular positioning to the intellectual interventions under consideration.

However, the positioning in itself also brings about a second type of effect: within a given context, certain types of positioning might help to diffuse the ideas and enhance the agent's career and material prospects. Other types of positioning might have adverse effects, limiting the further dissemination of the ideas proposed or halting the author's professional progress. To go back to our example of Sartre, we have argued that his positioning in 1945 'fitted' the context and contributed to his success, just as other forms of positioning which had been successful in the past – for instance, Gide's art for art's sake – were no longer appreciated. There are also plenty of examples of how positioning can help bring about symbolic and institutional recognition, sometimes belatedly, as in the case of Hayek who was ignored for several decades during the Keynesian aftermath of the Second World War, but achieved success later on. He inspired a revival of monetarist policy and collected numerous honours, including most notably the Nobel Prize, the Order of the Companions of Honour and the Presidential Medal of Freedom.

166

Positioning, obviously, always involves on the one hand an 'agent', *making* the intervention and *doing* the positioning, and on the other hand a 'positioned party', being attributed certain features. We purposefully use the term 'agent' rather than 'individual': although the agent can be a sole individual, it might also include several people or a larger group. Similarly, the positioned party can be an individual or a larger social entity, but it can also be something different, such as an intellectual school, an academic discipline or a political phenomenon. As can be inferred from the Sartre example, most striking cases of positioning involve self-positioning whereby the agent and positioned party coincide. In what follows, we will be paying particular attention to self-positioning, but we should keep in mind that self-positioning goes hand in hand with the positioning of other intellectuals or other entities.

Indeed, it is often in relation to a positioned party other than oneself – for instance, by contrasting one's own position with those of other individual(s) or a group – that self-positioning is at its most effective. We have discussed how, at the outset of the war, fascist intellectuals cemented their own position by blaming their progressive counterparts for the cultural and political malaise in which the French nation found itself. Likewise, referring to Sartre's 1945 'Présentation' again, Sartre's self-positioning was strengthened by the way in which he denounced writers such as Balzac and Flaubert who allegedly had not engaged when it really mattered. Positioning these literary authors as morally compromised, politically pernicious and indefensible was a dramatic platform that enabled Sartre to locate the journal, the editors and the contributors. Of course, self-positioning can also be achieved by the positioning of institutions or concepts rather than individuals, as is exemplified in Sartre's repeated celebratory references to Republican values and democracy, for instance in his *Qu'est-ce la littérature?*. Another example of the positioning of institutions and concepts, from a very different political vantage point, would be Carl Schmitt's attack on liberal democracy for promoting a neutral state that resolves differences, thereby allegedly failing to do justice to what he thought to be the natural enmity between people.[28]

Positioning may take place subtly. For instance, intellectuals' publishers, journal outlets and their choice of references might give subtle hints about what type of intellectual they are and where their allegiances lie. Sometimes, however, positioning is achieved overtly, and indeed intellectuals often use, just as we are doing now, the introduction or concluding part of their text or speech to situate their intellectual intervention and themselves in relation to others.

Intellectuals may use intellectual manifestos to bring about this effect or they launch a new journal or book series. As we have seen, the launch of *Les Temps modernes* on 1 October 1945 enabled the editors, especially Sartre, to position themselves as engaged intellectuals, tackling issues of contemporary social and political significance. Sartre's preface acted as a manifesto for the journal, positioning it and thereby positioning the editors and contributors as politically committed authors. Another example would be Bourdieu's launch of his book series *Liber/Raisons d'agir* in the mid-1990s; it was crucial in repositioning himself as a public and politically engaged intellectual and not just a professional sociologist. Besides new journals, intellectuals may use meta-theoretical or methodological works to locate themselves and their other writings. We discussed earlier how Sartre's *Qu'est-ce que la littérature?* presented a philosophical tract that located and cemented his distinct views about writing, centred round the interdependency of prose and democracy. Likewise, Michel Foucault's 'Nietzsche, genealogy, history',[29] although ostensibly a reconstruction of Nietzsche's conception of history, has often been treated as a methodological tract that acknowledged his indebtedness to the German philosopher and heralded a break with his archaeological period.

Equally explicit is the use of labels, which can act like brands. Intellectuals often use labels to flag their own position. These labels tend to capture the core idea in a succinct fashion. This is obviously the case for Sartre's 'existentialism' and his notion of the 'engaged intellectual' but also for, say, the 'reflexive turn' in anthropology, the 'strong programme in cultural sociology' or the 'new historicism' in literary studies. Of course, intellectuals use labels not just to refer to themselves but also to others, sometimes with the aim of criticizing or ridiculing their work. Take, for instance, 'humanism': whereas in the mid-1940s in France it had clearly positive connotations (used to full effect by Sartre, as we have seen), over the next couple of decades it gradually became a negative reference point, often used to denigrate any assumption of a coherent or transparent self.[30] Said's notion of 'orientalism' (and the related accusation of 'essentializing') provides another potent example: initially introduced in the specific context of literature, it caught on, spread to various disciplines and has invariably been used to denigrate allegedly flawed attempts to generalize about other cultures. The introduction of a label can facilitate the dissemination of ideas, but the clarity of its meaning and its distinctiveness might be undermined once others start subscribing to the same label. The term 'existentialism', which was initially used by journalists and then adopted by Sartre, was also used to refer to the ideas of a variety of other intellectuals (including Heidegger, Jaspers, Camus and de Beauvoir) and, eventually, to a broader culture of malaise or angst. After it had become so nebulous, Sartre himself abandoned the label. In a similar fashion Charles Peirce's 'pragmatism' demonstrates the precariousness of labels. Once William James, F. C. S. Schiller and literary figures started to adopt the term he had coined, Peirce switched to 'pragmaticism' to distinguish his intellectual orientation.[31] Likewise, Hayek adopted the term 'catallaxy' to refer to the spontaneous order produced by market interactions, after his earlier terms like 'free market' and 'liberal economics' had been adopted by the Chicago School, which had very different underlying philosophy and methods.[32]

Positioning can take two ideal-typical forms: an intellectual intervention may involve what we call 'intellectual positioning' or 'politico-ethical positioning'. Intellectual positioning locates the agent primarily within the intellectual realm. It might identify a specific intellectual orientation, defend that stance and elaborate on its significance. Claims about the importance often come down to claims about the originality or intellectual power of the intellectual orientation. Intellectual positioning can situate the agent and work within a broader tradition, linking it to important figures in the field, including possibly a mentor. 'Politico-ethical positioning', on the other hand, refers to a broader political or ethical stance which surpasses the narrow confines of the intellectual sphere. In practice, intellectual positioning and political-ethical positioning tend to be intertwined and sometimes explicitly so in the case for public intellectuals like Sartre. Whereas Sartre's earlier philosophical work, from his shorter technical pieces of the 1930s to *L'Être et le néant*, remained more or less confined within the contours of the intellectual realm, this changed dramatically in the mid-1940s. During this period, he connected the two types of positioning and made this link the cornerstone of his philosophy: his idea of committed literature and the writer's responsibility was as much a political project as an intellectual one. In general, public intellectuals emphasize their 'politico-ethical positioning' – other prototypical examples include Émile Zola's 'J'accuse!' and the pro-Dreyfus petition in the late 1890s or the Russell-Einstein manifesto and its call for peaceful resolutions to international conflict at the height of the Cold War[33] – but distinctive about Sartre was the explicit link he made between the two types of positioning, with his philosophy underscoring his political interventions.

The examples of Dreyfus, Sartre and Russell refer to politically tense situations, but politico-ethical positioning can also take place within the safe contours of an academic context, whether in the form of a critique – as in Habermas' depiction of French postmodern authors as 'crypto-conservative'[34] – or as a more constructive move – as in Michael Burawoy's plea for a more socially engaged 'public sociology'.[35] Some areas or topics are more likely to generate a merging of intellectual and politico-ethical positioning; this applies, for instance, to contemporary intellectual interventions in the fields of race and ethnic relations or gender where, due to the nature of the topic and the political sensitivities it raises, intellectual positioning often entails a strong politico-ethical component. In countries with less of a clear separation between the intellectual and political field (for instance, historically in Latin America), politico-ethical and intellectual positioning tend to be more explicitly intertwined,[36] and indeed in those countries leading intellectuals like the Argentinean Beatriz Sarlo tend to advocate and celebrate this link.[37] Even in countries with a clear differentiation between the political and intellectual sphere, a politically charged climate can lead to the blurring of the difference between politico-ethical and intellectual positioning, with the former taking a more central role in the latter. This was the case for the political context of the aftermath of the Second World War and the Cold War which led to a hardening of political positions among French intellectuals,[38] just as the student movement of the 1960s led to a growing scepticism in the American academy towards the political viability of mainstream social science and its attendant assumption of value neutrality.[39] In both cases, political and ethical concerns underscore intellectual positioning and self-positioning.

Performative tools, narratives and the profane

To take intellectual products as performative also involves taking into account the various material and symbolic props and devices that help to bring about effectively the intervention or positioning. Indeed, not every intellectual product manages to bring about a significant intervention or positioning, and the extent to which it does depends on a range of what we call 'performative tools': these are material and symbolic means that enable an effective intervention. For instance, the prestige and marketing strategies of the publisher of a book are performative tools that allow the book to have an impact, and so are the aura, authority and connections of the author and his or her rhetorical skills. We have discussed the significance of the German control of publishing during the war, not just through the banning of 'subversive' publications, but also by providing facilities and financing for established, charismatic intellectuals like Drieu la Rochelle who were politically on their side. In a similar vein, Gallimard's indebtedness to Sartre, as outlined in the previous chapters, was crucial in his willingness to back Sartre's key projects and to give him free reign. Sartre's connections in different worlds, from journalism to the theatre, as well as his rhetorical bravura have been well documented. They all constitute performative tools through which Sartre was able to position himself at the time. In the academic world, we can find plenty of other cases that demonstrate the significance of performative tools and their unequal distribution, as can be gleaned from the ranking of research institutions, publishers and journals.

Among the many performative tools that make possible effective positioning, rhetorical devices and in particular 'narratives' are worth further exploration.[40] Narratives are relatively coherent stories that accompany and make possible effective positioning. Narratives may refer to the authors themselves as in autobiographies, but they may also refer to other people or entities: by positioning itself as a Resistance novel, for instance, a book may invoke a narrative of a defiant, cohesive nation or of an exploitative, treacherous class. Positioning depends not just on what the narrative explicitly states, but also on what it implies and, crucially, what it leaves out. Narratives often involve recollections and reconstructions of the past, ranging from an individual's trajectories[41] to societal pasts.[42] The latter might involve claims about 'cultural trauma'; that is, about the nature of past wrongdoing, its severity and significance for today, and the identity of the perpetrators and the victims.[43] Narratives may also include references to the future: they may present a blueprint for a new beginning – be it a new life or a more just society – or they may depict the future as closed and contained in the past. We have seen how Sartre's articles, from 'La République du silence' to 'Qu'est-ce qu'un collaborateur?', presented a compelling narrative about the recent past, portraying the French nation in a heroic light and depicting collaborators and anti-Semites as outsiders. The articles also express hope for a future, egalitarian society, modelled on the camaraderie of the Resistance. We have seen how, with the help of these subtle narratives, Sartre provided a vocabulary that enabled a section of French society to come to terms with the trauma of the war and move forward. The narratives enable Sartre to connect with the public at the time, and it is this connection that contributed to his rise and that of existentialism. Besides Sartre, Marxism provides another striking example of how the past and the future are woven into intellectual narratives, with a historical pattern indicating how the injustices of the past might be resolved in a post-capitalist order. In performative terms, the strength of a narrative often depends on what is not said,[44] as became obvious in our analysis of Sartre's *Réflexions sur la question juive* which skirted around the complicity of the French in the deportation of the Jews. Ever since the revelations of Stalinist atrocities, the performative strength of Marxist interventions in France in the course of the second half of the last century has often lied in 'burying' these issues whenever possible, while subsequent critics such as the *nouveaux philosophes* reclaimed the past and its trauma to tarnish this political project and to condemn the alleged irresponsibility of a previous generation of French intellectuals.

Positioning and narratives draw on argumentation, especially in the intellectual field. It is through arguments that intellectuals differentiate themselves from others or associate themselves with them. In contrast with other forms of positioning in which visuals and unconscious associations play a significant role (e.g. advertising of a product), intellectual positioning stands or falls with explicit arguments. In the reconstruction of the conflict between collaborationist and Resistance intellectuals, we paid attention to the rhetorical and dramatic devices used at different ends of the political and intellectual spectrum to justify certain decisions and condemn others and which ultimately impacted considerably on both the cultural and political scene in post-war France. Particularly prevalent in intellectual positioning are meta-arguments. These are abstract assertions about other (intellectual) propositions, ranging from assertions about the political efficacy (or lack thereof) of a particular literary genre to broader statements about the role of the writer in society. Indeed, meta-arguments played an increasingly important role as Vichy started to unravel and the country prepared for the *libération* and the purge. These meta-arguments took on a judicial significance during the *épuration* itself where both prosecution and defence ended up speculating about both the political consequences of certain intellectual positions and the author's responsibility, while making those speculations central to their case. The more successful of those arguments were those that managed to resonate with the recent war experiences and feed into the general sense of the existential dilemmas those experiences entailed; they would eventually become integral to the French intellectual and political landscape of the mid-1940s. The prevalence of meta-arguments is, of course, not limited to the public intellectual arena and can also be found within the academy: for instance, critical theory, as developed by members of the Frankfurt school, drew on a meta-theoretical critique of existing social science, arguing that its aim should be to pursue emancipation rather than solely describe or explain.

Intellectuals often locate themselves in relation to a sacred realm, in opposition to the profane world of the market, party politics and everyday life. This is not merely the case for intellectuals who explicitly fulfil a religious function (for instance, the Old Testament prophets, as so vividly described by Weber), but also for secular intellectuals like the ones we have been discussing in this book. We have seen how, during the Second World War, the various arguments and meta-arguments by both sides alluded to a sacred realm, whether it was connected to national pride or purity of the writer. Both Resistance and collaborationist authors depicted literature and the act of writing as the last bastion of French Resistance, encapsulating the spirit of the nation. Collaborationist authors were forced to defend themselves against treason and accusations of selling out, writing *for* Germany in exchange for money and for a luxurious and sometimes extravagant lifestyle. They were at pains to show that this was not the case and that, throughout the war, they had remained loyal to the nation and that they had remained pure, untainted by economic and worldly incentives. Both Resistance and collaborationist intellectuals were mainly literary figures operating outside the academy, but references to the sacred are not limited to this category: in the modern university system, for instance, academics also often invoke a sacred realm when appealing to higher academic values such as intellectual autonomy, truth and excellence.

Relational logic

This brings us to the relational features of positioning. An intellectual intervention *in itself* does not involve a particular positioning; positioning only takes effect because of the *agents* operating within a particular *context*. There are three aspects of this relational logic. Firstly, the effects of an intervention in terms of positioning depend on the *individuals* who bring it about, on their already established status and positioning within the intellectual field. Petitions involving intellectuals, from the Dreyfus petition to those in which Sartre was involved, exemplify this: their significance relies as much on the status of the signatories as on their number. A similar intellectual intervention by a different agent might bring about a very different positioning, or not succeed as an act of positioning. The effect of an intervention depends on the length and nature of an agent's past pattern of interventions, with different trajectories or status likely to generate different effects. Richard Rorty[45] failed to see this point when he suggested that younger non-established scholars follow him in taking a humanist and iconoclastic stance as if their credibility would be as strong as his within the power game of the modern academy.

Secondly, the effects of intellectual interventions depend on those of the *other individuals* at play within the same field. Shifts in the positioning of other individuals affect our positioning and self-positioning. In particular, the position of an intellectual intervention might be undermined or reassessed because of an effective countermove or more subtly by the fact that a significant number of intellectuals have now moved onto different topics or issues. We have seen, for instance, how, in the mid-1940s, intellectuals became increasingly convinced of the writer's political responsibility and how this made Gide's notion of art for art's sake untenable. Further, once similar ideas were used in defence of collaborationist intellectuals, this notion and the people associated with it were conceived as pernicious. Another example from our discussion concerns a later period, when a new generation of intellectuals, born after the First World War, treated Sartre as increasingly insignificant and turned to different authors or proposed different interpretations of the same authors. Foucault, for instance, found inspiration in Nietzsche[46] and Lévi-Strauss relied on Durkheim and Saussure. Once even Sartre's previous allies, such as Merleau-Ponty, moved on to different intellectual traditions, his philosophical programme started looking outdated.

Thirdly, the actual effects in terms of positioning depend very much on the specific intellectual or socio-political *context* in which the intellectual intervention takes place, on the historically rooted sensitivities. This contextualization has been central to the explanation of the phenomenon 'Sartre' and we have provided plenty of examples. Throughout his book we have shown how, in the mid-1940s, Sartre's reformulation of his philosophy resonated with the French people, providing a simple vocabulary to assimilate the complex experience of the war. We have argued that this partly explains how he was able to make an inroad into the public domain at the time. The Cambridge school of history has analysed plenty of cases whereby understanding the context in which the intellectual interventions take place accounts for their power and significance at the time. For instance, by arguing in *Elements of Law* and *Leviathan* that the sovereign is the sole judge to assess a threat, Hobbes positioned himself in line with Charles I in the context of the ship-money crisis, defending not only the king's right to tax people in a military context but also his right (and *not* the public's or their representatives') to judge whether the Dutch were a sufficient threat to the crown to warrant increased military expenses.[47]

Given the significance of context, it follows that, through time, the same types of intellectual interventions might bring about different positioning even when the same people are involved. It also follows, crucially, that the same intellectual intervention might generate different positioning when transposed to different contexts. For instance, authors' self-presentation within the local field that is familiar to them might acquire different meanings and connotations in a different context. Therefore, even when intellectuals are involved in carefully constructed or calculated positioning and self-positioning, not all effects of their intellectual interventions are within their control. Indeed, intellectual interventions can amount to very different forms of positioning and self-positioning once they reach different audiences.

One extreme scenario is when intellectual interventions (and the intellectuals behind those interventions) are posthumously reassessed by others in pursuit of their own intellectual agenda. As Gary Taylor pointed out, what appear to us now to be iconic literary figures or key intellectual interventions were not necessarily considered as such at the time; it was sometimes only at a later stage that those intellectuals and interventions were identified as important.[48] Those who have been crucial in this process of 'remembering' often had their own agenda, positioning themselves in the competitive intellectual or political arena at the time. We discussed earlier how Sartre, to develop his own existentialist phenomenology, revisited, not just Heidegger and Husserl, but also Hegel. Subsequent intellectuals like Foucault and Deleuze centred their work round the 'discovery' of Nietzsche. Obviously, 'discoveries' of this kind do not take place in an institutional vacuum; in the French case historical research has shown that changes to the curriculum of the *agrégation* are often followed by new intellectual heroes and new fads.[49] There are many other examples of intellectual appropriation, some of which show the distortions that may accompany it. In the American academic setting of the mid-twentieth century, for instance, Herbert Blumer championed G. H. Mead as a key figure in American pragmatism to promote his own school of symbolic interactionism, thereby forging his own position within the sociological field which at the time was dominated by Talcott Parsons' structural-functionalism.[50] In the process, *Mind,*

Self and Society, a repetitive and flawed text based on student notes, became part of the canon whereas other writings – or indeed lectures – might have been more representative of Mead's ideas.[51] Sometimes this posthumous recognition can take several decades as in the case of Ferdinand de Saussure, whose *Cours de linguistique générale*,[52] also based on student notes, only received broader attention within the social sciences and humanities from the 1950s onwards when self-proclaimed structuralists searched for and identified their intellectual predecessors, reading Saussure through Jakobson's lens and focusing on Saussure's theory of signs and synchronic analysis.[53]

A related scenario – and in some respects a mirror image of the previous one – consists of the case where subsequent intellectuals, again in the pursuit of their own agenda, vilify earlier intellectual products. We have noted how, at the end of the war, Sartre used the alleged non-engagement of previous novelists as a foil to earmark his own intellectual agenda. Likewise, we mentioned how Sartre himself became a negative reference point for many others, ranging from Lévi-Strauss to Bourdieu. Analytic philosophy provides another interesting case, especially because it is supposedly unconcerned with past philosophers. For all their disdain towards the history of philosophy, earlier British analytic philosophers showed a remarkable interest in this sub-discipline: they repeatedly positioned their own intellectual agenda in opposition to what they saw as the dangers of foreign strands of thought, thereby coining the term 'Continental philosophy'.[54] Revealing a certain amount of smug patriotism, Russell, Ayer and several others depicted the alleged muddled thinking of Hegel and Heidegger as causally related to the emergence of totalitarian regimes, linking their own preoccupation with precision, logic and science to more responsible and liberal forms of government. Even subsequent British-based philosophers such as Berlin[55] or Popper,[56] who did not, strictly speaking, operate within the framework of analytic philosophy, made their case for piecemeal liberal democracy by depicting several German philosophies as pernicious, either because they allegedly promoted a problematic notion of liberty or because they proposed closed, utopian schemes that were immune from empirical refutation.

A final scenario – not unrelated to the previous one – is where subsequent intellectuals regard earlier intellectual interventions as irrelevant for contemporary purposes. In some cases, the omissions are very selective. While Bergson had been a towering figure in the early twentieth century, very few intellectuals of Sartre's generation properly engaged with Bergson's work. Sartre had done so initially,[57] but then proceeded also to ignore his legacy. To give a very different example, with the transition from communism in the early 1990s, Russian and East European intellectuals were, at least initially, keen to avoid the customary references to Marx and Marxist scholars, in the process implying that Marxist scholarship was no longer relevant to the contemporary societal context.[58] In other cases, *any* reference to the past is severely restricted altogether. For instance, once analytical philosophy obtained a relatively dominant position in several high-profile departments in the US, its proponents no longer expressed the need to distance themselves from Continental philosophy, with the exception, of course, of a few scattered outbursts.[59] Likewise, orthodox economics, in its neoclassical form and with its prevalence of econometrics and rational choice theory, tends to be equally indifferent to the wisdom or otherwise of previous 'classical' thinkers.[60] In both analytical philosophy and orthodox economics, the omission or silence implies that, however important 'great works' might have been at the time and however much depth and richness they might exude, they are extremely unlikely to add anything significant to contemporary concerns within the field and they are therefore at best of an antiquarian value.

Cooperation and individualization

It is rare for a single intellectual intervention to bring about the desired effect. In most cases several interventions – often repeating the same position – are necessary to get a message across. However, even repeated sole interventions would not be sufficient because one's positioning depends on so many other agents. Firstly, positioning depends on broader intellectual networks. The networks of an intellectual comprise a large number of agents, who engage with him or her and confirm his or her positioning, even if they disagree or are overtly hostile. The status and recognition of intellectuals is dependent partly on where they are acknowledged (in which journals or book series), and who precisely acknowledges them (what is their positioning and status). The previous chapters taught us how Sartre's rise as a public intellectual was partly due to these larger networks in which he was embedded, ranging from the world of publishing to journalism. We should also not ignore the role of the critics, especially those associated with the Communist Party, in creating and consolidating his public profile during this period.

Secondly, positioning is likely to be more effective when

accomplished in teams.[61] Teams are narrower than networks: teams of intellectuals actively cooperate in positioning themselves, for instance, by grouping around a school or research programme, often using a label which makes their work and agenda immediately recognizable. What we have in mind is close to Michael Farrell's 'collaborative circles' – that is, intense, small groups of innovative artistic and intellectual endeavour – but we do not share Farrell's predilection to generalize about the group formation of these circles or the roles that are fulfilled by their members.[62] Also, our study has been attentive to the fluidity of teams, the extent to which they may overlap and how people draw on different teams. Indeed, Sartre proved to be an interesting case because his positioning relied not just formally on the editorial board of *Les Temps modernes*, but also on other writers such as Camus who were somehow associated with 'existentialism'. There are numerous other examples of teams: the Frankfurt School, the Bloomsbury group, the Birmingham school of cultural studies, the strong programme in the sociology of knowledge, the strong programme in cultural sociology or new historicism. Teams are effective but they come at a cost: with the exception of the intellectual leaders, members of teams find it more difficult to position themselves as having an independent voice or as innovative. Ultimately the writings of the leaders will be remembered while the other works gradually fade away, unless other team members break away and actively reposition themselves as dissenting from the team leader.

Team membership is, however, crucial because positioning rarely goes uncontested. An intellectual might be able to position him- or herself for a certain period of time, but eventually rival intellectuals will mount a challenge, portraying him or her as outdated, insignificant, pernicious, erroneous, or as misrepresenting his or her self-proclaimed position. Even individuals who carefully position themselves may end up being pigeonholed differently by others and having to extricate from labels attributed to them. We have seen that, from the mid-1940s onwards, Sartre was the subject of criticisms from various quarters and that he struggled to shed accusations of being a bourgeois thinker or a nihilist. To give a more recent example, in spite of Richard Rorty's attempts to associate his project with John Dewey, others have subsequently dissociated Deweyan pragmatism from Rorty's and have labelled his work as 'postmodernist' or 'relativist'.[63] Positioning, therefore, is an ongoing achievement, requiring continuous attention and maintenance, not just from the individual, but from all his or her team members. Sometimes teams are formed to advocate and defend a certain position, in the process ignoring crucial differences. Some of the members of *Les Temps modernes*, for example, had different political orientations, with Aron on the centre right and Sartre clearly on the left, but they were able to set those differences aside and present a united front. Moving on to the economic sphere, the alliance of Hayekians and Friedmanites provides another example: they united around a neo-liberal political agenda in spite of differences, for instance, about the role of knowledge in the economy.[64]

Teams capture the cooperative side of intellectual life, but what we call 'individualization' is equally intrinsic to the realm of intellectuals. By intellectual individualization, we refer to the process by which intellectuals distinguish themselves from others, making themselves look different from them and possibly unique. Individualization is achieved through careful self-positioning and positioning, differentiating oneself from others. It may involve conflict because the act of differentiating tends to take place through criticisms of others. This is not to say that individualization and teamwork are necessarily mutually exclusive: intellectuals might collaborate with other team members to emphasize their distinct stance and to elaborate on how this stance differs from that of others. We have, however, already discussed the drawbacks of teamwork, and the extent to which it becomes difficult for individual members to maintain a distinct, visible profile. At some point, therefore, members of a team might wish to emphasize how they differ from the other members as well. This process of cooperation and individualization has been central to the reconstruction of Sartre' rise, as narrated in the previous chapters. Indeed, we have analysed how, with the help of underground publications, Resistance intellectuals were able to maintain a united front against collaborationist intellectuals, how at the end of the war different factions emerged within that front (Communists, progressive Catholics, existentialists, moderate liberals, etc.), and how eventually, within Sartre's camp, some of his previous allies (Aron, Camus, Merleau-Ponty) went their separate ways. In general, the more secure and established one's position, the less one needs to rely on teamwork and the more likely one will press for intellectual individualization.

Philosophical and methodological issues

Given its centrality in our exposition, it is important to clarify the precise status of the use of the term 'positioning' and with what type of explanation it should be associated. When initially used in military settings or in marketing, the concept of positioning brought up the image of a rational, calculating agent who is aware of the effects that are being produced. In the military the agent attempts to outmanoeuvre his or her opponent, whereas in marketing he or she carefully fills the untapped niche and projects the right brand. It is certainly possible to think of other social realms where intentional positioning is equally prevalent. Politics is one, and indeed we often assume that politicians skilfully position themselves, and reposition if need be. Interestingly, politicians often criticize each other for doing precisely that (e.g. the infamous accusation of 'flip-flopping') while positioning themselves as devoid of any such manoeuvring. However, moving away from marketing and politics, to what extent are intellectuals involved in intentional positioning?

At one level, the answer is straightforward. Given the premeditated nature of intellectual interventions, the amount of work that goes into them and the high levels of education of the authors, it is sensible to assume that the intellectuals are often involved in intentional positioning. That is, they will often be consciously aware of some of the effects produced and we can expect them to craft their interventions with those effects in mind. Almost every formal presentation of new intellectual work begins with a 'position statement' identifying the work on which it builds, the work that complements and supports it, and the work by other authors that it contradicts or supersedes. This is, of course, not to say that intellectuals are aware of all the effects produced given their potentially infinite number. Nor is it to say that the interventions of intellectuals necessarily comply with the various requirements of rational, self-interested action (e.g. clear preference ordering, transitivity, etc.). But it is to acknowledge that intentional positioning is widespread in the intellectual realm, and increasingly necessary when justifying new work for publication. Indeed, explicit positioning is built into the modern scientific and social-scientific paper, which usually begins with an explanation of how the present article relates to existing published work, and how it differs from and advances beyond past contributions.

The picture becomes more complicated once we are dealing with empirical research on intellectuals that involves specific case studies. While we may agree that intellectuals are often involved in intentional positioning, it often proves difficult to know in a particular instance whether at the time of the intervention the intellectual was conscious of the effects produced and whether the intended effect caused him or her to intervene in the way in which he or she did. It is often hard to identify with sufficient degree of certainty the motives or calculations underlying the intellectual intervention. The solution to this problem, as we see it, might be to search for more circumstantial evidence, but we should realize that there are many instances where that evidence is likely to be inconclusive. In those cases, the solution lies in abandoning a vocabulary of intentions for a vocabulary of effects. That is, in those cases, we suggest using positioning differently, denoting certain *effects* of a particular intellectual move within the intellectual field. So we are proposing that, unless compelling evidence is available, no claims are made about whether the agents involved were necessarily aware of those effects, let alone that this awareness played any role in making that particular intervention in the first place.

Whether or not the intellectuals anticipated those effects and whether this awareness had anything to do with the intervention, it is possible to trace the effects, assessing whether the intervention and the ideas in it were disseminated and whether the agents were rewarded accordingly. Crucially, it is possible to account for the diffusion of the ideas and institutional and symbolic rewards in terms of positioning. Effective positioning is likely to enhance the diffusion of ideas and corresponding institutional and symbolic rewards. This is not to say that the search for effects is immediately transparent to the sociologist of intellectual life or without any methodological difficulties. It can be an arduous task to establish, for instance, how a particular intellectual intervention helps to locate the author within a particular context, and indeed the task is likely to be more daunting if that context is unfamiliar to us. As our case study of Sartre and existentialism has shown, research of this kind also entails studying in depth the collective sentiments and sensibilities that characterize a particular epoch and which explain why certain intellectual interventions (and the positioning which they imply) connect with the public and others do not.[65] In other words, the study of an author's positioning needs to be accompanied by a hermeneutic understanding of the experiences, concerns and hopes of the audience within the socio-political context at the time. In our case study, we focused on how Sartre and existentialism were received within his own setting – that of the turbulent setting of France in the mid-1940s – but positioning theory can also be used to explore how intellectual interventions 'travel' from one context to another.[66] In some cases a particular positioning might be effective within a given local setting (and indeed lead to considerable rewards), but less likely to lead to the broader dissemination of the content that is being propagated. This is, for instance, the case in Latin-American social science where literary, humanistic approaches have a local appeal but are less likely to generate interest within an international market,[67] whereas in elite research universities in the US, the local system of incentives and rewards is conducive to the type of positioning that is likely to lead to broader diffusion within the subject area. Again, this example gives some indication of the in-depth analysis that needs to accompany the research into positioning. Yet, however laborious the task of tracing the effects in terms of positioning and strategic advantages might be, it remains an achievable intellectual exercise – imminently more accomplishable than the elusive search for what went on in people's minds.

By substituting a vocabulary of effects for a vocabulary of intentions whenever the empirical evidence for claims regarding intentionality is wanting, it is possible to use positioning theory to make sense of existing research findings while avoiding some of its pitfalls. With the framework of positioning theory, it becomes possible to reappraise existing research findings without replicating their errors. From this point of view, Camic has shown convincingly that Parsons' writings, by omitting certain allies and emphasizing others, were likely to be well received within the Harvard context and were instrumental in his professional rise in the local institutional setting in which he found himself. Harvard, with its prestige and central place within the American academy, provided an excellent basis for the diffusion of his ideas across the discipline of sociology. Likewise, we can use our framework to revisit Gross' biographical work on Rorty. From this vantage point, Rorty's flexibility in adapting to the demands for the 'new rigour' of analytical philosophy was crucial in obtaining first a junior and subsequently a senior position at a high-profile department like Princeton. If it had not been for this repositioning, Rorty might not have been in the comfortable position from which to launch his attack on epistemology and his appeal for an edifying, hermeneutically sensitive type of philosophy.

Two further methodological points are in order, one dealing with how positioning theory provides a persuasive explanation for the stability within intellectual trajectories, and the other with the evolutionary argument that underpins positioning theory. Regarding the first point, we have already commented on how the notion of positioning avoids the stability bias of Gross' and Bourdieu's writings on intellectuals: it accounts for a certain element of fluidity in how intellectuals project themselves and how they locate others. There are, however, limits to this flexibility. It is indeed rare for intellectuals to reinvent themselves on a regular basis, but I wish to explain this relative durability differently from Gross or Bourdieu. Rather than identifying factors that are linked to the individual and can be traced back to early childhood or early formation (see, for instance, the *habitus* or self-concept), we explain the relative solidity of positioning more sociologically by pointing out two distinctive features of the intellectual arena that make regular repositioning less likely. Firstly, as pointed out earlier, positioning is not a one-off event, but an ongoing achievement involving teams and indeed broader intellectual networks. It takes many years to achieve the work and contacts that bring about effective positioning, not to mention the formal training that often precedes it. In sum, substantial repositioning takes time and is costly. Secondly, given the focus of intellectuals on the internal coherence of the arguments presented (and indeed the internal coherence of someone's biography), repositioning might be noticed by other intellectuals who might demand justification. Not every explanation will be deemed acceptable and, if it is not, the credibility of the intellectual involved might be affected. In the absence of a major extraneous event (e.g. a war, a forced exile or a long detour outside the intellectual arena), radical repositioning is rarely attained without loss of credibility. The more the intellectual is known, the more likely the repositioning will have to be accounted for. In sum, repositioning entails reputational risks. Both factors – the costs and the reputational risks – explain why repositioning tends to be found among either firmly established intellectuals, such as tenured academics, or those who are just starting off and have not yet publicly cemented their position.

The second methodological point concerns the type of explanation that underscores our reliance of positioning theory. Our focus on the effects of intellectual interventions should not be mistaken for a functionalist argument. The latter purports to explain the recurrence of social practices by showing how they are beneficial to the social system in which they are embedded, even if, as the case may be, the individuals involved are unaware of those societal benefits or do not intentionally bring about those effects. In contrast, a research programme, centred round positioning theory, explores the selective advantages or disadvantages for the agents and for the intellectual interventions that different types of positioning might provide within a given intellectual and political context. As such, it is compatible, not with functionalist reasoning, but with an evolutionary logic, such as Harré's, that accounts for why some intellectual interventions are rewarded and diffused and others are not. As explained before, the individuals involved might be aware of the competitive advantages and disadvantages of various forms of positioning and strategize accordingly. Meanwhile, the interventions themselves always have the potential to affect and alter the intellectual and political fields in which they have emerged and which ultimately affect their dissemination. All this makes the transmission of intellectual products (as indeed the evolution of cultural artefacts in general) as somehow operating in between the contours of Darwinian and Lamarckian evolution.[68]

Transformation of the public intellectual

So far we have expanded on the theory underlying our historical reconstruction of Sartre's rise to public prominence. Seen through this theoretical lens, we can say that during the Second World War (and especially towards the end of it), Jean-Paul Sartre repositioned himself as an authoritative public intellectual. He became a politically engaged writer in the Dreyfusard tradition, distancing himself from his earlier apolitical attitude and from the notion of art for art's sake that had been associated with Gide and Drieu la Rochelle. At the end of the war, many intellectuals saw this depoliticized notion of writing as pernicious, associating it with the attitude of collaborationist writers. The trials of collaborationist intellectuals further fuelled the notion of the writers' responsibility, which fed into the frenzy around existentialism. Key intellectual interventions in 1944 and 1945 enabled Sartre to reposition himself as an *intellectuel engagé*, allowing him to occupy a central place in the immediate aftermath of the war. There has been a considerable debate as to whether Sartre was intentionally representing himself in a different light to gain advantage in the intellectual and political climate at the time. The evidence remains inconclusive,[69] showing the limitations of a vocabulary of intentions in the context of the intellectual sphere. There is no need to resort to arguments about intentional positioning. The effects speak louder than words: regardless of Sartre's intentions, his intellectual interventions gave him symbolic recognition and helped the diffusion of his ideas.

It is important, however, to recognize that Sartre was a particular type of public intellectual. He epitomised – and in some respects came to symbolize – a specific form of public engagement, one which, we will argue, is no longer quite as viable today as it was back then. Various sociological developments have made it less likely for his type of positioning to be credible and succeed. To understand this process, positioning theory will have to be complemented with a historical perspective. Whereas performativity and positioning capture

184

the creative ways in which individuals operate within the intellectual realm, we need to hone in on the structural and institutional background against which positioning takes place. It will be possible, then, to make a distinction between three types of positioning – the 'authoritative', 'expert' and 'embedded' public intellectual – each associated with a different societal context. Sartre embodies the first type of public engagement – the authoritative public intellectual – which, we shall see, is no longer as tenable as it was then.

Authoritative public intellectuals, like Sartre, rely on high cultural capital acquired from being trained in a high-profile discipline like philosophy and from being brought up in a very privileged background. They straddle neatly the inside–outside divide: they are so respected through privilege and intellectual achievement that they can oppose the establishment without ever substantially losing status or authority. They address a wide range of subjects without being experts as such. They speak from above – at, rather than with, their audience. And they have a strong moral voice, condemning, praising and spurring people on to act.

Authoritative public intellectuals thrive in a very particular setting. They thrive in societies in which a significant section of the population value intellectual life and in which nevertheless the cultural and intellectual capital is concentrated within a small elite. They thrive in a hierarchical educational context, with 'hierarchical' referring to a clear distinction not only between elite institutions and other higher education establishments but also between high- and low-status disciplines. They can exist independently of academic appointments because of independent resources, gained from family wealth or successful exploitation of the media of the time (book-writing and print journalism in the first half of the twentieth century, broadcasting in the second half and beyond). They tend to surface when the academic setting is more amorphous, with limited specialization, and especially when the social sciences are poorly professionalized. It is in this very specific context that authoritative public intellectuals like Sartre and Russell have a field day. Steeped in a high-profile discipline like philosophy and mathematics and with the confidence of the right *habitus* and an elite education, they can speak to a wide range of social and political issues without being criticized for dilettantism. The early part of the twentieth century, especially in parts of Europe, fits this ideal type remarkably well. It was the era of the philosopher as public intellectual.

What has changed since? Firstly, philosophy has lost to a certain extent its previous intellectual dominance. This is partly due to the rise, during the latter part of the twentieth century, of various philosophical currents, such as postmodernism and neo-pragmatism, which questioned, if not undermined, the erstwhile superiority of philosophy over other vocabularies. Within the Anglo-Saxon context, Rorty and Bernstein epitomise this strand, advocating Gadamerian hermeneutics and Dewey's pragmatism over epistemology.[70] But besides the developments within philosophy itself, other factors also came into play. The social sciences have emerged as a significant force and have professionalized, making it more difficult for philosophers or others without appropriate training and expertise in the social sciences to make authoritative claims about the nature of the social and political world without being challenged. Massive expansion of the ranks of professional social scientists means there are now lifelong specialists in the areas that public intellectuals used to comment on, who are better placed to contest such 'generalist' interventions as uninformed and superficial. For all its genius and perceptiveness, it would be difficult to imagine Sartre's *Réflexions sur la question juive* to have been met with such little critique when it came out if it had been published, say, twenty years later. Whereas this text was seen as a highly insightful piece of work in the 1940s, we now value it more as a quaint piece of French intellectual history rather than a valuable explanation of the phenomenon of anti-Semitism. Compare this with, say, *The Authoritarian Personality*, published only three years later and addressing related issues, but which has better stood the test of time, in part because of its sociological outlook and methodology.[71]

Secondly, with high educational levels for larger sections of society, the erstwhile distinction between an intellectual elite and the rest no longer holds to quite the same extent. With higher education also comes a growing scepticism towards epistemic and moral authority, an increasing recognition of the fallibility of knowledge and of the existence of alternative perspectives. Speaking from above and *at* their audience, as authoritative public intellectuals do, is no longer as acceptable as it used to be. Print and broadcasting media have become less deferential and more willing to challenge the statements of politicians and other public figures – a process assisted by the arrival of journalists with higher education and subject specialism. The rise of new social media in the twenty-first century intensified this 'democratization' of public intellectual interventions even further, partly because of the interactive nature of the technology involved, which means that no single party has intellectual monopoly, and partly because technically more people can enter the public sphere than they used to. Of course, we should not overestimate the dialogical and democratic potential of the new social media. The interactive potential of the technology does not always pan out in practice. The new social media have gatekeepers too just like newspapers and magazines, and we should keep in mind that very few bloggers have a large following. But the technology has made a difference, one which surely has further lessened the likelihood of authoritative public intellectuals.

Thirdly, there has since been a growing disquiet about 'philosophical systems' such as Marxism in whose name numerous authoritarian regimes have been established and legitimized. Although not all authoritative public intellectuals promoted a 'system' as such, let alone a Marxist one, the failure of the latter certainly put a serious dent in the status of philosophy within the wider public. Since the 1980s, those grand schemes, often the brainchild of philosophers, were gradually replaced by a rebranded free market ideology. Free markets are as much a 'grand narrative' as Marxism was, equally fanatical about the desirability of its utopian vision and equally adamant that an inevitable march of history would sweep across the globe. No other publication epitomises this doctrine of liberal supremacy more than Francis Fukuyama's *End of History and the Last Man*.[72] But unlike Marxism which conceived a different society for the future, the new free market ideology ultimately re-invoked the distant past, celebrating the era of unregulated capitalism and arguing why, with some modifications, it was the only viable strategy for the present. Whereas speculating about desirable futures had always been the hallmark of philosophical and political thought, the free market ideology with its attendant focus on the present put economics, rather than philosophy, centre stage and presented a view in which freely choosing individuals would generate a relatively open-ended future that intellectuals could not usefully shape or predict. Indeed, of all the social sciences, economics became particularly dominant from the 1980s onwards, acquiring credibility well beyond its limited predictive power.

If various societal forces have worked against the authoritative public intellectual, then what has emerged in its place? In the first instance 'expert public intellectuals' have come to the forefront. These are public intellectuals who draw on their professional knowledge, whether derived from their research in the social or natural sciences, to engage with wider societal or political issues that go beyond their narrow expertise. When, in the 1970s, Michel Foucault introduced himself as a 'specific intellectual', he had precisely this form of focused and expert-driven engagement in mind, and indeed his own research on the history of punishment, including *Surveiller et punir*, tied in with his campaigning for prison reforms.[73] Likewise, in the 1990s, Pierre Bourdieu drew on his research on poverty in France, including *La Misère du monde*, to enter the public arena and embark upon a political crusade against neo-liberalism, in particular against the policies of the French government at the time.[74] In some respects Noam Chomsky also falls in this category: although initially obtaining recognition for his theoretical contributions to the study of linguistics, he subsequently became a public figure as an expert on and critic of American foreign policy. While Foucault and to a lesser extent Bourdieu have sometimes been depicted as philosophers, they did, just like Chomsky, a considerable amount of empirical research, and in particular the work that formed the basis for their public engagement was respectively historical and sociological in nature. Indeed, philosophers rarely make expert public intellectuals. More precisely, if they have any tangible expertise, it is difficult to translate this into public engagement. Social scientists, on the other hand, are much better placed to act as expert public intellectuals, equipped as they are with well-rehearsed methods and specialized as they are in analysing contemporary social and political phenomena. Whereas authoritative intellectuals could exert influence outside their specialist subject entirely through demonstrated intellect and educational prowess, expert intellectuals' comparable influence relies on intellect *and acquired knowledge*, and mastery of the inductive technology (observational skill, statistical methods, lab machinery etc.) to acquire or verify that knowledge.

There is secondly the rise of what we would call the dialogical public intellectual. Contrary to both authoritative and expert public intellectuals, dialogical public intellectuals do not assume a superior stance towards their publics. Rather, they present themselves as equals to their publics, learning as much from them as *vice versa*. In contrast with Marxists, Foucault already took a more modest stance, employing the past as he did to shed light on the present, but without dictating an ideological agenda or imposing a political direction. Still, he positioned himself as an expert on the genealogy of how things came to be the way they are. Today, increasingly, intellectuals engage with their publics in a more interactive fashion, partly because of the technologies which make this dialogical format now possible and to a certain extent blur the distinction between public intellectuals and their publics; and partly because, with higher educational levels, the publics are no longer willing to accept entrenched hierarchies as they once did. In this context, what is striking about Michael Burawoy's recent plea for a public sociology[75] is not so much that it promotes critical engagement with the non-academic world – something which after all has been argued before – but that it advocates a dialogical model, whereby sociologists and their publics are, theoretically at least, equal partners and equally responsible for producing knowledge. Burawoy's utopian vision for sociology conceives an intellectual and social partnership between the sociological researchers and the communities they serve, whereby both parties are willing to learn from each other and collaborate, while striving for a common political goal. Anthropologists, having been forced to confront their colonial heritage, have adopted this dialogical stance much earlier, with the early traces going back to the 1970s.[76] The critical turn in cultural and social anthropology not only introduced reflexivity to the heart of this academic discipline, but also tied it to a different notion of knowledge acquisition in which anthropologists no longer positioned themselves as superior to the people who are being researched. More recently, intellectuals who use the new social media to get their message across often position themselves in contrast to those who rely on 'traditional' media by emphasizing how the new technologies permit frequent and intense interaction with the audiences. Of course, the situation is often more complex than the bloggers themselves tend to acknowledge. They are likely to continue to write for newspapers, magazines and other outlets, and their blogs might even simultaneously appear in print version. But the point is that they position themselves as 'democratic'; that is, in dialogue with their audience and ultimately blurring the distinction between themselves and that audience.

This brief historical excursion has given some indication of how certain types of positioning prosper in particular settings and how societal shifts can precipitate both their decline and the emergence of new types of positioning. The authoritative public intellectual, as typified by Sartre, was endemic to a particular societal setting which is no longer prevailing, even in a country like France which has often been depicted as providing an exceptionally fertile ground for the public intellectual. It should also be clear, however, that the erosion of the authoritative public intellectual, whether in France or elsewhere, does not imply the disappearance of the public intellectual altogether. On the contrary, new forms of public engagement have come to the surface, some of which might still rely on a hierarchical stance (the expert, as opposed to laypeople) while others explicitly do away with it.

189

NOTES

Introduction

1 E.g. Cohen-Solal (2005).
2 Idt (2001).
3 Hewitt (2006, pp. 7–8).
4 Sartre (1943). In English *Being and Nothingness*. Only one article mentioned the book that year (see Cohen-Solal 2005, p. 188).
5 See also Alexander et al. (2001).
6 Rousso (1991, p. 5).
7 Price (2005, pp. 282–303).
8 Rousso (1991, p. 7).
9 Ory and Sirinelli (1992, pp. 93–126).
10 See, for instance, Rousso (1991, p. 6)
11 Price (2005, pp. 288–93).
12 'le parti des 75,000 fusillés'.
13 Boschetti (1985).
14 Boschetti (1985, pp. 3–6).
15 Boschetti (1985, pp. 24–87).
16 Boschetti (1985, pp. 88–170).
17 Boschetti (1985, pp. 141–84).
18 Boschetti (1985, p. 11).
19 Louette (2001, p. 117).
20 Collins (1998).
21 Collins (1998, pp. 1–15).
22 See also Collins (2004).
23 Collins (1998, pp. 19–20).
24 Collins (1998, pp. 30–53).
25 See, for instance, Collins (1998, pp. 81–2).
26 Collins (1998, pp.754–84).
27 Collins (1998, pp. 764–82).
28 Collins (1998, p. 782).
29 For instance, both Ory and Sirinelli's *Les Intellectuels en France* (1992) and Michel Winock's *Le Siècle des intellectuels* (1988) elaborate on Sartre's

stardom at the end of the war but fail to explain it. Likewise, Annie Cohen-Solal's massive biography, *Jean-Paul Sartre: A Life* (2005), has a large section on this period, but again no coherent explanation.

30 Galster (2001b).
31 Michel Contat's contribution to *La Naissance du 'phénomène Sartre'* is a case in point, focusing on Sartre's remarkable 'desire for glory' (Contat 2001).
32 See, for instance, Lambin (2001, p. 351) and Judaken (2012, p. 90).
33 Sartre's communist critics at the time came close to providing this third type of explanation when they argued that existentialism appealed to a degenerate bourgeoisie, bereft of a moral compass (e.g. Lefebvre 1946).
34 E.g. Sirinelli (1988); Winock (2011). For a critique of this generational explanation, see for instance Stewart (2009).
35 See also Shils (1992, pp. 301–5).
36 See, for instance, Clark (1995); Baert and Shipman (2005).
37 Bourdieu (1993a, pp. 125–31).
38 See also Baert and Isaac (2011).
39 Bourdieu (1988, 1996).
40 Bourdieu (1991, 2000).
41 Camic (1983, 1987); Gross (2002, 2008); Lamont (2009).
42 E.g. Said (1994).
43 Baert and Shipman (2011, pp. 179–88); Small (2002).
44 E.g. Furedi (2004).
45 E.g. Jacoby (1987).
46 See also Posner (2001).
47 Jacoby (1987).
48 Robbins (1990).
49 Etzioni (2006).
50 Lamont (1987); Swartz (2003); Misztal (2007).
51 Latour (2007).
52 See also Kaplan (2001, pp. 143–51).
53 Bergson (1957[1907]).
54 See, for instance, Ory and Sirinelli (1992, pp. 5–8).
55 Harris (2010).
56 See, for instance, Judaken (2006, p. 4).
57 Duclert (2006, pp. 64–7); Whyte (2008, pp. 154–5).
58 See also Collini (2006, pp. 256ff).
59 See also Ory and Sirinelli (1992, pp. 13–18).
60 Benda (1927); Nizan (2001[1932]). Nizan's critique of Benda influenced Sartre's later writings.
61 Collini (2006, pp. 164).
62 Kleinberg (2005, pp. 19–110); Geroulanos (2010, pp. 37–206).
63 Corbin's translation of Heidegger's *Was ist Metaphysik?* was initially published in the journal *Bifur* in 1931, and Sartre later acknowledged reading it at the time. This text was included in the 1938 collection *Qu'est-ce que la métaphysique*, which also included two chapters of *Sein und Zeit* and other essays by Heidegger. See also Kleinberg (2005, pp. 116ff, 131ff).

1 Occupation, intellectual collaboration and the Resistance

1 'Drôle de guerre'.
2 Pétain announced: 'une collaboration a été envisagée entre nos deux pays. J'en ai accepté le principe.' The full text can be found in Azéma (1975, pp. 86–8).
3 Paxton (1972, p. 19).
4 Chef de l'État français. See also Paxton (1972, pp. 32–3).
5 'Je fais à la France le don de ma personne pour attenuer son malheur.'
6 He initially used the term 'national renovation'.
7 'Travail, famille, patrie' instead of 'Liberté, égalité, fraternité'.
8 The crime was called 'délit d'opinion'.
9 Statut des juifs.
10 Jackson (2001, pp. 300–1).
11 Sapiro (1999, pp. 47–59).
12 The *concours* is a competitive examination to enter elite educational institutions.
13 This hostile attitude towards *normaliens* was not necessarily shared by pro-fascist intellectuals in the occupied zone. Marcel Déat and Robert Brasillach were themselves *normaliens*.
14 Sapiro (1999, pp. 47–9).
15 Sapiro (1999, p.33).
16 Lambauer (2004, pp. 76–80), Sapiro (1999, pp. 32–42).
17 Lambauer (2004, pp. 80–3).
18 Named after the German Ambassador.
19 Sapiro (1999, pp. 161–79).
20 Paxton (1972, pp. 21–4).
21 Sapiro (1999, pp. 161–207).
22 Ory and Sirinelli (1992, pp. 126–32).
23 Paxton (1972, pp. 33–4).
24 Vinen (2006, pp. 67–9).
25 Vinen (2006, pp. 73ff).
26 Judt (1992, pp. 28–32).
27 Riding (2010, p. 130).
28 Judt (1992, pp. 15–25).
29 *Les Sept Couleurs* came out in 1939. Brasillach wrote it following his attendance at a Nazi congress in Nuremberg in 1937.
30 Sapiro (2004, p. 50).
31 Sapiro (1999, p. 35).
32 Lambauer (2004, p. 78).
33 Sapiro (1999, pp. 46–7).
34 Sapiro (1999, p. 36).
35 Sapiro (1999, p. 42).
36 Riding (2010, p. 229).
37 Riding (2010, p. 215).
38 Guéhenno (1947, preface, p. 59).
39 Paxton (1972, p. 17).
40 Paulhan (1940).
41 Vinen (2006, p. 113); Spotts (2008, p. 239).
42 Jean Bruller used his *nom de plume* Vercors. The book was translated into English as *Put out the Light* in 1944.

43 Atack (1989, p. 24).
44 Jackson (2001, p. 314).
45 The first issue of *Les Lettres françaises* appeared in September 1942. It was delayed because of the arrest of Decour, Politzer and Solomon.
46 In 1944 *Les Éditions de minuit* received the prestigious Prix Femina in recognition of its wartime contribution. It was the first and only time that this prize was awarded to a publisher rather than an author.
47 Riding (2010, p. 341).
48 Drieu la Rochelle (1943, p. 104) acknowledged Paulhan.
49 Sapiro (1999, pp. 24–5, 30).
50 Sapiro (1999, p. 30).
51 *The Flies.*
52 Riding (2010, p. 221).
53 *No Exit.*
54 *She Came to Stay.*
55 De Beauvoir (1986, p. 644).
56 Spotts (2008, p. 135).
57 Ory and Sirinelli (1992, pp. 136–7); Sapiro (1999, pp. 377–466).
58 *Myth of Sysiphus.* Spotts (2008, p. 93).
59 Schöttler (2004, p. 228). Bloch joined the Resistance and was captured and executed in 1944.
60 Riding (2010, pp. 228–9).
61 He was eventually arrested in 1944, deported and died in a concentration camp in 1945.
62 Judt (1992, pp. 15–25).

2 The purge of collaborationist intellectuals

1 See also Spotts (2008, pp. 134ff).
2 Assouline (1986, pp. 9–12).
3 See also Pickering (1985).
4 See also Bourdieu (1988, 1991); Cointet (2008: pp. 87–124); Verdès-Leroux (1996: pp. 370–3).
5 Rubenstein (1993); Sapiro (2011, pp. 544–50).
6 Judt (1992, pp. 61–63); Verdès-Leroux (1996, pp. 380–96); Sapiro (1999, pp. 571–81).
7 See also Sapiro (1999, pp. 581–92).
8 Chebel d'Appollonia (1991, pp. 83–5).
9 Assouline (1994, pp. 361–92).
10 The committee suspended Grasset for three months. At a much later stage – in July 1948 – the trial of the Grasset company took place and it was found guilty of collaboration with Nazi Germany (Lottman 1986, pp. 240–9).
11 Lottman (1986, pp. 244–8).
12 Lacroix (1945); see also Verdès-Leroux (1996, p. 367).
13 Verdès-Leroux (1996, pp. 373–80).
14 Rousso (1991, p. 20).
15 See also Vergez-Chaignon (2006, pp. 40–2, 72–4).
16 Lottman (1986, p. 134); Watts (1998, p. 19).

17 Kaplan (1986, pp. 176–7).
18 Lottman (1986, pp. 133, 137).
19 Sapiro (2011, p. 575).
20 Sapiro (2011, p. 595).
21 See Cointet (2008, pp. 392–7).
22 Sapiro (2011, pp. 544ff).
23 Spotts (2008, pp. 254–9).
24 *Le Figaro* (24.09.1945).
25 *Le Figaro* (30.01.1945; 25.01.1945).
26 'Enfin, un peu de justice ailleurs qu'en province; Le journaliste de la Gestapo Georges Suarez paiera de sa tête'.
27 'Cependant la liste est maintenant ouverte. A d'autres de payer, et que cela aille vite!' (*L'Humanité* 24.10.1944).
28 *L'Humanité* (30.12.1944).
29 'Traitre et délateur'.
30 *L'Humanité* (20.01.1945).
31 'Maurras, l'assassin vivra!'
32 'un verdict d'indulgence'. *L'Humanité* (26.01.1945).
33 For a thorough discussion of the trials and the arguments invoked, see, for instance, Assouline (1986); Kaplan (2000); Sapiro (2011, pp. 568–688); and Watts (1998).
34 'Mais les idées ne sont pas des jouets. Elles blessent et, souvent, elles tuent.' (*Le Figaro* 20.01.1945).
35 'Sinistre histoire d'un malheureux qui, sans presque s'en apercevoir, glissa du plan de la littérature sur celui des faits.' (*Le Figaro* 20.01.1945).
36 'Maurras semble ne s'être jamais soucié de savoir si ce qu'il écrivait pouvait avoir des conséquences concrètes.' (*Le Figaro* 26.10.1945).
37 Sapiro (2011, p. 573).
38 Watts (1998, p. 26); Rubenstein (1990, p. 154–5).
39 Kaplan (2000, pp. 160–9).
40 *Le Figaro* (27.01.1945).
41 *Combat* (25.01.1945).
42 *Combat* (20.01.1945).
43 Assouline (1986, pp. 56–9).
44 Kaplan (2000, pp. 160–9). See also the vivid description in *Le Figaro* (20.01.1945).
45 Cointet (2008, pp. 386–7). See also *Le Figaro* (20.01.1945).
46 'D'autant plus qu'on voyait trop bien vers quels crimes et vers quels châti-ments leurs éloquentes excitations avaient poussé de pauvres crédules. (. . .) Car, dans les lettres, comme en tout, le talent est un titre de responsabilité.' (de Gaulle 1959, p. 115).
47 *Combat* (24.10.1944).
48 *Le Figaro* (30.12.1944).
49 *Le Figaro* (20.01.1945).
50 'un écrivain et critique littéraire de talent' (*L'Humanité* 20.01.1945).
51 Kaplan (2000, pp. 176–7); Winock (1988, pp. 380–8).
52 *Le Figaro* (30.12.1944).
53 Sapiro (2011).
54 Watts (1998, pp. 24–5).
55 Judaken (2006, pp. 1–146).

56 'Je donne mon sang pour la France. Rien ne serait plus agréable et plus glorieux pour moi.' (*Le Figaro* 28.01.1945).
57 *Combat* (20.01.1945).
58 Watts (1998, pp. 27–8).
59 Assouline (1986, pp. 42–3).
60 Watts (1998, pp. 40–1).
61 Kaplan (2000, p. 152).
62 *Combat* (01.11.1944).
63 *Combat* (24.10.1944).
64 *Le Figaro* (24.10.1944).
65 *Combat* (30.12.1944); *L'Humanité* (30.12.1944).
66 'corrupteur salarié de l'opinion française' (*L'Humanité* 30.12.1944).
67 Watts (1998, p. 52).
68 Watts (1998, p. 43); Jennings (1993b, p. 18).
69 Compare with Jennings (1993b, pp. 12–15).
70 *Le Figaro* (24.10.1944).
71 Lindenberg (1993, pp. 140ff).
72 *Le Figaro* (30.12.1944).
73 'Toute la vie (. . .) j'ai lutté avec passion contre le péril allemand. Je l'ai dénoncé quand personne ne voulait y croire.' He argued that, after the defeat, support for Vichy was the only option. (*Le Figaro* 26.01.1945).
74 Jackson (2009, pp. 40–3).
75 Judt (1992, pp. 49–50).
76 Judt (1992, pp. 60–1).
77 Sapiro (2011, p. 582).
78 Brasillach (1942). The 'little ones' refers to Jewish children. See also Kaplan (2000, pp. 166).
79 Judt (1992, pp. 62).

3 Intellectual debates around the purge: responsibility, purity, patriotism

1 See also Sapiro (1999, 2007, 2011); Rubenstein (1993).
2 'politique de responsabilité' (*Combat* 27.10.44).
3 *Combat* (01.09.44; 08.09.44).
4 Watts (1998, pp. 60–1).
5 See also Assouline (1986, pp. 83–7).
6 'Comparer l'industriel à l'écrivain, c'est comparer Cain et le Diable. Le crime de Cain s'arrête à Abel. Le péril du Diable est sans limite.' (Vercors 1945).
7 See also Watts (1998, p. 61).
8 Benda (2003[1946]).
9 Wilkinson (1981, pp. 40ff).
10 Halbwachs (1950, 1952).
11 Judt (1992, pp. 45ff).
12 'Paris martyr, mais libéré par son peuple, lutte avec toute la France, avec celle qui se bat, je veux dire avec la France éternelle.' This was for instance cited in *Combat* (26.08.44).
13 See, for instance, *Combat* (26.10.44).

14 Rousso (1991); Suleiman (2006).
15 Sartre (1949a[1944]). It was reprinted in *L'Éternelle revue* a couple of months later.
16 'La cruauté même de l'ennemi . . .' (Sartre 1949a[1944], p. 12).
17 'Jamais nous n'avons été plus libres que sous l'occupation allemande.' (Sartre 1949a[1944], p. 11).
18 Sartre (1949a[1944], p. 11).
19 Sartre (1949a[1944], pp. 13–14).
20 Sartre (1949a[1944], pp. 11–12).
21 Sartre (1949a[1944], pp. 12–13).
22 Sartre (1949a[1944], p. 13).
23 'la République du silence et de la nuit' (Sartre 1949a[1944], p. 14).
24 '. . . cette élite que furent les vrais Résistants . . .' (Sartre 1949a[1944], p. 12).
25 See also Suleiman (2001).
26 Sartre (1949b[1944]).
27 Sartre (1949b[1944], pp. 15–16).
28 'Les Anglais et les Français n'ont plus un souvenir en commun, tout ce que Londres a vécu dans l'orgueil Paris l'a vécu dans le désespoir et la honte.' Sartre (1949b[1944], p. 17).
29 Sartre (1949b[1944], pp. 34–5).
30 Sartre (1949b[1944], pp. 29–30, 34–5).
31 Sartre (1949b[1944], pp. 28–9).
32 Sartre (1949b[1944], pp. 36–7).
33 Sartre (1949b[1944], pp. 18–20).
34 Sartre (1949b[1944], pp. 18–23).
35 Sartre (1949b[1944], pp. 30–3).
36 Sartre (1949b[1944], pp. 39–41).
37 Sartre (1949b[1944], pp. 23–8).
38 Sartre (1949b[1944], pp. 21–3).
39 Sartre (1949b[1944], pp. 34–5).
40 Sartre (1949b[1944], p. 42).
41 Sartre (1949b[1944], pp. 41–2).
42 Sartre (1949c[1945]).
43 Sartre (1949c[1945], pp. 43–4).
44 Sartre (1949c[1945], p. 46). See also Judaken (2006, pp. 118–22); Suleiman (2006, pp. 27–30).
45 Sartre (1949c[1945], pp. 46–8).
46 Sartre (1949c[1945], pp. 48–50).
47 Sartre (1949c[1945], pp. 58–9).
48 Sartre (1949c[1945], pp. 56–7).
49 Sartre (1949c[1945], p. 58).
50 Sartre (1949c[1945], p. 58).
51 Sartre (1949c[1945], p. 55).
52 Sartre (1949c[1945], pp. 52–5).
53 Sartre (1949c[1945], p. 54).
54 Sartre (1949c[1945], pp. 60–1).
55 Sartre (1949c[1945], p. 61).

4 The autumn of 1945

1 'Ce ne sont pas là des êtres ordinaires, des gens comme vous et moi qui travaillent pour vivre et élèvent une famille.' (*Témoignage chrétien* 02.11.1945).
2 *Figaro* (20.10.1945; 27.10.1945).
3 *Carrefour* (19.10.1945).
4 'Chacun est responsable de tout devant tous' (*Gavroche* 08.11.1945).
5 'J'ai appris de cette guerre que le sang qu'on épargne est aussi inexplicable que le sang qu'on fait verser.' (*Le Figaro* 08.09.1945).
6 'vedette de l'existentialisme' (*Gavroche* 25.10.1945).
7 *Gavroche* (08.11.1945).
8 *Témoignage chrétien* (16.11.1945).
9 Assouline (1984, pp. 297–324); Assouline (1985, pp. 361–92).
10 Assouline (1984, pp. 325–9); Assouline (1985, pp. 393–7); Cohen-Sohal (2005, pp. 218–19).
11 Hewitt (2006, pp. 15–16).
12 Sartre (1945a).
13 Sartre (1945a, pp. 8–21).
14 Sartre (1945a, pp. 20–1).
15 Sartre (1945a, pp. 3–8).
16 See the discussion of 'Qu'est-ce qu'un collaborateur?' in chapter 3.
17 Sartre (1945a, pp. 5–6).
18 Sartre (1945a, pp. 7–8).
19 Sartre (1945a, pp. 7–8).
20 Sartre (1945a, pp. 1–3).
21 Sartre (1945a, p. 7).
22 Sartre (1945a, p. 5).
23 Sartre (1945a, p. 3).
24 Sartre (1945b).
25 Sartre (1945b, pp. 193–5).
26 Sartre (1945b, pp. 208–11).
27 Sartre (1945b, pp. 203ff).
28 Sartre (1945b, pp. 207–9).
29 Sartre (1945b, pp. 198–203, 209–11).
30 Sartre (1945b, pp. 209–11).
31 Sartre (1996[1946]).
32 Contat and Rybalka (1974, p. 12). See also Baring (2014) for a detailed account of the use of the term 'existentialism' and related terms.
33 Cohen-Solal (2005, p. 253).
34 Sartre (1996[1946], pp. 88–9).
35 'L'existence précède l'essence' (Sartre 1996[1946], p. 26).
36 Sartre (1996[1946], p. 21).
37 Elkaïm-Sartre (1996).
38 See also Sartre (1996[1946], pp. 21–3).
39 See, for instance, Troisfontaines (1945; 1946).
40 See also Sartre (1996[1946], pp. 21–2).
41 Drake (2006, pp. 3–4); Sartre, Rousset and Rosenthal (1949, pp. 71ff).
42 Sartre (1944); Lefebvre (1945).
43 Sartre (1996[1946], pp. 31–3).
44 Sartre (1996[1946], pp. 23–5).

45 'En tout cas, ce que nous pouvons dire dès le début, c'est que nous enten-
dons par existentialisme une doctrine qui rend la vie humaine possible et
qui, par ailleurs, déclare que toute vérité et toute action impliquent un
milieu et une subjectivité humaine.' (Sartre (1996[1946], p. 23).
46 Sartre (1996[1946], pp. 74–6).
47 Sartre (1996[1946], pp. 36–8).
48 Sartre (1996[1946], pp. 54–7).
49 Sartre (1996[1946], pp. 37–45).
50 We are using loosely Mark Granovetter's distinction between strong and
weak ties (Granovetter 1973).

5 Sartre's committed literature in theory and practice

1 See also Baert and Shipman (2011, pp. 188–9).
2 Boullant (2003).
3 Swartz (2003).
4 Béraud and Coulmont (2008); Clark (1973); Masson (2008).
5 For instance, sociology degrees in France did not exist until 1958.
Philosophy training did include some sociology, and indeed Raymond
Aron's first book was an introduction to German sociological theory (Aron
1935). Of all the members of the initial team of *Les Temps modernes*, Aron
was the most familiar with the social sciences. He would later become
Professor of Sociology at the Sorbonne and the Collège de France.
6 Collini (2006, p. 164).
7 See also Sartre (1945a).
8 At a later stage he would help to set up a political party of his own, which
was short-lived (Cohen-Solal 2005: pp. 298–311).
9 Birchall (2004, pp. 123–43).
10 Sartre (1945a); Judaken (2006, p. 151).
11 *Qu'est-ce que la littérature?* is henceforth cited in parentheses in the notes,
with English page reference followed by French.
12 Sartre (1948b[1946–7], pp. 72–5; 2007[1950], pp. 12–15).
13 Sartre (1948b[1946–7], p. 70; 2007[1950], p. 11).
14 Sartre (1948b[1946–7], p. 75; 2007[1950], pp. 15).
15 Sartre (1948b[1946–7], pp. 89–106; 2007[1950], pp. 27–42).
16 Anon (1944).
17 E.g. Habermas (1987).
18 Sartre (1948b[1946–7], p. 13; 2007[1950], pp. 48–9).
19 Sartre (1948b[1946–7], p. 14; 2007[1950], p. 49).
20 Sartre (1948b[1946–7], pp. 87–103; 2007[1950], pp. 50–61).
21 Sartre (1948b[1946–7], pp. 189–96; 2007[1950], pp. 118–23).
22 Sartre (1948b[1946–7], pp. 120ff; 2007[1950], pp. 72ff).
23 Sartre (1948b[1946–7], pp. 139ff; 2007[1950], pp. 84ff).
24 See, for instance, Sartre (1948b[1946–7], pp. 276ff; 1950[2007], pp.
176ff).
25 Sartre (1948b[1946–7], pp. 276–357; 2007[1950], pp. 176–229).
26 Sartre (1948b[1946–7], p. 313; 2007[1950], p. 226).
27 Flynn (2012, pp. 235).
28 'Engagement' versus 'embarquement'. See also Goldthrope (1992, pp. 140–3).

29 Sartre (1948b[1946–7], pp. 304–5; 1950[2007], pp. 218–19).
30 E.g. Sartre (1948b[1946–7], p. 298; 1950[2007], p. 213).
31 Sartre (1948b[1946–7], pp. 314–16; 1950[2007], pp. 227–9).
32 Sartre (1948b[1946–7], p. 280; 1950[2007], p. 197). See also Sartre (2007[1950], pp. 197–204, 209–11).
33 *Réflexions sur la question juive* is henceforth cited in parentheses in the notes, with English page reference followed by French.
34 Sartre (1954[1946]).
35 Misrahi (1999); Vidal-Naquet (1999). Shortly after the publication of *Réflexions sur la question juive*, Sartre was invited to lecture by two Jewish organizations in France because several Jewish intellectuals appreciated the arguments. See, for instance, Lévinas' commentary at the time in *Les Cahiers de l'Alliance* (Lévinas 1999[1947]). Shortly after this, Lévinas (1947) distanced himself from Sartre's arguments.
36 See, for instance, Rabi (1947).
37 Sartre (1995[1948]). The phrase 'Jewish question', which appears in the French title, had also been used in anti-Semitic literature.
38 See, for instance, Rosenberg (1949).
39 See, for instance, Walzer (1995, pp. v–vi).
40 See, for instance, Hollier (1999a).
41 See also Walzer (1995, pp. v–xx; Schor (1999, pp. 107ff).
42 Adorno et al. (1950).
43 Sartre and Flapan (1966).
44 Sartre and Lévy (1991, pp. 65–76).
45 Contat and Rybalka (1970, p. 140); Rybalka (1999, p. 166); Sartre (1954[1946], pp. 11–12; 1995[1948], pp. 10–11).
46 Vidal-Naquet (1999, pp. 18–19); Birnbaum (1999, p. 98); Aron (1981, p. 108).
47 Walzer (1995: pp. vii–viii).
48 Sartre (1954[1946], p. 59; 1995[1948], p. 49).
49 Sartre (1954[1946], pp. 107–8; 1995[1948], p. 88).
50 Sartre (1954[1946], p. 100; 1995[1948], p. 81).
51 Sartre (1954[1946], pp. 28, 49, 54; 1995[1948], pp. 24, 41, 45).
52 Sapiro (1999).
53 Assouline (1986); Lottman (1986); Watts (1998).
54 See also Watts (1998, pp. 24–5).
55 Sartre (1954[1946], p. 7 ff; 1995[1948], p. 7 ff)
56 Sartre (1954[1946], p. 8; 1995[1948], pp. 7–8).
57 Sartre (1954[1946], p. 9; 1995[1948], pp. 8–9).
58 Sartre (1954[1946], p. 19; 1995[1948], p. 17).
59 Sartre (1954[1946], pp. 13–19; 1995[1948], pp. 12–17).
60 See also Sartre (1954[1946], pp. 156–160; 1995[1948], pp. 126–9).
61 See, for instance, Birnbaum (1999, pp. 94–5).
62 Sartre (1954[1946], p. 15; 1995[1948], p. 14).
63 Sartre (1954[1946], p. 16; 1995[1948], p. 14). The term 'Israel' and 'Israelite' were used at the time to refer respectfully to Jewish people. In the text Sartre often referred to 'Jews' rather than 'Israelites' but occasionally used the latter. The translator George G. Becker did not always follow Sartre's terminology, sometimes opting for 'Jews' and 'Jewish' when Sartre used 'Israel' and 'Israelite'.

64 Suleiman (1995).
65 Sartre (1954[1946], p. 73; 1995[1948], p. 60).
66 Sartre (1954[1946], p. 141; 1995[1948], p. 114).
67 Sartre (1954[1946], p. 142; 1995[1948], p. 115).
68 Sartre, (1954[1946], p. 153; 1995[1948], p. 124).
69 Sartre, (1954[1946], p. 156; 199 5[1948], p. 126).
70 E.g. Sartre (1954[1946], pp. 35–6; 1995[1948], pp. 29–30).
71 E.g. Sartre (1954[1946], pp. 25–6; 1995[1948], p. 22).
72 See also Birnbaum (1999, p. 101).
73 Sartre (1954[1946], pp. 29–30, 43; 199 5[1948], pp. 25, 36).
74 Sartre (1954[1946], pp. 29–30; 1995[1948], p. 25).
75 Sartre (1954[1946], p. 42; 1995[1948], p. 35).
76 For instance, Weil (1985) found an inverse correlation between education and anti-Semitism with the strength of the association varying from country to country.
77 Sartre (1954[1946], p. 184; 1995[1948], p. 149).
78 Sartre, 1954[1946], pp. 185–6; 1995[1948], pp. 150–1).
79 Sartre (1954[1946], p. 186; 1995[1948], p. 151).
80 Sartre (1954[1946], pp. 29–30; 1995[1948], pp. 25–6).
81 Sartre (1954[1946], pp. 30; 1995[1948], p. 26).
82 Sartre (1954[1946], pp. 31–2; 1995[1948], p. 27).
83 E.g. Sartre (1996[1946], pp. 41–3).
84 Hollier (1999b, p. 153).
85 Lévinas (1999[1947], p. 28).
86 Sartre (1954[1946], p. 72; 1995[1948], p. 60, *my italics*).
87 Hollier (1999b, p. 151).
88 Sartre (1954[1946], p. 20; 1995[1948], p. 18).
89 Sartre (1954[1946], p. 169; 1995[1948], p. 136, *my italics*).
90 Sartre (1954[1946], p. 21; 1995[1948], p. 18).
91 Sartre (1954[1946], p. 22; 1995[1948], p. 19).
92 Sartre (1954[1946], pp. 32–4; 1995[1948], pp. 27–8). See also Hammerschlag (2010, pp. 75ff).
93 Sartre (1954[1946], p. 170; 1995[1948], p. 137).
94 Sartre (1954[1946], pp. 169–89; 1995[1948], pp. 136–53).
95 Sartre (1954[1946], p. 22; 1995[1948], p. 19).
96 Sartre (1954[1946], pp. 10; 1995[1948], p. 10).
97 Sartre (1954[1946], p. 23; 1995[1948], p. 20).
98 Sartre (1954[1946], pp. 25–9, 134–45; 1995[1948], pp. 22–5, 109–17).
99 Sartre (1954[1946], p. 36; 1995[1948], p. 30).
100 Schor (1999).
101 Sartre (1954[1946], p. 72; 1995[1948], p. 60).
102 Sartre (1954[1946], pp. 66–70; 1995[1948], pp. 55–8).
103 See also Traverso (1999, pp. 81–3).
104 Hammerschlag (2010, pp. 81–93).
105 Judaken (2006, pp. 123–6).
106 Interestingly, Gaston Gallimard's personal trajectory during the war provided an additional impetus for him to withdraw from this commercial proposition: he had published openly fascist and anti-Semitic material during the war and was keen to 'move forward' (Assouline 1994).
107 Sartre (1949c[1945]).

108 Sartre (1954[1946], pp. 184–5; 1995[1948], pp. 149–50).
109 See also Birnbaum (1999, p. 101); Traverso (1999, pp. 77–8).
110 Judt (1992, pp. 45ff); Rousso (1991).
111 Sartre (1949a[1944]).
112 Suleiman (2006); Judaken (2006, pp. 106–22).
113 Sartre (1949c[1945]).
114 Traverso (1999, pp. 73–5).
115 Sartre is referring to the concentration camp Majdanek on the outskirts of Lublin in Poland.
116 Sartre (1954[1946], p. 57; 1995[1948], pp. 47–8).
117 Sartre (1954[1946], p. 70; 1995[1948], p. 58).
118 Sartre (1954[1946], p. 85; 1995[1948], p. 70).
119 Sartre (1954[1946], p. 86; 1995[1948], p. 71, *my italics*).
120 Sartre (1954[1946], p. 186; 1995[1948], p. 151, *my italics*).
121 Hollier (1999b, pp. 139–48).
122 Scriven (1993, pp. 72–86).
123 Scriven (1993, pp. 83–6).

6 Rise and demise: a synthesis

 1 Hewitt (2006, p. 11).
 2 Dufay (2006, pp. 49–65).
 3 Watts (1998, pp. 34–6).
 4 Cohen-Solal (2005, pp. 233–4).
 5 Assouline (1984; 1995, pp. 41–61).
 6 Cohen-Solal (2005, pp. 101–28).
 7 Hewitt (2006, p. 8).
 8 Cohen-Solal (2005, pp. 188–9).
 9 Lamont (1987, pp. 397–8).
10 See Cohen-Solal (2005, pp. 220–1).
11 Debray (1979, 1981).
12 Alexander et al. (2001); Eyerman (2001).
13 Alexander (2001, pp. 11–12); Eyerman (2001, pp. 3–4).
14 Wilkinson (1981, pp. 40ff).
15 Halbwachs (1950, 1952).
16 Rousso (1991); Suleiman (2006).
17 Suleiman (2001, pp. 218–31); Kelly (2004, pp. 96ff).
18 See Suleiman (2001: pp. 218–31).
19 See also Suleiman (2001).
20 Sartre (1945a, pp. 17ff).
21 Sartre (1943, pp. 85–111; 1996[1946], pp. 55–6, 80–1).
22 Sartre (1996[1946], pp. 56–62).
23 Mead (1959[1932]).
24 See also Sartre (1945a, pp. 8ff); Louette (2001, pp. 130–1).
25 Lindenberg (2001).
26 Judt (1992, pp. 60ff).
27 Kaplan (2000, pp. 158–9, 167–9).
28 de Beauvoir (1946).
29 Caroll (2007, pp. xi–xvi).

30 Sartre (1996[1946], pp. 59–62); see also Sapiro (2006).
31 Sartre (1945a, pp. 3ff).
32 Boschetti (1985); Collins (1998).
33 Bourdieu (2007, pp. 22–5).
34 McCumber (2001); Schrecker (1986).
35 Bozoki (1999); Eyal, Szelényi and Townsley (1998); King and Szelényi (2004).
36 *Wretches of the Earth.*
37 *The Coloniser and the Colonised.*
38 Schrift (2006, pp. 45–6).
39 Schrift (2006, pp. 40ff).
40 Lévi-Strauss (1955, p. 62; 1961).
41 For a detailed account of this process, see Chaplin (2007).
42 For his biography of Sartre, see Lévy (2000, 2004).
43 Barthes (1972, 1967).
44 Lévi-Strauss (1962, 1966). Synchronic analysis is opposed to diachronic analysis. Whereas the latter prioritizes temporal processes, the former does not.
45 Althusser et al. (1967, 1979).
46 Bourdieu (2004, 2007).
47 E.g. Foucault (1980, pp. 109–33).
48 *Les Mouches* (24.03.2013), Sartre avec Lacan (24.04.2012), Jean-Paul Sartre: une introduction (05.10.2011), Sartre aujourd'hui (12.06.2010), Sartre: Écrits Autobiographiques (16.05.2010).
49 For example, in *L'Humanité* (17.09.20.13), *Le Monde* (09.07.20.13).
50 Collini (2006).

7 Explaining intellectuals: a proposal

1 Camic (1987, 1992).
2 Skinner (1966, 1969).
3 Skinner (1966, p. 317).
4 Skinner (1969, p. 49).
5 See also Pocock (1985, pp. 4–7).
6 Camic (1992, p. 436).
7 Camic (1992, p. 437).
8 Alexander and Sciortino (1996).
9 Camic (1996, pp. 82–3); Gross (2008, pp. 258–63).
10 Durkheim (1982).
11 Durkheim (1992).
12 Collini (2008, pp. 187–95).
13 Gross (2008, p. 303).
14 Bourdieu (1991).
15 Gross (2008, pp. 263–4).
16 See also Bryant (2011).
17 Bourdieu (2000).
18 Gross (2008, p. 264).
19 Austin (1961, 1970).
20 On the performative turn in the social sciences, see, for instance, Alexander, Giesen and Mast (2006).

21 See, for instance, Ries and Trout (1981).
22 E.g. Davies and Harré (1990, 1999); Slocum-Bradley (2010, pp. 86ff).
23 van Langenhove and Harré (1999a).
24 Harré et al. (2009).
25 E.g. Schmidle (2010); Moghaddam and Rom Harré (2010); Montiel and De Guzman (2011).
26 van Langenhove and Harré (1993) and Osbeck and Nersessian (2010).
27 Latour (1987).
28 Schmitt (1996[1927]).
29 Foucault (1984[1971]).
30 See, for instance, Baring (2011) about Derrida's trajectory in relation to humanism and anti-humanism. For a broader history of French anti-humanism, see, for instance, Geroulanos (2010).
31 Peirce (1931–5, 5.414).
32 Hayek (1978, pp. 108–9).
33 Ory and Sirinelli (1992, pp. 13–40); Russell (2003[1955], pp. 318–21).
34 Habermas (1987).
35 Burawoy (2005).
36 See, for instance, Miller (1999).
37 Sarlo (2001).
38 Ory and Sirinelli (1992, pp. 155–86).
39 See, for instance, Ericson (1975).
40 See, for instance, Moghaddam and Harré (2010).
41 See also Harré and van Langenhove (1999b).
42 See also Berman (1999).
43 See Alexander et al. (2001).
44 See also Berman (1998).
45 Rorty (1999).
46 See also Eribon (1989) and Foucault (1984[1971]).
47 Tuck (1989).
48 Taylor (1991, 1996).
49 Schrift (2008).
50 Blumer (1966, 1969).
51 Carreira da Silva and Brito Viera (2011).
52 Saussure (1917).
53 Ungar (2006).
54 Akehurst (2008, 2010).
55 Berlin (1969).
56 Popper (1945, 1957).
57 Sartre (1963[1936]).
58 See, for instance, Szakolczai and Wydra (2006); Dmitriev (2006).
59 Kuklick (2003, pp. 199–281).
60 Dasgupta (2002, p. 61).
61 See also Goffman (1959).
62 Farrell (2001) distinguishes, for instance, between the formation stage, the rebellion stage, the creative stage, the collective action stage, the disintegration stage and the reunion stage. He identifies the role of the gatekeeper, the novice, the peacemaker, the lightning rod, the radical boundary maker, the executive manager, and so on.
63 See, for example, Sleeper (1986).

64 Cockett (1994).
65 In this sense, positioning theory shows affinities with Frickel and Gross' attention to how intellectual movements 'resonate' with the 'concerns' of the people operating in the field(s) (Frickel and Gross 2005, pp. 221–5).
66 We hinted at this towards the end of the last chapter when we discussed briefly Sartre's reception in the US.
67 See, for instance, Gonzàles (2000).
68 See also Harré (1993); Ingold (1986, pp. 368ff).
69 See, for instance, Galster (2001).
70 Rorty (1980, 1992).
71 Adorno et al. (1950).
72 Fukuyama (1992).
73 Foucault (1975). See also Eribon (1989, pp. 237–51). For a brief comparison between Foucault and Sartre, see Catani (2013, pp. 144–6).
74 Bourdieu (1993b). See also Swartz (2003).
75 There is a whole cottage industry surrounding public sociology, but the canonical text remains Burawoy's 2004 Presidential address for the ASA, subsequently published in the *American Sociological Review*. See Burawoy (2005).
76 See, for instance, James Clifford and George Marcus (1986).

REFERENCES

Adorno, Theodor et al. (1950) *The Authoritarian Personality.* New York: Harper and Row.

Akehurst, Thomas (2008) The Nazi tradition: the analytical critique of continental philosophy in mid-century Britain. *History of European Ideas* 34, 4: 548–57.

Akehurst, Thomas (2010) *The Cultural Politics of Analytic Philosophy; Britishness and the Spectre of Europe.* London: Continuum.

Alexander, Jeffrey (2001) Toward a theory of cultural trauma. In *Cultural Trauma and Collective Identity*, eds. J. Alexander et al. California: University of California Press, pp. 1–30.

Alexander, Jeffrey (2011) *Performance and Power.* Cambridge: Polity.

Alexander, Jeffrey et al., eds. (2001) *Cultural Trauma and Collective Identity.* California: University of California Press.

Alexander, Jeffrey, Bernard Giesen and Jason Mast, eds. (2006) *Social Performance; Symbolic Action, Cultural Pragmatics, and Ritual.* Cambridge: Cambridge University Press.

Alexander, Jeffrey and Giuseppe Sciortino (1996) On choosing one's intellectual predecessors: the reductionism of Camic's treatment of Parsons and the institutionalists. *Sociological Theory* 14, 2: 154–71.

Althusser, Louis (1967) *Lire le Capital.* Paris: Collection Théorie.

Althusser, Louis (1979) *Reading Capital.* London: Verso.

Anon (1944) La Littérature, cette liberté. *Les Lettres françaises* 15, p. 8 (unsigned).

Aron, Raymond (1935) *La Sociologie allemande contemporaine.* Paris: Alcan.

Aron, Raymond (1981) *Le Spectateur engagé.* Paris: Julliard.

Assouline, Pierre (1984) *Gaston Gallimard: A Half-Century of French Publishing.* London: Harcourt Brace Jovanovich.

Assouline, Pierre (1985) *L'Épuration des intellectuels.* Brussels: Complexe.

Assouline, Pierre (1994) *Trois hommes d'influence: Biographies de Gaston Gallimard, D.-H. Kahnweiler et Albert Londres.* Paris: Balland.

Atack, Margaret (1989) *Literature and the French Resistance: Cultural Politics and Narrative Forms, 1940–1950.* Manchester: Manchester University Press.

Austin, John (1961) *How to Do Things with Words.* Oxford: Clarendon Press.

Austin, John (1970) *Philosophical Papers.* Oxford: Oxford University Press.

Azéma, Jean-Pierre (1975) *La Collaboration 1940–1944*. Paris: Seuil.

Baert, Patrick and Joel Isaac (2011) Intellectuals and society: sociological and historical perspectives. In *The International Handbook of Contemporary Social and Political Theory*, eds. G. Delanty and S. Turner. London: Routledge, pp. 200–11.

Baert, Patrick and Alan Shipman (2005) University under siege? Trust and accountability in the contemporary academy. *European Societies*, 7, 1: 157–85.

Baert, Patrick and Alan Shipman (2011) Transformation of the intellectual. In *The Politics of Knowledge*, eds. Fernando Rubio Dominguez and Patrick Baert. London: Routledge, pp. 179–204.

Baring, Edward (2014) Anxiety in translation. *History of European Ideas*. DOI: 10.1080/01916599.2014.926658.

Baring, Edward (2011) *The Young Derrida and French Philosophy, 1945–1968*. Cambridge: Cambridge University Press.

Barthes, Roland (1967) *Writing Degree Zero*. London: Cape.

Barthes, Roland (1972) *Le Degré zéro de l'écriture: suivi de Nouveaux essais critiques*. Paris: Seuil.

Benda, Julien (1927) *La Trahison des clercs*. Paris: Grasset.

Benda, Julien (2003[1946]) *La Trahison des clercs*. 2nd edn. Paris: Grasset.

Béraud, Céline and Baptiste Coulmont (2008) *Les Courants contemporains de la sociologie*. Paris: Presses Universitaires de France.

Bergson, Henri (1957[1907]) *L'Évolution créatrice*. Paris: Presses Universitaires de France.

Berlin, Isaiah (1969) *Four Essays on Liberty*. Oxford: Oxford University Press.

Berman, Laine (1998) *Speaking through the Silence: Narratives, Social Conventions, and Power in Java*. New York: Oxford University Press.

Berman, Laine (1999) Positioning in the formation of a 'national' identity. In *Positioning Theory: Moral Contexts of Intentional Action*, eds. Rom Harré and Luc van Langenhove. Oxford: Blackwell, pp. 138–59.

Birchall, Ian (2004) *Sartre against Stalinism*. New York: Berghahn Books.

Birnbaum, Pierre (1999) Sorry afterthoughts on 'Anti-Semite and Jew'. *October* 87 Winter: 89–106.

Blumer, Herbert (1966) Sociological implications of the thought of G. H. Mead. *American Journal of Sociology* 71, 5: 535–44.

Blumer, Herbert (1969) *Symbolic Interactionism: Perspective and Method*. Berkeley: University of California Press.

Boschetti, Anna (1985) *Sartre et 'Les Temps modernes'*. Paris: Minuit.

Boullant, François (2003) *Michel Foucault et les prisons*. Paris: Presses Universitaires de France.

Bourdieu, Pierre (1988) *Homo Academicus*. Cambridge: Polity.

Bourdieu, Pierre (1991) *Political Ontology of Martin Heidegger*. Cambridge: Polity.

Bourdieu, Pierre (1993a) *La Misère du monde*. Paris: Seuil.

Bourdieu, Pierre (1993b) *The Field of Cultural Production*. Cambridge: Polity.

Bourdieu, Pierre (1996) *State Nobility: Elite Schools in the Field of Power*. Cambridge: Polity.

Bourdieu, Pierre (2000) *Pascalian Meditations*. Cambridge: Polity.

Bourdieu, Pierre (2004) *Esquisse pour une auto-analyse*. Paris: Raisons d'agir.

Bourdieu, Pierre (2007) *Sketch for a Self-Analysis*. Cambridge: Polity.

Bourdrel, Philippe (1988/1991) *L'Épuration sauvage 1944–1945 I & II*. Paris: Perrin.

Bozoki, Andras (ed.) (1999) *Intellectuals and Politics in Central Europe*. Budapest: Central European University Press.

Brasillach, Robert (1942) Éditorial. *Je suis partout*, 25 September 1942.

Bryant, Joseph (2011) Perennial challenges in the sociology of philosophy: theoretical and methodological notes on Neil Gross. *Richard Rorty. Transactions of the Charles S. Peirce Society* 47, 1: 3–27.

Burawoy, Michael (2005) For public sociology. *American Sociological Review* 70, February: 4–28.

Camic, Charles (1983) *Experience and Enlightenment: Socialization for Cultural Change in Eighteenth-Century Scotland*. Chicago: University of Chicago Press.

Camic, Charles (1987) The making of a method: a historical reinterpretation of the early Parsons. *American Sociological Review* 52, 4: 421–39.

Camic, Charles (1992) Reputation and predecessor selection: Parsons and the institutionalists. *American Sociological Review* 57, 4: 421–45.

Camic, Charles (1996) Alexander's antisociology. *Sociological Theory* 14, 2: 172–86.

Carreira da Silva, Filipe and Monica Brito Viera (2011) Books and canon building in sociology: the case of *Mind, Self and Society*. *Journal of Classical Sociology* 11, 4: 356–77.

Carroll, David (2007) Forward. In *Camus at Combat: Writing 1944–1947*, ed. J. Lévi-Valensi. Princeton: University of Princeton Press, xii–xxvi.

Catani, Damian (2013) *Evil: A History of Modern French Literature and Thought*. London: Bloomsbury.

Chaplin, Tamara (2007) *Turning on the Mind: French Philosophers on Television*. Chicago: University of Chicago Press.

Chebel d'Appolonia, Ariane (1991) *Histoire politique des intellectuels en France (1944–1954): Tome 1, des lendemains qui déchantent*. Paris: Complexe.

Clark, Burton (1995) *Places of Inquiry: Research and Advanced Education in Modern Universities*. Berkeley: University of California Press.

Clark, Terrence Nichols (1973) *Prophets and Patrons: The French University and the Emergence of the Social Sciences*. Cambridge, Mass.: Harvard University Press.

Clifford, James, and George Marcus, eds. (1986) *Writing Culture: The Poetics and Politics of Ethnography*. Berkeley: University of California Press.

Cockett, Richard (1994) *Thinking the Unthinkable: Think-Tanks and the Economic Counter-Revolution*. London: Fontana.

Cohen-Solal, Annie (2005) *Jean-Paul Sartre: A life*. New York: New Press.

Cointet, Jean-Paul (2008) *Expier Vichy: L'épuration en France (1943–1958)*. Paris: Perrin.

Collini, Stephan (2006) *Absent Minds: Intellectuals in Britain*. Oxford: Oxford University Press.

Collini, Stefan (2008) *Common Reading: Critics, Historians, Publics*. Oxford: Oxford University Press.

Collins, Randall (1998) *The Sociology of Philosophies: A Global Theory of Intellectual Change*. Cambridge, Mass.: Harvard University Press.

Collins, Randall (2004) *Interaction Ritual Chains*. Princeton, N.J.: Princeton University Press.

Contat, Michel (2001) Sartre et la gloire. In *La Naissance du phénomène 'Sartre'*, ed. I. Galster. Paris: Seuil, pp. 29–41.

Contat, Michel and Michel Rybalka (1970) *Les Écrits de Sartre: chronologie, bibliographie commentée*. Paris: Gallimard.

Contat, Michel and Michel Rybalka (1974) *The Writings of Jean-Paul Sartre: Volume 1: A Bibliographical Life*. Evanston, Il: Northwestern University Press.

Dasgupta, Partha (2002) Modern economics and its critics. In *Fact and Fiction in Modern Economics: Models, Realism and Social Construction*, ed. U. Maki. Cambridge: Cambridge University Press, pp. 57–89.

Davies, Bronwyn and Rom Harré (1990) Positioning the discursive production of selves. *Journal for the Theory of Social Behaviour* 20, 1: 43–63.

Davies, Bronwyn and Rom Harré (1999) Positioning and personhood. In *Positioning Theory: Moral Contexts of International Action*, eds. R. Harré and L. van Langenhove. Oxford: Wiley-Blackwell, pp. 32–52.

de Beauvoir, Simone (1946) Oeil pour oeil. *Les Temps modernes* 5, February.

de Beauvoir, Simone (1986) *La Force de l'âge*. Paris: Gallimard.

Debray, Régis (1979) *Le Pouvoir intellectuel en France*. Paris: Ramsay.

Debray, Régis (1981) *Teachers, Writers, Celebrities: The Intellectuals of Modern France*. London: New Left Books.

de Gaulle, C. (1959) *Mémoires de guerre. Le salut 1944–1946*. Paris: Plon.

Drake, David (2006) Sartre et le parti communiste français après la liberation. *Sens Public* 3.

Drieu la Rochelle, Pierre (1943) Bilan. *La Nouvelle Revue française*.

Duclert, Vincent (2006) *Dreyfus est innocent: Histoire d'une Affaire d'État*. Paris: Larousse.

Dufay, François (2006) *Le Soufre et le moisi: la droite littéraire après 1945*. Paris: Perrin.

Durkheim, Emile (1982[1895]) *The Rules of Sociological Method: and Selected Texts on Sociology and its Method*. London: Macmillan.

Durkheim, Emile (1992) *Suicide: A Study in Sociology*. London: Routledge.

Elkaïm-Sartre, Arlette (1996) Situation de la conférence. In *L'existentialisme est un humanisme*, Jean-Paul Sartre. Paris: Gallimard, pp. 9–17.

Eribon, Didier (1989) *Michel Foucault*. Paris: Flammarion.

Ericson, Edward (1975) *Radicals in the University*. Stanford: Hoover Institute.

Etzioni, Amitai (2006) Introduction: Are public intellectuals an endangered species? In *Public intellectuals: An endangered species?* eds. A. Etzioni and A. Bowditch. Oxford: Rowman and Littlefield, pp. 1–27.

Eyal, Gil, Szelényi, Iván and Townsley, Eleanor (1998) *Making Capitalism without Capitalists: The New Ruling of Elites in Eastern Europe*. London: Verso.

Eyerman, Ron (2001) *Cultural trauma, Slavery and the Formation of African American Identity*. Cambridge: Cambridge University Press.

Farrell, Michael (2001) *Collaborative Circles: Friendship Dynamics and Creative Work*. Chicago: University of Chicago Press.

Flynn, Thomas R. (2012) Political existentialism: the career of Sartre's political thought. In *The Cambridge Companion to Existentialism*, ed. Steven Crowell. Cambridge: Cambridge University Press, pp. 227–51.

Foucault, Michel (1975) *Surveiller et punir: Naissance de la prison*. Paris: Gallimard.

Foucault, Michel (1984[1971]) Nietzsche, genealogy, history. In *The Foucault Reader*, ed. Paul Rabinow. New York: Pantheon, pp. 76–100.

Foucault, Michel (1980) *Power/Knowledge: Selected Interviews and Other Writings 1972–1977*, ed. Colin Gordon. New York: Harvester Wheatsheaf.

Frickel, Scott and Neil Gross (2005) A general theory of scientific/intellectual movements. *American Sociological Review* 70 April: 204–32.

Fukuyama, Francis (1992) *The End of History and the Last Man*. London: Hamish Hamilton.

Furedi, Frank (2004) *Where Have All the Intellectuals Gone? Confronting 21st Century Philistinism*. London: Continuum.

Galster, Ingrid (2001a) *Sartre, Vichy et les intellectuels*. Paris: L'Harmattan.

Galster, Ingrid (ed.) (2001b) *La Naissance du phénomène Sartre*. Paris: Seuil.

Geroulanos, Stefanos (2010) *An Atheism that is not Humanist Emerges in French Thought*. Stanford, CA: Stanford University Press.

Goffman, Erving (1959) *The Presentation of Self in Everyday Life*. New York: Doubleday.

Goldthorpe, Rhiannon (1992) Understanding the committed writer. In *The Cambridge Companion to Sartre*, ed. Christina Howells. Cambridge: Cambridge University Press, pp. 140–77.

Gonzàles, Horacio (2000) *Historia Crítica de la Sociologia Argentina. Los Raros, los Clássicos, los Científicos, los Discrepantes*. Buenos Aires: Colihue.

Granovetter, Mark (1973) The strength of weak ties. *American Journal of Sociology* 78, 6: 1360–80.

Gross, Neil (2002) Becoming a pragmatist philosopher: Status, self-concept and intellectual choice. *American Sociological Review* 67, 1: 52–76.

Gross, Neil (2008) *Richard Rorty: The Making of an American Philosopher*. Chicago: University of Chicago Press.

Guéhenno, Jean (1947) *Journal des années noires*. Paris: Gallimard.

Habermas, Jurgen (1987) *The Philosophical Discourse of Modernity*. Cambridge: Polity.

Halbwachs, Maurice (1950) *La Mémoire collective*. Paris: Presses Universitaires de France.

Halbwachs, Maurice (1952) *Les Cadres sociaux de la mémoire*. Paris: Presses Universitaires de France.

Hammerschlag, Sarah (2010) *The Figural Jew: Politics and Identity in Postwar French Thought*. Chicago: University of Chicago Press.

Harré, Rom (1993) *Social Being*. 2nd edn. Oxford: Blackwell.

Harré, Rom et al. (2009) Recent advances in positioning theory. *Theory and Psychology* 19, 1: 5–31.

Harré, Rom and Luc van Langenhove (1999a) Introducing positioning theory. In *Positioning Theory: Moral Contexts of Intentional Action*, eds. Rom Harré and Luc van Langenhove. Oxford: Blackwell, pp. 14–31.

Harré, Rom and Luc van Langenhove (1999b) Reflexive positioning: autobiography. In *Positioning Theory: Moral Contexts of Intentional Action*, eds. Rom Harré and Luc van Langenhove. Oxford: Blackwell, pp. 60–73.

Harris, Ruth (2010) *The Man on Devil's Island: Alfred Dreyfus and the Affair that Divided France*. London: Allen Lane.

Hayek, Friedrich (1978) *Law, Legislation and Liberty, Volume 2: The Mirage of Social Justice*. Chicago: University of Chicago Press.

Hewitt, Nicholas (2006) The selling of Sartre: existentialism and public opinion, 1944–7. *Journal of Romance Studies* 6, 1/2: 7–18.

Hollier, Denis (1999a) Introduction. *October* 87, Winter: 3–6.

Hollier, Denis (1999b) Terminable and interminable. *October* 87, Winter: 139–60.

Idt, Geneviève (2001) L'Émergence du 'phénomène Sartre', de la publication du 'Mur' (juillet 1937) à l'attribution du prix populiste (avril 1940)'. In *La Naissance du 'phénomène Sartre'*, ed. I. Galdster. Paris: Seuil, 47–85.

Ingold, Tim (1986) *Evolution and Social Life*. Cambridge: Cambridge University Press.

Jackson, Julian (2009) *Living in Arcadia: Homosexuality, Politics and Morality in France from the Liberation to Aids*. Chicago: University of Chicago Press.

Jackson, Julian (2001) *France: The Dark Days, 1940–1944*. Oxford: Oxford University Press.

Jacoby, Russell (1987) *The Last Intellectuals: American Culture in the Age of Academe*. New York: Basic Books.

Jennings, Jeremy (1993b) Introduction: Mandarins and Samurais: the intellectual in modern France. In *Intellectuals in Twentieth-Century France*, ed. Jeremy Jennings. New York: St Martin's Press, pp. 1–32.

Judaken, Jonathan (2006) *Jean-Paul Sartre and the Jewish Question*. Lincoln: University of Nebraska.

Judaken, Jonathan (2012) Sisyphys's progeny: existentialism in France. In *Situating Existentialism*, eds. J. Judaken and R. Bernasconi. New York: Columbia University Press, pp. 89–122.

Judt, Tony (1992) *Past Imperfect: French Intellectuals, 1944–1956*. Berkeley: University of California Press.

Kaplan, Alice (1986) *Reproductions of Banality: Fascism, Literature, and French Intellectual Life*. Minneapolis: University of Minnesota Press.

Kaplan, Alice (2000) *The Collaborator: The Trial and Execution of Robert Brasillach*. Chicago: University of Chicago Press.

Kaplan, Francis (2001) Un Philosophe dans le siècle. In *La Naissance du 'phénomène Sartre'*, ed. I. Galster. Paris: Seuil, pp. 142–58.

Kelly, Michael (2004) *The Cultural and Intellectual Rebuilding of France after the Second World War*. London: Palgrave/Macmillan.

King, Lawrence and Iván Szelényi (2004) *Theories of the New Class: Intellectuals and Power*. Minneapolis: University of Minnesota Press.

Kleinberg, Ethan (2005) *Generation Existential: Heidegger's Philosophy in France, 1927–1961*. Ithaca: Cornell University Press.

Kuklick, Bruce (2003) *A History of Philosophy in America, 1720–2000*. Oxford: Clarendon Press.

Lacroix, Jean (1945) Charité chrétienne et justice politique. In *Esprit*, February.

Lambauer, Barbara (2004) Otto Abetz, inspirateur et catalyseur de la collaboration culturelle. In *Les Intellectuels et l'occupation*, eds. Albrecth Betz and Stefan Martens. Paris: Éditions Autrement, pp. 64–89.

Lambin, Bianca (2001) Sartre avant, pendant et après la guerre. In *La Naissance du 'phénomène Sartre'*, ed. I. Galster. Paris: Seuil, pp. 349–52.

Lamont, Michèle (1987) How to become a dominant French philosopher: the case of Jacques Derrida. *American Journal of Sociology* 93, 3: 584–622.

Lamont, Michèle (2009) *How Professors Think: Inside the Curious World of Academic Judgement*. Cambridge, Mass.: Harvard University Press.

Latour, Bruno (1987) *Science in Action*. Cambridge, MA: Harvard University Press.

Latour, Bruno (2007) *Reassembling the Social: An Introduction to Actor-Network-Theory*. Oxford: Oxford University Press.

Lefebvre, Henri (1945) Existentialisme et marxisme: Réponse à une mise au point. *Action* 40, 8 June.

Lefebvre, Henri (1946) *L'Existentialisme*. Paris: Sagittaire.

Lévinas, Emmanuel (1999[1947]) Existentialism and anti-Semitism, *October* 87, Winter: 27–31.

Lévinas, Emmanuel (1947) Être juif, *Confluences* 7, 15–17: 253–64.

Lévi-Strauss, Claude (1955) *Tristes tropiques*. Paris: Plon.

Lévi-Strauss, Claude (1961) *Tristes tropiques*. New York: Criterion Books.

Lévi-Strauss, Claude (1962) *La Pensée sauvage*. Paris: Plon.

Lévi-Strauss, Claude (1966) *The Savage Mind*. London: George Weidenfeld and Nicolson.

Lévy, Bernard-Henri (2000) *Siècle de Sartre: enquête philosophique*. Paris: Grasset.

Lévy, Bernard-Henri (2004) *Sartre: the Philosopher of the Twentieth Century*. Cambridge: Polity.

Lindenberg, Daniel (1993) French Intellectuals and a German Europe: An Aspect of Collaboration. In *Intellectuals in Twentieth-Century France*, ed. Jeremy Jennings. New York: St Martin's Press, pp. 140–56.

Lindenberg, Daniel (2001) Sartre et le nouveau 'mal du siècle'. In *La Naissance du 'phénomène Sartre'*, ed. I. Galster. Paris: Seuil, pp. 101–7.

Lottman, Herbert R. (1986) *The People's Anger: Justice and Revenge in Post-Liberation France*. London: Hutchinson.

Louette, Jean-François (2001) Piliers d'un success: portrait de Sartre en pont. In *La Naissance du 'phénomène Sartre'*, ed. I. Galster. Paris: Seuil, pp. 111–40.

McCumber, John (2001) *Time in the Ditch: American Philosophy and the McCarthy Era*. Northwestern University Press.

Masson, Philippe (2008) *Faire de la sociologie: les grandes enquêtes françaises depuis 1945*. Paris: La Découverte.

Miller, Nicola (1999) *In the Shadow of the State: Intellectuals and the Quest for National Identity in Twentieth-Century Spanish America*. New York: Verso.

Misrahi, Robert (1999) Sartre and the Jews: a felicitous misunderstanding, *October* 87, Winter: 63–72.

Misztal, Barbara (2007) *Intellectuals and the Public Good: Creativity and Courage*. Cambridge: Cambridge University Press.

Moghaddam, Fathali and Rom Harré, eds. (2010) *Words of Conflict, Words of War: How the Language we use in Political Processes Sparks Fighting*. New York: Praeger.

Montiel, Christina and Judith De Guzman (2011) Intergroup positioning in the political sphere: contesting the social meaning of a peace agreement. *Journal for the Theory of Social Behaviour* 41, 1: 92–116.

Nizan, Paul (2001[1932]) *Les Chiens de garde*. Marseille: Agone.

Ory, Pascale and Jean-François Sirinelli (1992) *Les Intellectuels en France: de l'affaire Dreyfus à nos jours*. Paris: Armand Colin.

Osbeck, Lisa and Nancy Nersessian (2010) Forms of positioning in interdisciplinary science practice and their epistemic effects. *Journal for the Theory of Social Behaviour* 40, 2: 136–60.

211

Paulhan, Jean (1940) L'Espoir et le silence. *La Nouvelle Revue française* 28, 1, June: 721–43.

Paxton, Robert (1972) *Vichy France: Old Guard and New Order, 1940–1944.* London: Barrie and Jenkins.

Peirce, Charles Sanders (1931–5) *Collected Papers of Charles Sanders Peirce, Volume 5.* Cambridge, Mass.: Harvard University Press.

Pickering, Robert (1985) Writing under Vichy: ambiguity and literary imagination in the non-occupied zone. In *Vichy France and the Resistance*, eds. Roderick Kedward and Roger Austin. London: Croom Helm, pp. 260–4.

Pocock, J. G. A. (1985) *Virtue, Commerce and History.* Cambridge: Cambridge University Press.

Popper, Karl (1945) *The Open Society and its Enemies.* London: Routledge and Kegan Paul.

Popper, Karl (1957) *Poverty of Historicism.* London: Routledge and Kegan Paul.

Posner, Richard (2001) *Public Intellectuals: A Study in Decline.* Cambridge, Mass.: Harvard University Press.

Price, Roger (2005) *A Concise History of France.* Cambridge: Cambridge University Press.

Rabi, Wladimir (1947) Portrait d'un philosémite. *Esprit* 138, October: 532–46.

Riding, Alan (2010) *And the Show Went On: Cultural Life in Nazi-Occupied Paris.* London: Duckworth.

Ries, Al and Jack Trout (1981) *Positioning: The Battle for your Mind.* London: McGraw-Hill.

Robbins, Bruce (1990) Review: intellectuals in decline? Russell Jacoby, The last intellectuals: American culture in the age of academy. *Social Text* 25/26: 254–9.

Rorty, Richard (1980) *Philosophy and the Mirror of Nature.* Oxford: Blackwell.

Rorty, Richard (1992) *Consequences of Pragmatism.* Brighton: Harvester Wheatsheaf.

Rorty, Richard (1999) *Philosophy and Social Hope.* London: Penguin.

Rosenberg, Harold (1949) Does the Jew exist? Sartre's morality play about anti-semitism, *Commentary* 7, 1: 8–18.

Rousso, Henry (1991) *The Vichy Syndrome: History and Memory in France since 1944.* Cambridge, Mass.: Harvard University Press.

Rubenstein, Diane (1990) *What's Left? The* École Normale Supérieure *and the Right.* Madison, WI: University of Wisconsin Press.

Rubenstein, Diane (1993) Publish or perish: the *épuration* of French intellectuals. *Journal of European Studies* 3, 1: 71–99.

Russell, Bertrand (2003) *Collected Papers of Bertrand Russell, Volume 28: Man's Peril, 1954–1955.* London: Routledge.

Rybalka, Michel (1999) Publication and Reception of *Anti-Semite and Jew.* October 87, Winter: 161–81.

Said, Edward (1994) *Representations of the intellectual: the 1993 Reith lectures.* London: Vintage.

Sapiro, Gisèle (1999) *La Guerre des écrivains 1940–1953.* Paris: Fayard.

Sapiro, Gisèle (2004) La Collaboration littéraire. In *Les Intellectuels et l'occupation*, eds. A. Betz and S. Martens. Paris: Éditions Autrement, pp. 39–63.

Sapiro, Gisèle (2007) The writers' responsibility in France: from Flaubert to Sartre. *French Politics, Culture and Society* 25, 1: 1–29.

Sapiro, Gisèle (2011) *La Responsabilité de l'écrivain: Littérature, droit et morale en France (XIXe-XXIe siècle)*. Paris: Seuil.

Sarlo, Beatriz (2001) *La Batalla de las ideas (1943–1973)*. Buenos Aires: Ariel Historia.

Sartre, Jean-Paul (1963[1936]) *L'imagination*. Paris: Presses Universitaires de France.

Sartre, Jean-Paul (1943) *L'Être et le néant*. Paris: Gallimard.

Sartre, Jean-Paul (1944) À Propos de l'existentialisme: Mise au point. *Action* 17, 29 December: 11.

Sartre, Jean-Paul (1949a[1944]) La République du silence. In *Situations, III*, J.-P. Sartre. Paris: Gallimard, pp. 9–14.

Sartre, Jean-Paul (1949b[1944]) Paris sous l'occupation. In *Situations, III*, J.-P Sartre. Paris: Gallimard, pp. 15–42.

Sartre, Jean-Paul (1949c[1945]) Qu'est-ce qu'un collaborateur? In *Situations, III*, J.-P. Sartre. Paris: Gallimard, pp. 43–61.

Sartre, Jean-Paul (1945a) Présentation. *Les Temps modernes*, 1 October: 1–21.

Sartre, Jean-Paul (1945b) La Nationalisation de la littérature. In *Les Temps modernes*, 2 November: 193–211.

Sartre, Jean-Paul (1996[1946]) *L'Existentialisme est un humanisme*. Paris: Gallimard.

Sartre, Jean-Paul (1954[1946]) *Réflexions sur la question juive*. Paris: Gallimard.

Sartre, Jean-Paul (1948b[1946–7]) *Qu'est-ce que la littérature?*. Paris: Gallimard.

Sartre, Jean-Paul (1948[1947]) Qu'est-ce que la littérature? In *Situations, II*, J.-P. Sartre. Paris: Gallimard, pp. 57–330.

Sartre, Jean-Paul (1995[1948]) *Anti-Semite and Jew*. New York: Schocken.

Sartre, Jean-Paul (2007[1950]) *What is Literature?* London: Routledge.

Sartre, Jean-Paul, David Rousset and Gérard Rosenthal (1949) *Entretiens sur la politique*. Paris: Gallimard.

Sartre, Jean-Paul and Simha Flapan (1966) Jean-Paul Sartre et les problèmes de notre temps: Interview recueillie par Simha Flapan, *Cahiers Bernard Lazare* 4 April: 4–9.

Sartre, Jean-Paul and Benny Lévy (1991) *L'Espoir maintenant: les entretiens de 1980*. Lagrasse: Verdier.

Schmidle, Robert (2010) Positioning theory and terrorist networks. *Journal of the Theory of Social Behaviour* 40, 1: 65–78.

Schmitt, Carl (1996[1921]) *The Concept of the Political*. Chicago: University of Chicago Press.

Schor, Naomi (1999) Jean-Paul Sartre's 'Anti-Semite and Jew'. *October* 87, Winter: 107–16.

Schöttler, Peter (2004) La continuation des *Annales* sous l'occupation: une 'solution élégante'? In *Les Intellectuels et l'occupation*, eds. Albrecth Betz and Stefan Martens. Paris: Éditions Autrement, pp. 243–61.

Schrecker, Ellen (1986) *No Ivory Tower: McCarthyism and the Universities*. Oxford: Oxford University Press.

Schrift, Alan (2006) *Twentieth-Century French Philosophy: Key Themes and Thinkers*. Malden, MA: Blackwell.

Schrift, Alan (2008) The effects of the *agrégation de philosophie* on twentieth-century French philosophy. *Journal of the History of Philosophy* 46, 3: 449–73.

Scriven, Michael (1993) *Sartre and the Media*. London: Macmillan.

213

Shils, Edward (1992) The idea of the university: obstacles and opportunities in contemporary societies. *Minerva* 30, 2: 301–13.

Sirinelli, Jean-François (1988) *Génération intellectuelle: khâgneux et normaliens dans l'entre-deux-guerres*. Paris: Fayard.

Skinner, Quentin (1966) The ideological context of Hobbes's political thought. *The Historical Journal* 9, 3: 286–317.

Skinner, Quentin (1969) Meaning and understanding in the history of ideas. *History and Theory* 8, 1: 3–53.

Sleeper, R. (1986) *The Necessity of Pragmatism: John Dewey's Conception of Philosophy*. New Haven: Yale University Press.

Slocum-Bradley, Nicci (2010) The positioning diamond: a trans-disciplinary framework for discourse analysis. *Journal for the Theory of Social Behaviour* 40, 1: 79–107.

Small, Helen (2002) *The Public Intellectual*. Oxford: Wiley-Blackwell.

Spotts, Frederic (2008) *The Shameful Peace: How French Artists and Intellectuals Survived the Nazi Occupation*. New Haven: Yale University Press.

Stewart, Ian (2009) Conservative political science or existentialist manifesto: problems in interpreting Raymond Aron's *Introduction à la philosophie de l'histoire*. *European Review of History* 16, 2: 217–33.

Suarez, Georges (1940) *Le Maréchal Pétain*. Paris: Plon.

Suarez, Georges (1941) *Pétain ou la démocratie? Il faut choisir*. Paris: Grasset.

Suleiman, Susan (1995) Sartre's *Réflexions sur la question juive*, pp. 201–18. In *The Jew in Text*, ed. Linda Nochlin. London: Thames and Hudson.

Suleiman, Susan (2001) Choisir son passé. In *La Naissance du 'phénomène Sartre'*, ed. I. Galdster. Paris: Seuil, pp. 213–37.

Suleiman, Susan (2006) *Crises of Memory and the Second World War*. Cambridge, Mass.: Harvard University Press.

Swartz, David (2003) From critical sociology to public intellectual: Pierre Bourdieu and politics. *Theory and Society* 32, 5/6 December: 791–823.

Szakolczai, Arpad and Harald Wydra (2006) Contemporary East Central European social theory. In *Handbook of Contemporary European Social Theory*, ed. G. Delanty. London: Routledge, pp. 138–52.

Taylor, Gary (1991) *Reinventing Shakespeare: A Cultural History from the Restoration to the Present*. Oxford: Oxford University Press.

Taylor, Gary (1996) *Cultural Selection: Why Some Achievements Survive the Test of Time*. New York: Basic Books.

Traverso, Enzo (1999) The blindness of the intellectuals: historicizing Sartre's 'Anti-Semite and Jew'. *October* 87, Winter: 73–88.

Troisfontaines, Roger (1945) *Le Choix de J.-P. Sartre*. Paris: Aubier-Montaigne.

Troisfontaines, Roger (1946) *Existentialisme et pensée chrétienne*. Paris: Aubier-Montaigne.

Tuck, Richard (1989) *Hobbes*. Oxford: Oxford University Press.

Ungar, Steven (2006) Saussure, Barthes and structuralism. In *The Cambridge Companion to Saussure*, ed. Carole Sanders. Cambridge: Cambridge University Press, pp. 157–73.

van Langenhove, Luc and Rom Harré (1993) Positioning in scientific discourse. In *Anglo-Ukrainian Studies in the Analysis of Scientific Discourse*, ed. Rom Harré. Lewiston: Edwin Mellon Press, pp. 1–20.

van Langenhove, Luc and Rom Harré (1999a) Introducing positioning theory. In

Positioning Theory: Moral Contexts of International Action, eds. R. Harré and L. van Langenhove. Oxford: Wiley-Blackwell, pp. 14–31.

van Langenhove, Luc and Rom Harré (1999b) Positioning and the writing of science. In *Positioning Theory: Moral Contexts of International Action*, eds. R. Harré and L. van Langenhove. Oxford: Wiley-Blackwell, pp. 103–15.

Vercors (1945) *Carrefour*. Number 25. 10 February.

Verdès-Leroux, Jeannine (1996) *Refus et violence: Politique et littérature à l'extrême droite des années trente aux retombées de la Libération*. Paris: Gallimard.

Vergez-Chaignon, Bénédicte (2006) *Vichy en prison: les épurés à Fresnes après la Libération*. Paris: Gallimard.

Vidal-Naquet, Pierre (1999) Remembrances of a 1946 Reader. *October* 87 Winter: 7–23.

Vinen, Richard (2006) *The Unfree French: Life under the Occupation*. London: Allen Lane.

Walzer, Michael (1995) Preface. In *Anti-Semite and Jew*, J.-P. Sartre. New York: Schocken, v–xxvi.

Watts, Philip (1998) *Allegories of the Purge: How literature Responded to the Postwar Trials of Writers and Intellectuals in France*. Stanford, CA: Stanford University Press.

Weil, Frederick (1985) The variable effects of education on liberal attitudes: A comparative-historical analysis of anti-semitism using public opinion survey data. *American Sociological Review* 50, 4: 458–74.

Whyte, George (2008) *The Dreyfus Affair: A chronological history*. London: Palgrave Macmillan Wilkinson, James (1981). *The Intellectual Resistance in Europe*. Cambridge, Mass.: Harvard University Press.

Wilkinson, James (1981) *The Intellectual Resistance in Europe*. Cambridge, Mass.: Harvard University Press.

Winock, Michel (1988) *Le Siècle des intellectuels*. Paris: Seuil.

Winock, Michel (2011) *L'Effet de génération*. Vincennes: Editions Thierry Marchaisse.

215

INDEX

216